The
Workshop

DESIGNING · BUILDING · EQUIPPING

The Workshop

DESIGNING · BUILDING · EQUIPPING

JIM KINGSHOTT

GUILD OF MASTER CRAFTSMAN PUBLICATIONS LTD

First Published in 1993 by
Guild of Master Craftsman Publications Ltd,
Castle Place, 166 High Street, Lewes, East Sussex BN7 1XU

Reprinted 1994

© Jim Kingshott 1993

ISBN 0 946819 42 4

Designed by Ian Hunt Design.

Typeset by G. Beard & Son Ltd.

Printed and bound in Great Britain by
Hillman Printers (Frome) Ltd

Dedication

TO JOHN

Acknowledgements

I would like to express my grateful appreciation to the following people: my wife, Jo, for reading the manuscript and correcting the numerous mistakes; Liz Inman for her inestimable encouragement; Ian Kearey, who not only edited the manuscript, but allowed me to talk over all the different ideas I had and made some invaluable suggestions of his own. Last but not least, I would like to thank the people who offered to have their workshops photographed, even if the offer was not taken up.

CONTENTS

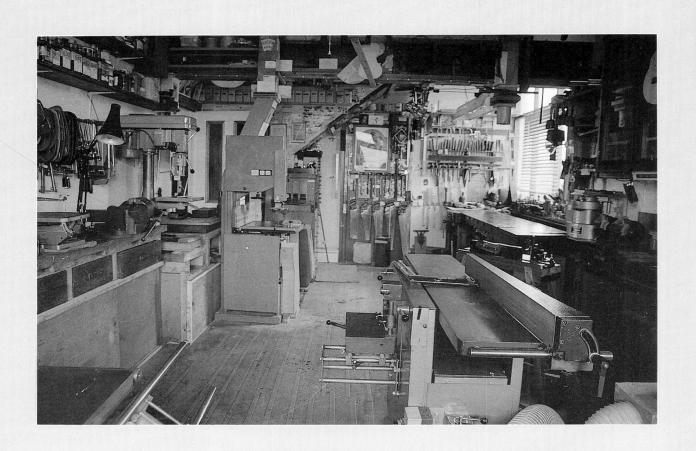

PREFACE

Almost as long as I can remember I have had some sort of workshop. The first was in the corner of my parents' coal shed: it was so dark that I took some slates off the roof and replaced them with glass. I would then have been about 12 years old. That was the first modification to my working conditions, and the process has continued ever since.

Every time I have changed workshop it has been an improvement on the last one. Today I have what to many woodworkers would seem the ultimate, but I can still see little improvements that I will make one day when I have the time, or the money. It may be helpful if I briefly relate the history of the different workshops that I have owned and how they came into being.

As a child growing up during the war things were anything but normal for me. Father was called up and went abroad to fight in the desert, Italy and Sicily, and mother had to work on what was called the war effort. That left me to be brought up by my maternal grandmother. My grandfather had run an antiques business until he died in 1940; there was still much of his stock about the place, and a very good workshop in which one of my uncles still worked. I gravitated to this workshop at every opportunity. While I was not allowed to touch the tools, I was more at ease there than in any other place. I remember to this day the comfort that the smell of the wood and polish gave me, and the security of knowing that most of the furniture had been around for a hundred years, and would probably be around for another hundred. These early experiences must, I suppose, influence me even now when deciding just how to arrange the workshop or what to put in it.

With this sort of start it is not surprising that the first thing I did on returning to live with my parents after the war was to make a corner of their coal shed into a workshop. It was an old stone outhouse, with all sorts of paraphernalia stored in it: there was the coal at one end and grain bins with the chicken feed at the other. Between these two extremities were scattered gardening tools, bicycles and all the usual rubbish that a family collects and needs to store somewhere.

I cleaned out one end of the building, whitewashed the walls and installed a small bench. Each Christmas and birthday I had asked for tools as presents, so I set up in the shed and started a lifetime of woodworking. There was no electricity or gas for lighting; we had to use paraffin which made working after dark very difficult. I saved up all my pocket money and bought a newfangled pressure lamp, a great improvement over the old lamps with a wick.

I started my apprenticeship at the age of fourteen; a local gentleman who lived in the manor house asked me to do some work for him. One thing led to another, and he allowed me to use the loft over his garages as a workshop. This was a big improvement, as not only did I have a large window under which I could put my bench, but there was electricity; an engine connected to a generator charged a room full of lead acid batteries that supplied 120v DC to the house and outbuildings, including my workshop. Apart from making a new bench and some drawers in which to store tools, I could not alter things very much. The main drawback to this workshop was that it was in a loft, reached by a near-vertical set of steps. It was a major task to get furniture in or out of the place.

A few years later we moved house. This looked more promising as there was a basement which was to be my very own domain, to do with almost as I pleased. Like nearly every basement in a Victorian house, this one was damp. The last thing needed where furniture is being made or repaired is moisture, so I spent a good deal of time and money treating the walls with damp-proofing and trying to dry the place out, but never really succeeded. Like my original workshop in the coal shed, this one was without a window. I still have a mania about natural light: you can't have too much of it in the workshop.

The next change of home workshop was when I got married. We moved into a small semidetached house with a large garden, and the first job was to build a workshop. Money was tight, so I went on the scrounge for secondhand materials. What I could get would dictate how the shop would be built. I managed to find just enough 8ft x 4ft asbestos cement sheets to make a building 8ft x 12ft. A concrete base was laid and the shop was erected using 2in x 2in framing clad with the cement asbestos sheeting. The inside was lined with a very cheap insulating board sold under the name of Essex board; this material was made from waste paper pressed into a ¼in thick hardboard. I have always liked a real fire in my

workshop – I know there is a hazard involved, but it is worth the risk, and I am very careful. A slow-burning combustion stove was installed, and the glue pot merrily singing away on that stove is still a fond memory some 35 years on.

There were three windows, a large one over the bench and a smaller one at each end. The shop door was opposite the kitchen door, convenient for the occasional cup of tea. There was electricity laid on, and some small machinery installed. The only problem was one of the condensation on steel tools, which caused rusting. I fought a never-ending battle cleaning tools and polishing away fine rust. Many happy hours were spent in that building.

For a number of years after that I had to work from commercial premises and did not have a workshop at home. However, when my business was large enough to move on to a factory site I again had a workshop at home. This came into being in a roundabout way; we had lived in a flat over the business, and when it moved into a factory we sold the premises. This left us needing a home. The GPO had built a new automatic telephone exchange in the village and the house in which the exchange had been previously situated was allowed to become derelict. We managed to buy it at public auction. While I was working on the refurbishment, I used one of the ground floor rooms as a workshop; this room eventually became my own home workshop (*see* Appendix A).

INTRODUCTION

When I was asked to write a book about setting up and equipping a workshop, I jumped at the opportunity. The chance to encourage and help others to take up this fascinating occupation of working wood appealed to me enormously; however it was not until I put pen to paper that I began to realise just how wide a subject this is. It has been necessary to restrict the depth of information given, otherwise there would be a need for several volumes. I have tried to include things that are not easily found in general woodworking books; this should provide the would-be workshop owner with a base on which to start.

There has been difficulty of gender when writing: I have used the term 'craftsman' and referred to things in a masculine way. This I have done because of convention and for ease and clarity, and should in no way be construed as anti-feminist. Some of the best woodworkers I know are female and there is no reason why there should not be more.

I have included a large number of illustrations: the machines and power tools are from my own workshop, and are certainly not of the very latest design, but they show exactly what the machine or tool looks like. The suppliers mentioned will be only too willing to send brochures illustrating their latest products, so you will have up-to-the-minute information on which to base your decisions.

One's workshop is such a very personal thing that I would not wish to be dogmatic about anything that I have stated. The suggestions and observations are for guidance only. Persons who have been working in the craft for some time will have developed their own likes and dislikes which I respect and in no way would disagree with; however we all have to start somewhere, and I hope this book will be a good starting point.

CHAPTER ONE

PRELIMINARY STEPS

SERIOUS CONSIDERATIONS

I have always believed that the craftsman needs the best tools available, sometimes very special tools. However, even armed with the finest tools, his potential will still be very limited unless he has the right environment in which to work. The workshop is just as important as the tools, and getting the conditions right must be the aim of every woodworker. Finding or building and equipping a workshop can be a challenging and interesting task. Even so, one must bear in mind that, like acquiring a fine kit of tools, this is just a means to an end, as it is the finished woodwork that is the ultimate goal.

It is easy to become sidetracked into making a workshop that is a showplace, but the acquisition of the workshop should be a spur to getting on and producing even better work. The workshop probably has more influence than anything else over the work produced by the woodworker and if he is to produce the best he is capable of, there must be no minor irritations. He needs to be happy, comfortable and at peace with the world, and at one with the work in hand.

Things like efficient lighting, heating and ventilation, are expected in any modern building, but there are more subtle things to be considered. I know of one restoration shop occupied by two young craftsmen who had a radio on while they worked, one chap likes loud modern music, while the other man prefers light music played quietly. Now, whenever one of these two has music to suit his taste, the other is irritated. The obvious thing is not to have the

radio on at all, but then both craftsmen have a minor grumble about the lack of music.

NOT AN IMPOSSIBILITY

To acquire your own ideal workshop may at first seem impossible. We nearly all have restrictions due to family or financial commitments. However, Rome was not built in a day, and if you are able to improve your working conditions little by little, it is surprising what can be achieved over a period of time. To that end, each factor that has a bearing on the work being carried out is studied in detail to see if it can be improved. If there is an alteration that is worthwhile, it is undertaken, and if necessary modified again and again, until the goal is achieved. Even then, as the years pass certain things will need to be altered. It is possible that your interests will change and require a different set-up. We all age and find that the body is not as supple as it

Fig 1.1 The outside lavatory that is used as a workshop. There is insufficient room in it for the bench, so this has to be located under the lean-to.

once was: it becomes a nuisance to have to bend down or stretch, so some fittings in the shop may need to be changed.

WHERE TO START?

Each individual requires something different from a workshop. At the start it is difficult to know just what one wants. A common problem is lack of space. However, this may not be as insurmountable as it first appears. A woodworker in Hull uses the outside lavatory as his shop (*see* Figs 1.1, 1.2 and 1.3). I am told on good authority that he has produced quality work in it. I have also seen some remarkable furniture made on a kitchen table. So you see – where there is a will there is a way!

There is a great diversity of trades in the woodworking industry, and while many of them require similar workshops, there will also be differences, some quite large. The boat builder has a totally different requirement to a musical instrument maker, but both are woodworking craftsmen requiring somewhere to work.

Most of the woodworking trades are very old and over the years

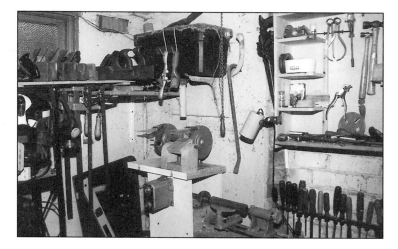

craftsmen have refined the tools and accoutrements needed. It is a good starting point to see what has been established as normal trade practice, and then possibly, modify this to suit your own purpose.

WHERE WILL THE WORKSHOP BE?

The best way to set about establishing a workshop is to break the task down into a number of logical steps. One of the first, and for many people a major hurdle, is fitting in with the rest of the family. Modern homes tend to be on the small side, and any space taken deprives somebody else. Even gardens

Fig 1.2 To make room for a grinder it had to be mounted over the headstock of the lathe. Note also how pot hooks are used to hang tools around the cistern.

Fig 1.3 In this restricted space tidiness is of paramount importance.

Fig 1.4 Timothy Constable, seen here at work in his shop, converted a dentist's chair into this very useful bench, the height of which is easily adjusted to suit the work in hand.

have become very small because of the price of building land. It is therefore expedient to have the approval of the rest of the household before even surveying to see where to site the shop.

A friend worked in a very small garage attached to his house with a door into the kitchen from inside the garage. When he retired, he found it a bit too small. He had mentioned this a number of times to his wife, who had always replied that he should consider himself lucky, as not every family would agree to the car living outside while the garage was used as a workshop. Then my friend was left to fend for himself while his wife went to look after her mother. When his wife returned and asked him how he had managed on his own, his reply was, 'However do you manage in this very small old-fashioned kitchen? Don't you think it's time we put in a new kitchen?' Of course his wife was delighted with the idea, so the kitchen

was extended at the rear of the house. While they were about it they extended the garage.

If you only intend to undertake light work which does not create much noise or dust, two of the biggest nuisances are avoided. However, modern woodwork nearly always involves the use of some machinery. This can cause annoyance not only to the family, but also to neighbours. It is pointless to build and equip a fine workshop only to find that it can only be used part of the time. Even a small limitation on use can be a bind: you have just got to the stage of assembling a job that you have worked on for several weeks, but you must stop because it is the children's bedtime. No hammer blows must be heard, and certainly no machine noises after seven o'clock which leaves you waiting impatiently to get back to the job in hand. Get this sort of problem out of the way before you even start planning.

The first step in the planning exercise is to decide where the shop is to be situated. Several things need to be taken into consideration: distance from the main services, i.e. how far will the electric cables have to be laid? Will you need gas for heating If so, this will need to be piped in. For some types of work you may consider the supply of piped water a necessity.

There is also a factor that I now find an embarrassment in my own workshop – natural light. It may be nice to be surrounded by trees, but when they are in full leaf it can be quite dark in their shade.

If the workshop is to be some distance from the house, there can be a problem in the winter. Remember that the toilet facilities are in the house, as are the tea and other essential services. This is no problem on a sunny summer evening, but it is a different story in the middle of a snowy January day.

You may be lucky and get the use of a ground floor room in the house. This can involve you in some simple soundproofing and the installation of a very effective dust extractor, but it is so convenient.

There are several things that should be borne in mind if you are planning to use a room in the house for a workshop. You may at some time wish to sell the house, so do not carry out alterations that will be difficult to rectify. Suspended wooden floors are not designed to carry heavy machinery, but covering the floor with flooring-grade chipboard will spread the load sufficiently to accommodate the machines usually found in the home workshop. If you intend to purchase ex-industrial machinery on the secondhand market you will need to put in proper machine beds (*see* Chapter 4).

The lighting in the average domestic room will not be what is required in the workshop: lights will be needed over the bench and each machine, preferably fluorescent tubes. This will mean additional installation, probably under the floor of the room above. Unless the type of woodwork to be done is of a very light nature, only a ground floor should be considered: punching mortises through a few oak stiles will soon have the ceiling down in the room below.

AN IDEAL PLACE

There is still one popular place to site the workshop that I have yet to mention – the garage. Now this can be ideal – perhaps a bit small if you want to build joinery, but then some garages are quite a size. The first thing to decide is where the car is to live once you have occupied the garage. Even if the garage is of the two-car size, the vehicle must still be precluded, as the amount of water it will bring in is unacceptable. Of course, if the garage is big enough there is no reason why an area cannot be partitioned off.

The materials from which the building is constructed will have some bearing on its suitability. The type of garage that is attached to the house and has an internal door leading into the house would be most desirable. A detached brick or block building would be fine.

Precast concrete and sheet-clad buildings will need a good deal of work done on them before being suitable: both these forms of construction – unless they are lined – cause a lot of condensation, which causes tools to rust and affects any timber in the shop. A garage floor will probably be sound enough to support any machinery you might wish to install. There may even be a separate electricity supply, e.g. the garage has its own fuse panel. If you live in a second floor flat, why not try to rent a garage.

CHAPTER TWO
THE FLOOR PLAN

DON'T BE TOO EAGER

The average woodworker faced with the prospect of a new workshop wants to get into it as soon as possible. This is quite understandable, but the old saying 'make haste slowly' is very apt here. Acquiring a new workshop is a major step. Even if moving into a ready-made building or room, some preliminary planning is essential; apart from the financial cost of mistakes, there is the frustration of things not being right when you do occupy the shop. A few hours spent planning and deciding exactly what is wanted will be repaid many times over later on. There is nothing worse than having those 'if only' thoughts when it is too late to do anything about it. Planning for the installation of equipment, and deciding what size building will be required needs to be approached in a methodical way.

Once these decisions are made the work can be undertaken with a clear target in mind. There is nothing worse than having to keep retracing one's steps because things are not working out.

EXACTLY WHAT YOU WANT

Not many of us are in the ideal situation where we can have exactly what we want. Even so, when planning a workshop it is best to start with this premise and then modify it to suit what we can have. This may seem a cockeyed way of going about things, but one has to start somewhere. What better way than to start with the ideal? In this way important things will not be overlooked, and compromises can often effectively be worked out without sacrificing the ultimate aim.

If we start with a floor area of a certain size and try to fit our equipment into it piecemeal, the result will probably be unsatisfactory.

PRELIMINARY STEPS

The first thing is to list exactly what is to be done in the workshop, i.e., surface planing and thicknessing timber with a maximum length of 10ft by machine. If you think about this, a space of at least 20ft long will be needed, and this does not allow any room for manoeuvring the length of timber. (There are ways of getting over this situation that will be explained later.) This illustrates exactly the reason for making a list; it is the only way to arrive at the layout needed. The following is an example; you will of course have different criteria.

■ Lengths of timber 8ft long must be prepared (sawn and planed).

■ Spindle moulding of 8ft lengths of timber.

■ Mortise stiles with a maximum length of 6ft 8in.

■ Mortises of ¼ – ¾in wide need to be cut.

■ Bench 7ft long x 2ft 3in wide (must have access all round).

■ Installation of a pillar drill capable of boring holes up to 2in in diameter. There should be room around the pillar drill for lengths of wood up to 6ft long to be worked.

■ A bandsaw capable of deeping a board 9in wide, to be installed.

■ There should be room on the band saw for lengths of wood 8ft long.

■ 8ft x 4ft sheets of ply need to be cut down to smaller panels.

■ All machines should be connected to a dust extractor installation.

■ A fluorescent light should be installed over each machine and the bench.

■ A lathe capable of turning spindles 4ft long and with a faceplate capacity of 15in should be installed.

■ There must be a large window in front of the bench.

It is obvious that this list is incomplete; it could easily go on for several pages – even the ideal floor finish could be specified.

THE FLOOR PLAN

A suitable scale at which to draw the plans must first be decided upon. 1in to 12in gives a very usable size without being unwieldy. If you already have the machines you intend to use, measure their size in plan view, and if you are proposing to buy the machines the supplier's brochure will give the sizes

Draw all the machines, benches, racks and any other item that will require floor space to the determined scale. Next, write on each what it is and cut it out. With machines, put an arrow on the cutout representing the direction that wood passes through when working.

The different types of work the workshop will be used for will affect the positioning of machines. A logical progression is usually to be found: for most work this means that the timber is first cut to length, then ripped to size.

Next it is planed and thicknessed. After setting out, joints are cut, then mouldings, rebates and grooves worked. Machines are positioned to facilitate the easy handling of timber through these steps. In many small

workshops a universal woodworking machine is installed; this can sometimes save room, but it should not be assumed that this is always the case.

Narrow strips of paper are cut to scale; these depict the longest pieces of timber that are to be worked. The cutouts representing the machines and other items are positioned on a large sheet of paper. They are moved about, and their ideal positions can be located using the strips representing the timber. You will probably end up with an enormous floor area. Now decisions have to be made on where to compromise. The reasons for the excessive amount of floor area need to be investigated; it will probably be found that it is not the physical space that the machines take up, but more usually, the working room needed for handling the timber that takes up most of the area.

If you are planning the installation in an existing building, a floor plan to the same scale as the cutouts will be required. Doors and windows need to be marked on this plan, and the space any doors take up when open should be indicated. It is possible to open a door to give room for long pieces of timber. A machine can be positioned in line with a door or a window that opens, and this will enable the timber to be passed out of the workshop when there is insufficient room within the shop.

Where the door or window is in an external wall there will be a reluctance to open it during cold weather; this problem can be overcome by hanging strips of plastic about 4in wide, weighted at their lower end, over the opening (see Fig.12.1). Timber can now be passed through this plastic barrier without letting much of the warm air out.

The technique of placing machines so that a door or window can be used to accommodate long lengths of timber can be further developed. Where a purpose-made building is to be used and there is not a convenient door or window where required, a special aperture can be made. This can have convenient lockable flaps, allowing machines to be installed close to the wall.

BIG IS NOT BEAUTIFUL

One should not be disappointed if restricted to a smaller shop than that desired. The smaller the shop the less walking about required. This last point is one worth bearing in mind when planning, as the smaller shop imposes a discipline on the occupant to keep the place tidy. This means less time spent locating things that have been mislaid. A further bonus for the small shop is that the heating bill will be smaller. With fuel costing what it does today, this is no mean consideration.

I once worked in a shop located in an old aeroplane hanger, where there were only six employees. The amount of rubbish in that workshop had to be seen to be believed. All six of us were guilty of accumulating all sorts of items – there were the offcuts of wood that were too useful to be thrown out, although they were never used, and old fittings like draw pulls were kept against the day when they might be needed. So many things accumulated that it was impossible to find what one wanted; it was easier to get another from the stores. Whenever a sizable job came into the shop, we had to clear a space to work on it. Our employer never seemed to be aware how much the inefficiency was costing him.

THE WORKING FLOOR PLAN

Having gone through the procedure described above, the final positions of all items will have been decided upon. A master drawing on good quality cartridge paper should now be made.

Most towns have a print shop that will make dyeline copies of drawings; get at least two copies of your drawing. Failing this make two tracings on foil. Modern drafting foils are tough, but some of them go brittle and break up. Astrafoil takes a fine ink line, and one can work very accurately.

The electrical installation is drawn on one of the prints or tracings; different coloured lines can be used for each separate cable run. All switches, power points, isolators and main switch gear can be shown. Fuses are numbered and labelled. This may seem a bit over the top to you at this stage, but come the day when something goes wrong or you need to alter the installation, you will bless the day you made this drawing. The other print or tracing is used as a working drawing. The original is stored away against the day when the print becomes mislaid or torn.

HOW HIGH?

Having given all this thought to the layout at floor level, it would be remiss if we overlooked the important item of head room. If you are occupying an existing building, there is little that you will be able to do; with a new proposed building, planning permission excepted, the sky is the limit. However desirable headroom is, remember all that empty space up there requires heating. Hot air rises, and all your precious warmth will be up on the ceiling, not around your feet where you need it.

How much headroom will you require? In many small shops tenons are run in using a jig on the table saw; this requires that the rail being tenoned is stood on end on the saw bench. The maximum length of rail being handled is therefore dictated by the height of the ceiling. Perhaps provision can be made for extra height only in this part of the shop. I know of one small workshop with a flat roof which has what looks like a wooden chimney on it over the saw; the ends of long rails go up it when they are being tenoned. In shops where joinery is made, there is a need to manoeuvre quite large frames: the biggest frame to be assembled in the shop will be affected by the ceiling height, and the frame has to be turned over when cleaning up. Of course, a very large frame can be assembled outside the workshop in fine weather.

There is another point that may need to be considered when thinking about the ceiling. Stair builders wedge down off a beam when assembling staircases. This feature is often built into a special stairmaker's bench. However, the ability to use the ceiling over the bench to wedge against is a very useful facility to have, as all sorts of work can be held this way. It may be worth giving some thought to providing a beam of some sort.

ORIENTATION

One of the most important things in my workshop is the window over the bench. While I enjoy the view from it, the light that comes through it is a commodity that money cannot buy. If you contemplate doing fine complex woodwork, this natural light is a boon. A window that faces north, while not getting any sun, will provide the best working light.

One of the best ways of providing natural light that I have come across is the roof light. Some modern, double-skin transparent polyester sheets would be ideal for this. There is one drawback to roof lights; the sun pitching through them can make the workshop unbearably hot. However, some form of sun blind should not be beyond the ingenuity of the average woodworker. There is also a product painted by gardeners on the outside of their greenhouses during the summer; this is sold under the trade name of 'Summershade'. It degrades, and the glass clears after about four months.

The position of windows or roof lights will dictate the best position for placing certain pieces of equipment. If planning a new building, position of equipment will dictate the position of windows, Bearing this last statement in mind, it might be possible to turn the whole building around to orientate it to the desirable north light. One thinks of Victorian photographic studios with their glass wall and roof – what a workshop one of these would make even with the heat loss through the glass.

CHAPTER THREE

CONSTRUCTION FORMS AND MATERIALS

WHICH MATERIAL?

When deciding what sort of materials to use in the construction of a workshop, there will be several factors to be considered. If there is any possibility that the occupant will move house, then a portable building would be most suitable. Perhaps the site on which the building is to be erected is rented; there may be some restrictions in the tenancy agreement. The local planning authority may require a material that will not clash with the surroundings.

To my mind the best structure would be built from bricks with a tile roof – of course this is probably going to be the most expensive to build. (My experience of workshops is restricted to those built in the temperate zone. In other countries where there is an extreme climate, this would have an influence on the type of structure required.) With most materials the tried and tested are best. New materials come and go; only the best stand the test of time.

BRICKS

Every child knows the story of the three little pigs. The third little pig built his house of bricks, which withstood everything the wolf could do to destroy it. What better recommendation could any building material have?

The brick was brought to this country by the Romans and has a history that can be traced back to before 6000 BC. The Roman brick was thinner than our present ones and many of them survive to this day.

A brick is defined in BS 3921 Part 2 as a walling unit not exceeding 337.5mm in length, 225mm in width or 112.5mm in height. As the brick is such an important item, I will deal with it at some length. Should you contemplate building with bricks it is important to choose those most suitable for the purpose, and to be able to judge their quality. Bricks of the standard building variety are obtainable in several grades and types. The standard size of a brick was $8\frac{3}{4}$in long, x $4\frac{3}{16}$in wide and x $2\frac{5}{8}$in high. With the mortar joint, this makes a size of 9in x $4\frac{1}{2}$in x 3in. The metric brick now being made in this country is 215mm long, 102.5mm wide and 65mm high. (*see* Fig 3.1). This size may seem small, but it has come about through thousands of years of use. It is the ideal size. A larger brick, similar in bulk to a modern building block, may seem more effective at first. However, the brick can be picked up with one hand. A building block cannot: the bricklayer has to put his trowel down and use both hands to pick up the block. With the brick he can manipulate the mortar with his trowel in one hand and place the bricks with the other. One only needs to watch a skilled bricklayer at work to appreciate the speed at which bricks can be laid.

There are two distinct ways of shaping the material the brick is made from. A mould can be used. This is a box the size of the brick, which has no lid; the material is rammed into the box and scraped off level at the top.

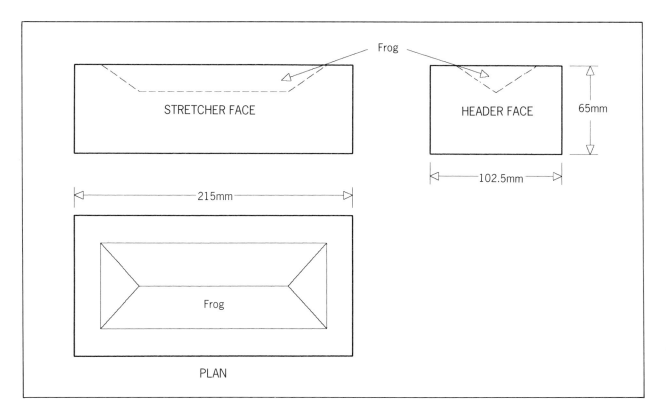

The moulded material is turned out, and the next brick formed, and so on. This produces a pressed brick, and is the most common method of manufacture accounting for nearly two-thirds of the 8000 million produced in this country each year. The other method produces bricks known as wirecuts. Material is extruded in a continuous ribbon the length and width of a brick. This ribbon is cut into pieces the thickness of a brick by a wire, very similar to the way cheese is cut.

Of the many materials that bricks can be made from, the one that usually comes first to mind is clay. This term covers a wide range of substances. Brick clay, or aluminium silicate, forms the basis of the various brick earths. When wet, clay possesses plastic properties. If sufficient heat is applied it gives off its moisture and takes on a permanent rigid form; there is no known process that can restore the original plasticity. Silica is present in various brick earths in the

form of sand and flint, or chemically combined with alumina and water. If silica is present in excessive quantities it causes the brick to be brittle.

Limestone or chalk when present acts as a flux, causing the particles in the clay to unite and form a strong brick. In excessive quantities it causes the brick to partly melt in the burning and become misshaped. Where iron occurs in the form of pyrites, it has to be removed as it oxidises and splits the brick. Iron also affects the colour. Magnesia also has an effect on the colour, giving a yellowish tint. Most brick earths usually contain various salts. If these are present in excessive quantities the brick absorbs moisture from the atmosphere; this causes efflorescence, which appears on the surface of the brickwork as a white powdery deposit.

Bricks are burnt in a kiln or a clamp. The process is fourfold; first driving off the moisture, burning out any carbonaceous matter, raising to peak temperature, followed by

Fig 3.1 The standard metric brick.

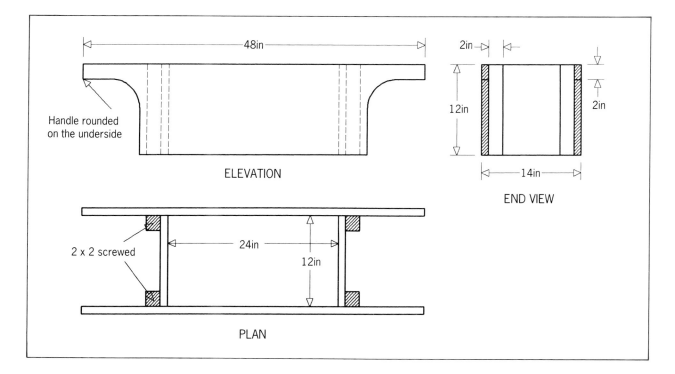

ELEVATION

END VIEW

Handle rounded
on the underside

48in

2in

12in

2in

14in

2 x 2 screwed

24in

12in

PLAN

Fig 3.2 The ballast gauge box. The box is placed on a flat surface where the concrete is to be mixed, and it is filled with ballast. Using the handles two people can lift the box clear of the mixing area leaving a heap of ballast of measured quantity.

annealing, which is accomplished by holding peak temperature for a given time.

Concrete bricks are made in various sizes and colours, using an aggregate with coloured cement. These bricks are very hard. The aggregate is usually a fine ballast, although sometimes fine broken brick is used instead. Units larger than the standard brick are usually referred to as a block.

VARIETIES OF BRICKS

Stocks are used extensively throughout the country, especially in the south where they are called London stocks. Stocks can be obtained in colours ranging from a yellow through various shades of red to purple. There are several distinguishing points: pressed bricks have sharp corners and a single or double frog. (The frog is that depression on the flat side of the brick). There is usually a distinguishing mark like the maker's name. The wirecut stocks have marks from the wires on both flat sides; they tend to be uniform in shape and size

and reasonably dense; there is no frog.

Red bricks are made in a variety of shades. They have a sand face that can either be coarse or fine, and can be obtained in colours that range from a very dark plum to a light red. These bricks are largely used for face work.

Gault Bricks are white and made from a bluish coloured clay situated between upper and lower green formations. The clay contains an amount of chalk that acts as a flux. It produces a good hard white brick.

Fletton bricks are made in very large quantities by the London Brick Company. The bricks are machine-made from clay obtained from the Oxford formation. A Fletton brick is uniform in shape and size, and has very sharp corners. There is usually a single frog. The bricks are cheap compared with many other varieties. Several surface finishes are available for face work.

Staffordshire Blue bricks are made from a very dense marl clay. This brick is very hard, of a deep blue-greyish colour. The brick is virtually impervious, acid-proof and durable.

Midhurst Whites are calcium silicate bricks with a smooth white surface. Used for internal and external work, they are impervious to gases and soot. They can be washed down and will keep their white appearance. These bricks are of uniform shape and size, usually with one frog.

There are many other varieties of brick; those described are merely a cross section of the different types available. A visit to your local builder's merchant can be quite instructive and many large DIY stores have small stocks of the common varieties of brick. From the descriptions and details given above, you should be able to make a sensible choice from what you are offered.

BS 3921, Part 2 gives the following description that clarifies some terms which may be encountered:

Varieties

Common Suitable for general building work but having no special claim to give an attractive appearance.

Facing Specially made or selected to have an attractive appearance when used without rendering or plaster.

Engineering Having a dense and strong semi-vitreous body conforming to defined limits for absorption and strength.

Qualities

Internal Suitable for internal use only; may need protection on site during bad weather or during the winter.

Ordinary Less durable than special quality but normally durable in the external face of buildings.

Special For use in conditions of extreme exposure where the structure may become saturated and frozen.

Fig 3.3 The cement gauge box. Use with ballast gauge box for 6:1 mix.

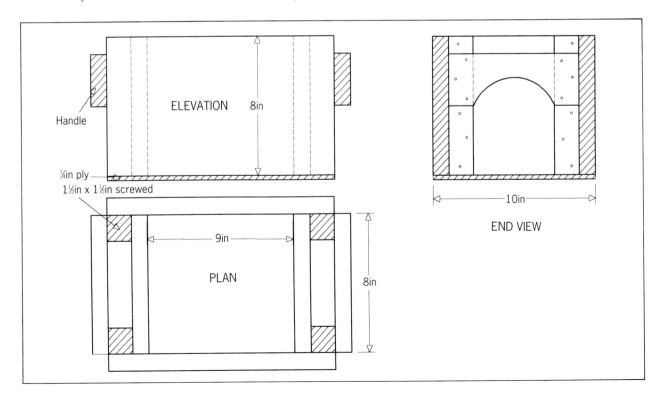

Handle

ELEVATION   8in

¼in ply
1½in x 1½in screwed

9in

PLAN

8in

10in

END VIEW

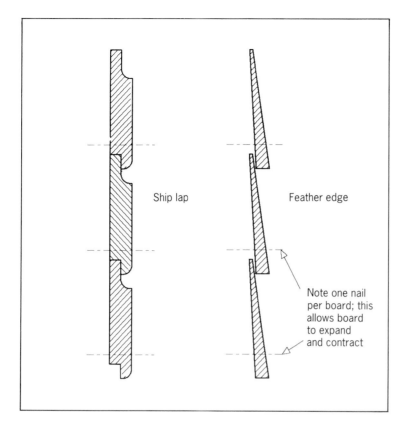

Ship lap

Feather edge

Note one nail per board; this allows board to expand and contract

Fig 3.4
Weatherboarding.

BLOCKS

Building blocks are made from a number of different materials. The blocks are usually 450mm x 225mm, with thicknesses of 75mm, 100mm, 140mm and 215mm. Some are weatherproof, and blocks can be made in a variety of colours by using coloured cement concrete; there are also several surface finishes. A very attractive block is made with an imitation stone surface; some blocks are in fact made from reconstituted stone. Blocks tend to vary depending on the locality. As transport tends to be a big item in their cost, they are usually supplied by a local manufacturer.

Where blocks that are porous are used, they will have to have some weatherproofing finish applied to them. This is usually some form of cement rendering, often with a rough cast or pebble dash finish. There are specialist contractors that will spray the finished walls with aerated

cement. Rough surface finishes can be a nuisance where they can collect soot and dust from the atmosphere; there is also the problem of algae which can make large, dirty, dark green patches on the surface of the wall. Some forms of surface finish, emulsions, etc. contain a fungicide to combat this problem.

British Standard 6073 applies to Concrete Wall and Partition Blocks.

MORTAR

Cement mortar is used in the building of a brick wall to keep the bricks apart, *not* to stick them together. The bricks, no matter how accurately they have been moulded, will not build a wall that is true and strong if piled one upon another, so mortar is used to bed each brick true and level on top of the one below. Good mortar does have some adhesive properties, but this is not its primary function. Cement mortar works short, that is to say it breaks up when it is rolled with the trowel. This feature makes it difficult to work with, so lime or some other plasticizer is added to overcome this problem, there are several brands of liquid plasticizer that replace lime in the mix on the market.

The following is the normal mix used for good quality brickwork; all measures are by volume: cement 1 part, sand 4 parts, lime ¼ part. Water used for mixing mortar must be clean. When mixed, the mortar should be used within two hours of mixing. Under no circumstances must water be added after the initial mixing – the mortar hardens by a chemical action, *not* by drying out, and additional water will weaken the strength of the mortar.

Before leaving the subject of bricks and mortar, the following British Standard Specifications may be of use: Portland cement BS 12, Building Lime BS 890, Natural Aggregates BS 882.

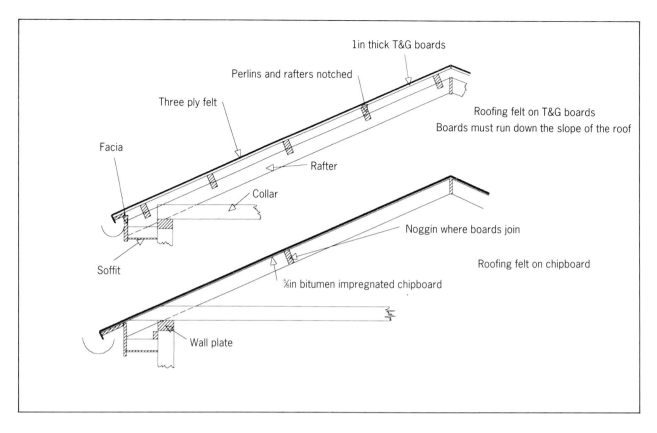

Perlins and rafters notched

1in thick T&G boards

Three ply felt

Roofing felt on T&G boards
Boards must run down the slope of the roof

Facia

Rafter

Collar

Noggin where boards join

Roofing felt on chipboard

Soffit

⅝in bitumen impregnated chipboard

Wall plate

Fig 3.5 Details of bitumen felted roof.

TIMBER FRAME

Assuming that you will be constructing the building yourself, not purchasing a prefabricated unit (*see* Chapter 8), this method of construction is ideal for building a portable workshop; just how portable it is will depend on the size of the individual units. The size of the timber used for the frame is determined by the span of the building and the outside cladding. It will be best if we first look at the various materials that can be used to clad the outside.

WEATHERBOARDING

There are two distinct types of weatherboarding (known as clap-board in the USA), feather edged and shiplap. Drawings of the sections of these are given in Fig 3.4. Of the two, shiplap is superior, but costs considerably more than the feather edged. The species of timber that the boards are cut from has a bearing on

the durability and, of course, the cost. The best shiplap is made from cedar; this is almost rot-proof, but is very pricey. The cheapest boards are cut from larch; this timber has large knots that tend to drop out as the boards dry. A few years ago, before the onset of Dutch elm disease, elm made very durable weatherboarding. The waney-edged boarding that many people considered so attractive was normally cut from elm; other timbers do not seem to cut this way.

Weatherboarding should be fixed with galvanized nails. A layer of building paper, a tough manila paper impregnated with bitumen, or reinforced felt should be inserted between the boards and the framework. The insertion of this membrane will keep the workshop dry.

When the framework is clad with weatherboarding, the studs should be spaced no wider apart than 2ft centre to centre.

SHEET MATERIAL

The choice of a ridged sheet material to clad the framework has some bearing on the structural strength. This means that the studs in the framework can be spaced further apart than when using weatherboard. However, it is still good practice to have a moisture barrier between the sheets and the framework.

All cladding should be fixed with rust-proof screws or nails, galvanized, zinc plated or sheradized are adequate. Some plywood manufacturers have a marine quality ply that will not meet the British Specification because of some minor defect. This material can make very good cladding.

There are several steel products that are made for cladding, the best known of which is the **corrugated** variety, which has been available for the last hundred years. This is usually referred to as corrugated iron, but it is actually made from mild steel. Unfortunately steel rusts and there must be some coating on it to protect it from the atmosphere. Added to this there is the question of thickness: over the past few years, to reduce the price, most suppliers stock the thinner gauges. Where sheets have a galvanized finish it should comply with BS 3083.

There are several different designs of **ridged sheet**. These are flat sheets that have two or three ridges running up their length. This ridge adds stiffness to a flat sheet, but does not require as much steel as those that are fully corrugated. Many of these have a plastic coating instead of being galvanized. I do not know how long this type of finish will last, but I doubt that it is as good as proper hot-dipped galvanizing.

There is an **aluminium sheet** cladding, but I have no personal experience of its use. Aluminium does oxidize and deteriorate when exposed to the atmosphere, and would need some form of protection.

Before it was found that asbestos was carcinogenic, the cement asbestos sheet was a popular form of cladding. Several manufacturers market **substitute cement asbestos sheets** and if these are as good as the old cement asbestos they would be well worth investigation.

Plastic sheeting, both with a corrugated section and various ribbed sections, is available. The clear variety can be very useful where there is a need to let some light in, preferably on a roof. However, these plastics tend to become very brittle with age and will break up with the slightest impact.

Bitumen impregnated particle board is not a good cladding on its own: this material is intended for use as a roof covering to be covered with roofing felt.

All sheets that have a shape in cross section (corrugated, etc.) need special fixings. The corrugated iron sheet is fixed with the spring head nail. The heads of these special nails are designed to stop the ingress of water. Some types have an additional washer under the head. There are several types that have a plastic cap that is pushed on after they are driven in. It is important that the correct variety is used for the type of sheet being fixed.

THE ROOF

At one time the roof of a timber-framed building would have been boarded and covered with roofing felt. While this is still a very good roof, the cost of 1in thick boarding is prohibitive and many of the sheet materials previously mentioned can be used. There is a factor that needs careful consideration when choosing the cladding for the roof: some form of insulating should be incorporated. In summer the workshop can become unbearably hot due to the sun heating

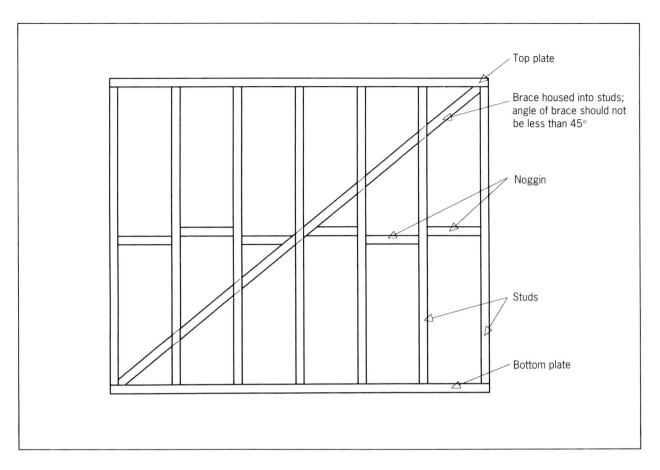

Top plate

Brace housed into studs;
angle of brace should not
be less than 45°

Noggin

Studs

Bottom plate

Fig 3.6 Framework
suitable for
weatherboarding.

the roof. When winter comes there is the opposite effect, and most of the heat in the workshop can disappear through the roof.

There is a 2in thick board made from compressed straw – one proprietary brand goes by the name of 'Stramit board' this material makes a very well insulated flat roof. The one drawback is that it is very heavy. When this board is cut to size, the cut edge must be immediately sealed or the straw starts to come out in capacious quantities. Sealing is carried out using 4in wide gummed paper tape.

ROOFING FELT
There are several types and different weights of bitumen roofing felts, for a variety of uses. The basic product is a felt made from animal and vegetable fibre impregnated with asphaltic bitumen. Different surface finishes

are applied: plain felt has the surface treated with mica or talc; there is a sand surface where the surface is covered with sand while the bitumen is in a semi-molten state; mineralized felt has the face surface covered with slate or similar granules, the undersurface being finished with talc. Roofing felt is supplied in several weights; the heavy grade used to cover a roof is usually described as three-plies. Reinforced felt is a layer of felt and hessian impregnated with bitumen. Its main use is that of a moisture barrier.

Felt is fixed down with large-headed clout nails sold for this purpose, which need to be spaced at about 4in centres. All overlapping joints in the felt should be made with lapping compound, a thick liquid bitumen that is painted on to the lower layer before the upper layer is put into place. During cold weather

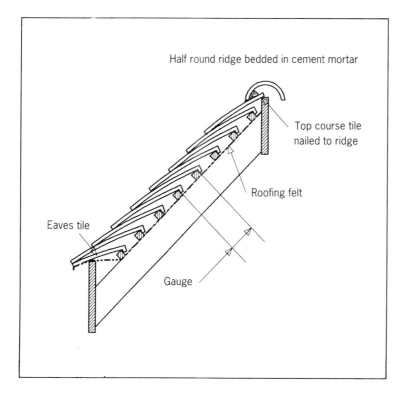

Half round ridge bedded in cement mortar

Top course tile nailed to ridge

Roofing felt

Eaves tile

Gauge

Fig 3.7 Section through a plain-tiled roof.

the compound needs to be warmed so that it thins down sufficiently to spread evenly. It is usual to paint over the nails with this compound to make sure that water does not percolate in under their heads.

INSULATING BOARDS

The thermal insulation of the workshop is very important, especially so where the building is not occupied all the time. There is nothing worse than looking forward to an evening in the shop only to find that it is so cold that the temperature only becomes bearable when it is time to stop work. With the portable building, the space between the studs can be filled with polystyrene sheeting or glass wool. The inside lining can also afford some insulation – Tentest or Sundealer board would be ideal. This material could also be fixed inside the roof. Where there is a pitched gable roof, a ceiling will help energy conservation; it will save having to heat the space up in the roof, and acts as an additional thermal barrier.

THE FRAMEWORK

Once the type of cladding material has been chosen, a suitable framework to support it must be designed. Ridged and flat sheets offer quite a lot of strength to the structure, whereas weatherboarding gives no structural strength whatsoever. The vertical studs for the walls should be spaced out to suit the cladding, e.g. where a 4ft wide sheet of ply is being used, three studs per sheet would be fine.

When using corrugated steel the size to be used needs to be determined first. The most common types are eight or ten corrugations of 3in pitch (known as 8/3in, or 10/3in). Lengths are obtainable from 5ft in increments of 6in up to 8ft and then in 1ft increments to 10ft. The thicknesses obtained in Birmingham gauge are 16, 18, 20, 22, 24, 26; these equate to .0625in, .0495in, .0392in, .03125in, .02476in, .01961in. When working out the width covered, remember that at least one corrugation is lost in the lap.

Sheets require a fixing at a maximum of 3ft centres in their length. This will mean that noggins need fixing between the studs (*see* Fig 3.6). The number of fixings needed across the sheet will vary with the gauge; thin sheets require more than thick sheets. A nail in every other corrugation is the maximum that is required.

For a small workshop up to a floor area of 8ft x 12ft, the framework for the walls could be made of 2in x 1½in when covered on both sides with a sheet material. A minimum of 2in x 2in is needed for weatherboarding; 3in x 2in should be used up to a size of 24ft x 18ft, anything larger will need 4in x 2in. These sizes are arbitrary. If secondhand timber of a nearly similar size is available, that would be suitable. It is possible to reinforce the upright members where roof trusses are supported.

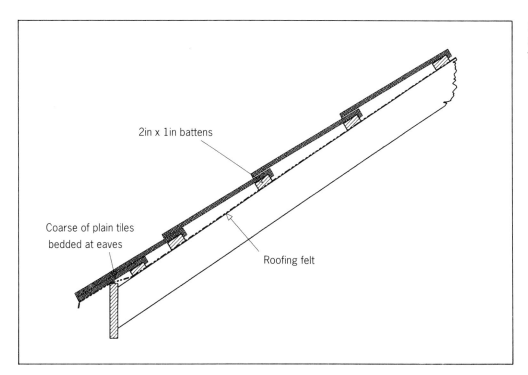

Fig 3.8 Section through a roof with interlocking tiles.

2in x 1in battens

Coarse of plain tiles bedded at eaves

Roofing felt

THE ROOF

The structure of the roof will of course depend on what is to weather it: the weight of clay or cement tiles, compared with sheet material and felt, is considerable, and obviously this weight needs supporting. There are also snow loads to be considered. Roof span is a very influential factor on the size of the various timber members required. To start with, I will describe a roof for a medium-sized workshop with a tiled roof.

Tiles come in two very distinct types (*see* below) A traditional roofing tile produces a very heavy roof because at most points on the roof there are three layers of tile (*see* Fig 3.7) To reduce this weight most tile roofs are now clothed with interlocking tiles, where only one thickness occurs over most of the area covered (*see* Fig 3.8). To reduce the size of the timbers required, the rafters should be trussed. There are several designs of truss that can be used. The Timber Development Association have designed several trusses that have become standard in

Fig 3.9 Timber connectors such as these are used in the construction of timber roof trusses.

the building trade. There are similar trusses designed by the Forest Products Research Laboratory, FPRL. A series of design sheets is issued by the association (*see* appendix).

Before describing the method of roofing using these trusses, an account of the method of connecting the members is necessary. The joints are bolted, and a timber connector is used as well as the bolt (*see* Fig 3.9). A timber connector is in fact a stress plate which distributes the stresses over a larger area than that of the bolt. There are firms that will make trusses to order, but because of the

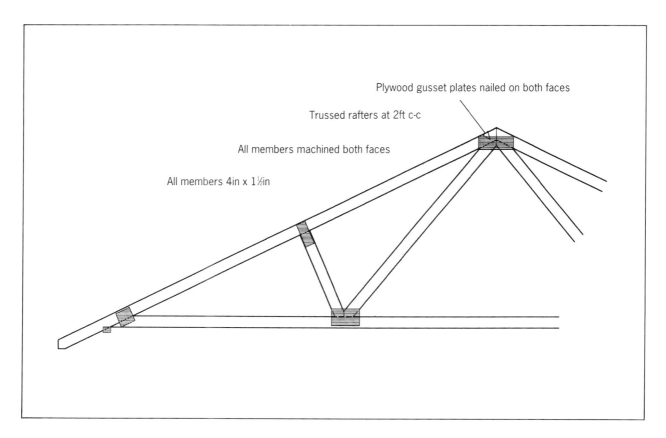

Plywood gusset plates nailed on both faces

Trussed rafters at 2ft c-c

All members machined both faces

All members 4in x 1½in

Fig 3.10 Roof truss for spans up to 20ft.

stress imposed on the joints when handling these heavy units they are best made on site. Trusses are required at 6ft centres, with common rafters between spaced at 18in centres (*see* Fig 3.11).

Plain tiles have been used in Britain for several centuries; they are 10½in long x 6½in wide. For normal conditions of exposure, with a roof pitch of 40° and over, a lap of 2½in is satisfactory and should be considered an absolute minimum. Near the coast or in exposed locations, e.g. on top of a hill, a 3in or 3½in lap should be given. The battens on which the tiles are hung have a gauge of 4in when the lap is 2½in, i.e. from the top of one batten to the top of the next will be 4in.

Interlocking or single lap tiles are usually hung on a roof with a pitch of 35°. There are many different patterns, which vary in size from 11½in x 8½in to 16½in x 14in. One of the most suitable is the Single Roman; this is 15in x 10in, and is one of the lightest in weight.

Tiles are hung on 1in x 1in or 2in x 1in batten. The gauge varies with the type of tile. There should be a layer of reinforced felt between the battens and the rafters. If there is no ceiling in the workshop it would be best if the rafters were covered with an insulating board before the felt and battens were fixed. The ridge of a tiled roof is finished off with the half-round ridge tile; these are bedded on with cement mortar.

FLAT ROOFS
A truly flat roof would not be used : some slope must be given so that water will run off it. The usual structure for a span of 12ft would be 9in x 1½in joists at 2ft centres. Firing pieces are nailed to the upper surface of the joist to give a fall of 2in in 10ft

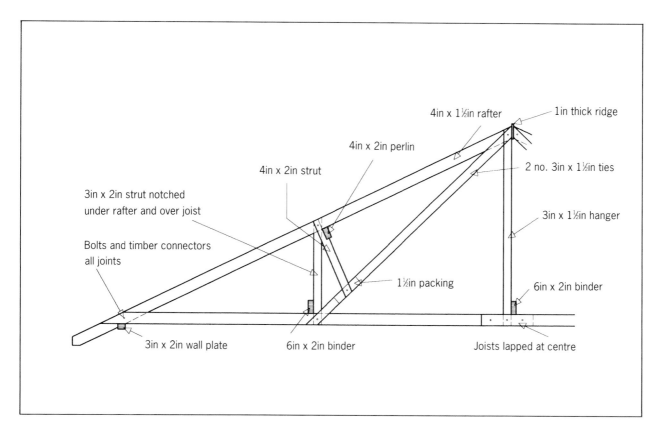

4in x 1½in rafter

1in thick ridge

4in x 2in perlin

2 no. 3in x 1½in ties

4in x 2in strut

3in x 2in strut notched
under rafter and over joist

3in x 1½in hanger

Bolts and timber connectors
all joints

1½in packing

6in x 2in binder

3in x 2in wall plate

6in x 2in binder

Joists lapped at centre

(this is the minimum fall). Sheet material is fixed on top of the firing pieces to support the weatherproofing material. There are several materials that can be used for this purpose; the easiest to use is roofing felt. With the very small fall on this roof, there would be three layers bonded together with roofing compound. Asphalt makes a good flat roof, but this needs special equipment, and would best be laid by a specialized contractor.

Fig 3.11 Roof truss for spans up to 26ft.

WEIGHTS OF DIFFERENT CLADDING	lb per sq ft
Ordinary machine made tiles, 10½in x 6½in laid 4in gauge	13.0
Ordinary handmade tiles, 10½in x 6½in laid 4in gauge	14.5
Cement tiles, 10½in x 6½in laid 4in gauge	14.5
Interlocking tiles, Roman, Pan, Marseilles, etc	7.5
Galvanised corrugated sheet, including lap, 22BG	2.7
3 layers of three-ply felt including compound	1.5
Asphalt ¾in thick	9.0
Asphalt 1in thick	12.0
¾in rough boarding	2.25
1in rough boarding	3.0
Reinforced felt	1.0
½in insulating fibreboard	0.75
Plasterboard	2.0
Plasterboard with setting coat	3.0

These figures are accurate enough to calculate loads for various structures. Some vary with moisture content so a mean average has been taken.

CHAPTER FOUR

CONVERTING AN EXISTING BUILDING

WHERE TO START

It is human nature for the woodworker who acquires a room or building to use as a workshop to be impatient to move in and start working wood. The first step, however, should be to make plans as described in Chapter 2. Moving into a separate building and moving into a room in the house present diverse problems – the room in the house usually requires more planning and thought than a separate building, so I will deal with that first, but things that are common to both situations will be covered.

A ROOM OF YOUR OWN

A room can mean anything from a small utility room, originally intended to house the washing machine, etc., to a billiards room large enough to hold a Ball in. Something in the middle of these two extremes is probably what you require. However, beggars can't be choosers and anything is better than nothing.

Access

The first thing to consider is access. Getting timber, machines, furniture and other essential items that are to be worked on in and out of the workshop will be a continuing task; if everything has to be manoeuvred along a passage and round corners, not only will this be an unwelcome chore, but damage to walls and decorations will follow.

A door from the workshop direct to the outside world is very desirable. A window can be converted; if the proposed door opening is the same width as that of the window it is to replace, this is not a very difficult job. The lintel over the window opening will support the wall above the opening, the wall below the window can be knocked out and a frame and door inserted in the opening. If a good job is made of this work, the door can improve the room even when it is no longer used as a workshop. A fully glazed door would be desirable in a domestic room, but would be a liability in a workshop. Removing a window will affect the natural light entering the shop: for this reason the door should be glazed above the lock rail; this is usually called a half glass door. If the workshop is to be used to make musical instruments or similar light or small items, access is of much less importance.

Natural Light

Anyone who has had to work where there is poor illumination will be more than aware of the restriction that this places on the quality of fine work. There are some very good modern artificial light sources available. The very fact that we call these artificial suggests that they are not considered as good as natural light, so the more glass the better.

Windows can be where most of the warmth escapes from the workshop. Modern double glazing prevents this; it can be costly, but a woodworker could instal secondary double glazing. Not only can this be better than most of the special aluminium units, but it will also act as a sound barrier. If the

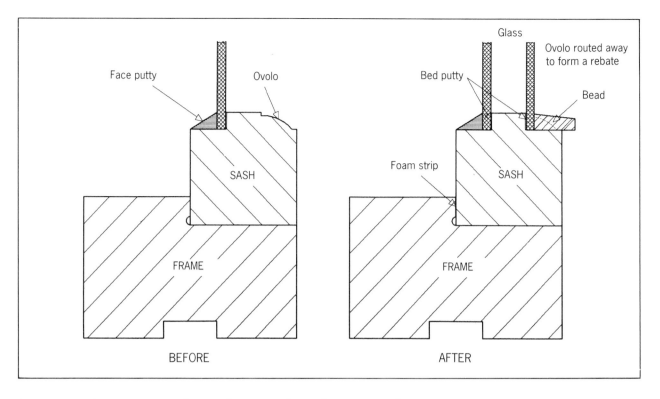

Face putty   Ovolo   SASH   FRAME   BEFORE

Glass   Ovolo routed away to form a rebate   Bed putty   Bead   Foam strip   SASH   FRAME   AFTER

Fig 4.1 A simple method of double glazing.

house next door, or its garden is close to the workshop, noise from woodcutting machinery can be a problem, so double glazing can have a dual role.

Double glazing is a task that can be left until you have installed yourself in the workshop. There are two ways to double glaze a conventional casement window. The simplest is to rout a rebate on the inside of the sash where there is normally an ovolo moulding (*see* Fig 4.1). Glass can be held in this rebate with a small wooden bead, and putty should be used to bed the glass and form a good seal. This method can also be used on box sash windows, but there may be some problems sealing around the sash. With casement windows a foam rubber seal can be used in the rebate into which the sash closes. Self-adhesive foam strip, usually called draught excluder, is sold in rolls especially for this purpose.

Windows not only allow the occupant of the room to look out, but also allow those outside to look in.

Where there are tools, expensive items of furniture or other attractive items, this is a security risk. Besides, not everybody likes what they are doing to be seen by the rest of the world. Curtains are out of the question; the amount of dust in a woodwork shop would soon make them just dirty bits of rag. Venetian blinds are an answer, but the slats would soon have a thick layer of dust on them and they need regular cleaning.

Obscure Georgian wired glass was fitted for the secondary glazing in my workshop, with one exception: the centre sash in the window over the bench has clear wired glass, so that I can see out. This window has a Venetian blind over it. There were two reasons for choosing the wired glass: first, the wire acts as a deterrent to the casual housebreaker, and second, Georgian glass is at least ¼in thick and reinforced, so it does not break when accidentally knocked with the end of a length of timber. The uneven surface of this glass is, however, inclined to hold the dust that settles on it.

Ventilation

The variations in climate in Britain require that some means of ventilating the workshop will be needed. As previously stated, I have experience only of workshops in the UK. The suitability of the ambient air condition for working wood in other locations will probably be different. Being able to open windows in the summer makes working conditions more pleasant, and if you have an external door this can also be left open during warm weather. It may be necessary to instal some form of forced air ventilation; a simple way of achieving this is to instal a fan unit in a window. There are units that will extract stale air from the top and blow fresh air in at the bottom: one could easily be installed if it was found that the air in the shop became dead after working in there for a while. This can be left until there is a need for it.

There is a further item when considering the condition of the air in the workshop. As wood is a hydroscopic material, it is affected by the moisture content of the air. Depending on the type of work undertaken and the locality of the workshop, there may be a need for some form of air conditioning. For the normal size of home workshop, a small portable unit would be sufficient. Air conditioning is discussed more fully in Chapter 6.

The floor

There are several factors to be considered on this topic. I have already mentioned the load-bearing characteristics of floors (see page 7). It is most important that woodworking machines are secure and stable – the floor breaking up under a circular saw while it is in use is a mind-boggling image. Some knowledge of the different forms of floor structure is necessary in order to judge the suitability of a floor.

There are two distinct types of ground floor: **suspended** and **solid**. Within these two types there are a few variations. The type of floor will depend on the age of the building: suspended timber ground floors were common until 1939, but the cost and availability of suitable timber has meant that most ground floors are now solid. There has also been a tendency over the past 30 years to reduce the amount of timber used in the floor to a minimum, which of course has an effect on the strength. Added to this, the quality of timber used has also been reduced. If you have a recently built house, don't panic – the floor will probably be solid.

Fig 4.2 shows a typical suspended floor, and the position of each member mentioned in the following discussion. It will be helpful if you can lift a floorboard and inspect the underfloor structure. It may be necessary to take up the floorboards when additional electrical installations are put in, and perhaps two birds can be killed with one stone. Have a good look under the floor with your torch and a mirror. First, what size are the floor joists? Older floors will probably be 4in x 2in, while newer properties may have 3in x 2in or 4in x 1½in joists. How far apart are the joists? You can see this clearly if you have taken a board up. If no boards have been lifted, the distance apart of the rows of nails fixing the floorboards will show the joist spacing.

The one thing that is important and cannot be seen by lifting just one board is the number and distance apart of the sleeper walls. Is there bare earth or concrete between the sleeper walls? Some cheap terraced housing built in the 1920s did not have site concrete: the sleeper walls stand directly on the earth. Most of the floors constructed in this fashion

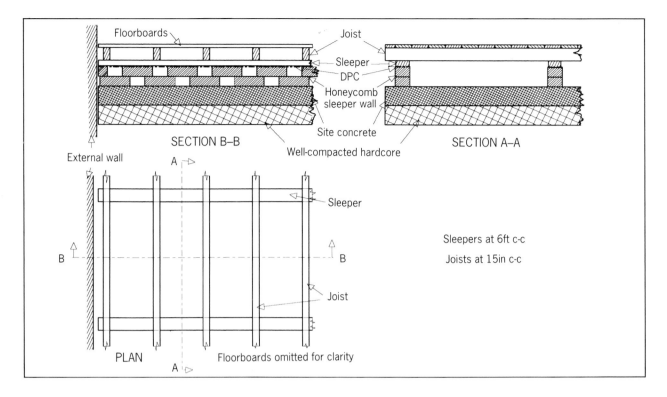

Floorboards
Joist
Sleeper
DPC
Honeycomb
sleeper wall
Site concrete
SECTION B–B
Well-compacted hardcore
SECTION A–A

External wall
A
Sleeper

Sleepers at 6ft c-c
Joists at 15in c-c

B
B

Joist

PLAN
A
Floorboards omitted for clarity

Fig 4.2 Suspended timber ground floor.

have been replaced, as they were subject to dry rot and have long since perished. The thickness of the boards will be in the range $\frac{3}{4}$in – 1in nominal, the finished thickness being $\frac{9}{16}$in – $\frac{13}{16}$in.

Armed with this information, some way of estimating the load-bearing potential of the floor is needed. There is no replacement for experience here, but common sense will dictate if a floor is really unsuitable. The best conditions would probably be:

■ Sleeper walls 4ft – 5ft apart, on concrete.

■ Joists 4in x 2in spaced 15in centres.

■ $\frac{7}{8}$in finished thick floorboards.

A floor constructed as above would safely support a dead load of 90lbs per square foot, if it was evenly spread and not a point load. However the following conditions may be found:

■ Sleeper walls 6ft – 7ft apart on concrete.

■ Joists 3in x 2in spaced 18in centres.

■ $\frac{9}{16}$in finished thick floorboards.

The maximum dead load that should be imposed on this floor is 40lbs per square foot.

From the above it is possible to make a fairly accurate estimate of what a floor will support. If the loads that the floor will have to support are greater than those which you estimate it will safely support, there are two alternative solutions. The first is to spread the load over a larger area. This can be accomplished by covering the floor with a thick sheet material; flooring quality chipboard would serve. This method is particularly useful where the item to be installed has feet or legs: these will impose a load on a very small area, so something that will distribute this point load over a wider area must be used. This can even be a $\frac{1}{4}$in thick steel plate.

When dealing with a point load, the position of the joists will have to be

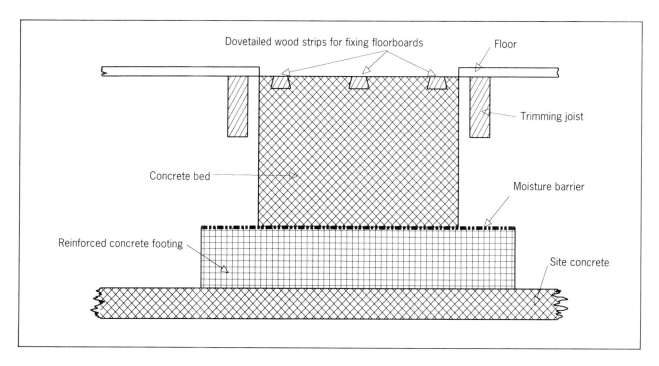

Dovetailed wood strips for fixing floorboards

Floor

Trimming joist

Concrete bed

Moisture barrier

Reinforced concrete footing

Site concrete

Fig 4.3 Schematic section through machine bed.

considered. If the load falls between two joists the boards will be subjected to a very strong bending stress. Common sense must prevail: don't just overload the floor and keep your fingers crossed. Where spreading the load will still not allow the installation of a heavy machine, a proper bed will have to be made.

MAKING A MACHINE BED

The floor where the machine will stand is removed. Where joists have to be cut out, the ends that remain under the floor will need to be supported by a new sleeper wall. Timber shuttering 6in deep is erected in the hole on the site concrete; this should be arranged box-fashion so that a slab of concrete considerably bigger than the hole in the floor can be cast. Concrete is laid in the bottom of the box formed by the shuttering. Reinforcing in the form of welded steel fabric to BS4483 needs to be inserted after a layer of concrete 3in thick has been laid. This slab needs to be 1ft bigger on each side than the finished machine bed, e.g. taking a bed 3ft x 4ft, a slab 5ft x 6ft would be laid.

When the concrete is hard, a waterproof membrane is applied: this can be a liquid waterproofing agent that is painted over the concrete in three separate applications, each applied after the previous coat has dried. A polythene sheet not less than 500 gauge, but preferably 1000 gauge, can be used as a membrane. Hot poured bitumen in a layer at least 3mm thick will also serve. Building regulation C3(1) requires that: 'Such part of a building as is next to the ground shall have a floor so constructed as to prevent the passage of moisture from the ground to the upper surface of the floor'.

The form work around the concrete slab can now be struck. When the membrane is in place, new shuttering is made to fit between the top of the concrete slab and the underside of the floorboards. The box so formed will allow a block the size of the machine bed to be cast. Concrete is placed in the box so that the top of the bed is level with the surface of the floor. If the floor is wooden boarded and you want to maintain its appearance, level the concrete to the underside of the

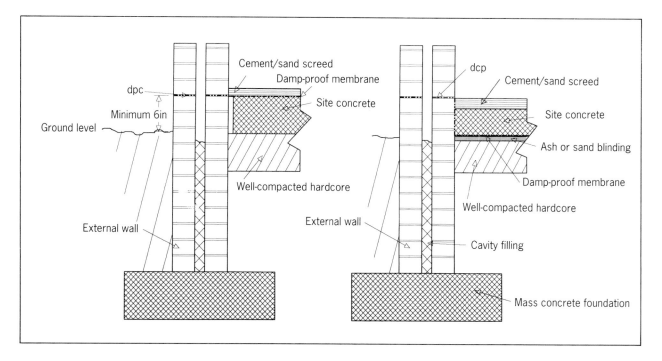

Fig 4.4 Typical solid floor at external wall.

boards. Dovetail-shaped strips of wood can be inserted into the wet concrete. When the concrete is hard, floorboards can be fixed back over the opening, nailing them to the strips of wood (*see* Fig 4.3) Some machines have provisions in their base for bolts to hold them firmly to the floor. Rag bolts can be set in the concrete bed when laying it, to coincide with these holes. A hardboard template should be made to ensure that the bolts are in the correct position, as, if they are not, severe difficulties will be caused. The problem is not usually apparent until a heavy piece of machinery is lifted and tried in place. There you are with all your helpers lifting this machine, jiggling it this way and that only to find that a bolt has to be chopped out of the concrete and repositioned. Even heavy machines need fixing down – it is surprising how much they can 'walk' over years of continual use. Coach screws can be used for this purpose on wooden floors.

Solid floors

If you are fortunate enough to have a solid floor in the room, then there is little to worry about. Unless you have machines that have their weight quoted in tons there will be no need to instal special beds. Fig 4.4 shows the section through a typical domestic solid ground floor, and you will see that this form of construction lends itself to our requirements. However, it would be unwise to subject it to a very heavy point load; some form of weight distribution, as discussed under 'suspended floors' would be advisable. If you have found a suspended floor in very poor condition, replace it with a solid floor. This is not such a colossal task as it may at first seem, and if the old floor is on the way out this job will need to be undertaken in the near future anyway.

FLOOR COVERING

The floor covering or the surface floor finish in the workshop is important. I have seen several home workshops with carpet on the floor. This is very unsuitable for most woodworking activities: a carpet or mat will collect all the sawdust and rubbish, and it is easy to trip over an edge – as you fall, you put your hands out to break the fall and are likely to stick them into a machine!

Floors must be flat and have a non-slip surface. Cement floors are hard on the feet, and should you drop an edged tool it will land so that an important corner is damaged. This is governed by the same law that states that if you drop your toast it will land buttered side down.

A wooden floor takes a lot of beating, but working on an uncovered wooden floor has two drawbacks. First, if it is a nice-looking block floor, workshop use will soon damage its appearance. This could be a problem if the room is returned to domestic use. Second, a plain boarded floor has gaps between the boards where they have shrunk, and sawdust and odd panel pins etc. will lodge in this gap and become a nuisance. Some form of hard-wearing covering is therefore desirable. There are several coverings sold in roll form that are worth considering; modern plastics come in the form of 'Cushionfloor' and similar brand names. Old-fashioned heavy grade linoleum is very durable but can become polished by sawdust – a slippery workshop floor is the last thing that is required.

Covering the floor with tempered hardboard and coating it with deck paint can be very successful. My present workshop floor has this covering, and apart from repainting it twice and trying out an adhesive strip called 'Safewalk' it is as good as the day I put it down 10 years ago. Deck paint is obtainable from yacht chandlers, and gives an anti-slip surface. There are several floor paints made for industrial floors, some of which are epoxy based; most of them are only obtainable in large quantities. 'Safewalk' is a very useful product; I used strips 1in wide, 4in apart, and they work fine, even when painted over with deck paint.

WALLS

The decoration on the walls of a domestic room can vary from smooth emulsion paint to a textured plaster surface. Textured surfaces, even that of anaglypta wallpaper, are unsuitable for a workshop – a smooth light-coloured surface is what is required. Your workshop is a place where you must be at ease and feel relaxed. Given the criterion stated at the start of this chapter, the choice of decoration must be one that you are happy with.

Dark or dull colours will absorb light – I might appear to be harping on about this subject of light but it is very important, and should not be overlooked. A white ceiling will reflect light down into the working area. I have worked for some years very happily in a workshop with honey-coloured walls and a white ceiling; given the time over again, I would choose exactly the same.

ELECTRICITY

The supply to the workshop is an important consideration at this stage. The workshop needs its own supply from the main distribution board, and the chances of a domestic room having this are remote. *See* Chapter 6 for full details.

REVERSION

When converting the room to a workshop, remember that it will probably return to its original use one day – it is therefore a good policy to alter things as little as possible. This is not all that easy if you want to put in hefty machines, and it may pay in the long run to find alternatives that do not require alterations to the structure.

A SEPARATE BUILDING

Exactly what constitutes a building is a debatable point. We are not talking here about the typical garden shed –

Fig 4.5 Newspapers rolled up and laced together with string. This makes a very good thermal insulation when fixed between the studs of a timber building before the inside lining is fitted.

but then I suppose there are sheds and sheds. The minimum size worth looking at will depend on the type of work you intend to produce. If you do knife carving only, a disused privy could suffice – this is not intended to be facetious but to make the point that only you will know the size you need. The exercise described in Chapter 2 may help you decide.

Having found a building of suitable size, the type of structure needs consideration, e.g. a timber-framed building clad on the outside with weatherboarding will need a lot of work to make it suitable, but a brick building with a tile roof would be almost ready for immediate occupation. The first step is to list all the things that need doing – and on completing this, it may be decided it will not be worth the bother!

For example, returning to that timber-framed building with the weatherboarding – what type of boarding is it (*see* Chapter 2)? Is it weatherproof? If not, how much work will be needed to make it so? Some form of lining will be needed; hardboard will probably be the cheapest.

Before fixing, the hardboard should be laid out and soaked with water from a garden hosepipe. It is then nailed to the framework in a soaking condition. Wetting the hardboard makes it expand. As it shrinks it becomes as tight as a drum skin and makes a good flat wall. If it is fixed in a dry condition it absorbs moisture from the atmosphere and expands. Because it is fixed to the framework and there is nowhere for it to expand to, the surface bows in or out between studs, leaving a wall with a wave-like surface.

Thermal insulation should not be forgotten. A very effective insulation can be made by using old newspapers rolled up and held in place under lengths of string (see Fig 4.5). Before lining with the hardboard, a moisture barrier should be fixed inside the timber frame. Polythene sheet works well here.

WINDOWS

Apart from double glazing windows, there is the question of their position and size. There is little difficulty in putting in another window in a timber-framed building. With a brick-built structure, things may not be so easy. However the chances are that it will be a single-storey building. There will be little weight, if any, above the window, so making a hole to receive a new one is not a big job, although you must be confident that you know what you are doing before you start. Getting one of these from the library and studying it should be sufficient education. I have always found the average woodworker an adaptable character, able to turn his hand to most things.

LOCATION AND ACCESS

The position of the building in relation to other buildings is important. This has been well covered on page 7, but there are one or two other factors that need thinking about. For instance like all other human beings, woodworkers need toilet facilities from time to time – and a tin can in the corner is not the best answer.

THE ROOF

The roof can vary from a couple of purlins and corrugated sheets to a boarded and tiled structure. Providing that the roof is stable and watertight, it will do. There is always a storage problem in the workshop, so if there is space up in the roof to store timber, it should be used.

Something should be done with a roof that is just clad with a single layer of sheet material. The heat transfer through this part of the workshop will be a constant problem: in the winter most of the heat will go out this way, and in summer the workshop can become unbearably hot from the sun. The easiest solution may be to instal a ceiling with a layer of glass wool on top of it as insulation.

SECURITY

An isolated building these days risks being burgled or vandalised; there may even be a need for shutters on the windows. I know of several craftsmen who have even had a workshop in their garden broken into. It must be worthwhile installing an alarm system: while the police seem to ignore them when they go off, one will at least let you know what is happening if you are around at the time. Security type door locks are well worth installing; make sure that the edge of the door and the frame where the lock keep is installed are reinforced with metal, as these are the first places to give if a door is forced with a jemmy. A large, well-trained dog is the best investment although someone who has broken in and is attacked by the dog may have a case against the owner!

CHAPTER FIVE
SAFETY

DON'T BE ALARMED

Some of the subjects covered in this chapter are unpleasant, but they are best faced squarely and precautions taken to stop the worst happening. Please do not think that the risks are being exaggerated, and move on to the next chapter. I remember going some years ago, to a meeting of a professional body of woodworkers, where there were at least 30 members present. Of those, only two of us could order 10 pints, i.e. had a full complement of fingers. Having once spent a while searching in the sawdust for a workmate's fingers with a plastic bag of ice, I have learned to be very careful.

Today, because of the woodcutting machinery regulations, most operatives still have all their fingers. The factory inspector is not prepared to overlook even the slightest infringement. The problem here is that these regulations and their enforcement do not apply to the home workshop, where there are no employees. You must take account of these and enforce them yourself.

ON YOUR OWN

The average home workshop occupant will be on their own 90 per cent of the time. This in itself is a safety risk, particularly so when there is no one within hailing distance. What would you do if there was an accident? Think about it, and have some plan of action, which you hope will never be acted upon. With woodcutting machinery there can be horrendous accidents. The sensible woodworker faces this fact and does not assume that accidents only happen to other people.

Having earned my living in the trade for nearly 50 years, during which time I worked in large wood mills, and in small ones with two or three employees, I have only witnessed two bad accidents. Both were caused by the operatives doing something that was not supposed to be done – and these were men who had served an apprenticeship and were fully trained to operate the machines.

The home woodworker is often self-taught, and does not have the benefit of professional training, so he may expose himself to risks of which he is unaware. There are several important items that should be installed in the workshop to reduce the risk, and if the worst happens, deal with it to minimize the damage.

ELECTRICITY

What can be done to protect the craftsman using electrically powered tools? To give an example, the belt sander needs two hands to control it properly; it is used on large flat surfaces where it is moved back and forth in long sweeps; as it travels back and forth it needs a good deal of slack flex if its use is not to be restricted. It is very easy for the wire to be picked up by the belt and wound up in the drive. The abrasive soon cuts the insulation away, exposing the bare conductor wire. The machine becomes electrified, and so does the operator. With any luck he will drop the machine, but what happens if the wire is wrapped around his wrist and he is unable to?

There is a small electric device called a residual current circuit breaker (RCCB) that can turn the current off if the worst happens; it is essential in a one-person shop. This item compares the current flowing into the circuit with that flowing out. Where there is a difference, some electricity must be leaking out and the component turns the supply off in microseconds. This is a rather simplified version of what happens, but you will see why it is so important.

Because we cannot see electricity, it is easy to become blasé about it. This was brought home to me with force a few years ago: my son and I were making some adjustments to the drive on a table saw. I was lying on the floor with my hands up inside the works – the electric isolator on the machine had been turned off, so one assumed that the machine was electrically dead. Suddenly I received a tremendous electric shock from the frame of the machine that was pressed against my shoulder. My other shoulder was against a central heating radiator which, being connected to the water system, was an ideal earth. There I was, wedged in, with electricity passing across my body through the region of the heart. I could not move or speak, but was perfectly aware of what was happening. It seemed ages before my son pulled me out, though he assured me it was only a matter of seconds. Apart from the electric shock I suffered physical shock, which seriously affected me for several hours. The electrical installation in the workshop had an earth trip that I mistakenly thought would protect me in this situation. I consulted an expert electrician, who installed an RCCB.

The main switch

There is another essential electrical item: it is installed just inside the workshop entrance door. It has a label proclaiming in large letters "MAIN SWITCH. STOPS ALL MACHINES"

(*see* Fig 5.1). All the members of the household should know what this switch does and where it is, so they do not have to go searching around for it. Should there be an accident where clothing becomes entangled with revolving parts, or any other occurrence where you are unable to turn off the machine yourself, it can be very quickly done by somebody else. This switch also makes a very useful isolator. When leaving the workshop it is so easy to just throw the switch; everything is then dead, and there can be no fires caused by defective insulation or similar hazards.

Fig 5.1 Main electricity switch with prominent notice, and BCF fire extinguisher.

The switch gear on machines should be easily reached from the operating position. Most of my machines have the off switch positioned so that I can press it with my knee when standing in the operating position. I nearly always turn the machine off in this way, so should I have to shut down quickly, it is a reflex action to press my knee against the button. If the machine is large and does not have just one operating position, a second switch should be installed – this is particularly necessary on a thicknesser.

MACHINE GUARDS

Like so many other things, safety is a case of using one's common sense. The small booklet issued by the Health and Safety Executive Book, 41, *Safety in the use of woodworking machines*, is obtainable from HM Stationery Office and should be studied.

Some machines sold on the amateur market do not comply with the woodcutting regulations. The guards that the regulations stipulate should be regarded as a minimum. If you have to remove a guard to carry out an operation, you are doing something that the machine was not designed to do and you are placing yourself at risk.

A very good example of this is the riving knife on a circular saw. It is not there to stop the back of the saw marking the wood, it is to stop the wood pinching, one of the main causes of accidents on this type of machine. The saw revolves towards the operator. This means that the saw's teeth are travelling downwards where they cut the wood, forcing the wood down on to the saw table, and everything is nice and stable. The teeth at the back of the saw are therefore travelling upwards. If the saw kerf closes and pinches on the saw blade the wood is thrown upwards. The peripheral speed of the teeth on a circular saw is 9,500 feet per minute. Perhaps that figure does not mean much, but it is around 108 mph. Just think what happens when a piece of wood is picked up at this speed. There is no time to think 'Oh dear, the wood is pinching' – the end of the wood farthest away from the operator goes up in the air. It is snatched from the operator's hands, which, because of their position and the force being applied to the wood, go into the blade revolving at 108 mph. *Don't ever remove the riving knife.*

Perhaps you think this is overstating the danger of woodworking machinery. The point about danger is to recognize it: one can then avoid most situations where an accident is likely to occur. Anyone would think you a fool if you walked down the centre of a busy city street – this is because we are all aware of the dangers involved.

A young friend who is a very good mechanical engineer uses metal cutting machines all day long. His hobby is woodworking, and recently he was surface planing some wood. Needing to check the length of one piece, he placed it on the out table of the surface planer. Taking his measuring tape, he placed the hook over the end of the timber with his left hand. The tape reel was in his right hand, which he moved instinctively without looking at the other end of the timber. The hand went past the end of the timber into the unguarded cutter block. The bridge guard had been removed because it was a nuisance when planing wide boards.

There is another danger of which you should be aware. Offcuts of wood can be thrown by the revolving saw blade at its peripheral speed. This is a particular risk when rebating on the saw by running in from each face.

When the saw releases the lath so cut, this sliver of wood is between the saw and the fence. The saw can throw the offcut down the workshop at 108 mph – just like an arrow. Never stand in line with the saw when it is being used, or allow anybody else to. (Incidentally, rebating in this way contravenes the woodcutting regulations. Although the regulations only apply to commercial premises employing people, they are worth complying with for your own benefit.)

All woodcutting machine cutters travel at speeds similar to those mentioned above. This is particularly worth remembering with regard to spindle moulders and similar machines that have the blades attached to a revolving spindle. Although the cutters may only be small pieces of steel, centrifugal force imposes heavy G loads upon them, which can throw the cutter out of the machine – you can imagine what a piece of sharp steel going across the workshop at a speed in excess of 100 mph can do! Make sure all cutters and blocks are fixed properly and never allow anything to interrupt the fitting of cutters. If called away in the middle of changing a cutter, it is so easy to forget that nuts have not been properly tightened up; on returning the machine is started, and the worst happens.

FIRE PREVENTION

Just stop and consider for a moment; if you wanted to start a fire, what would you use? Flammable liquid and shavings, probably – just what the average workshop contains. Therefore precautions must be taken to reduce the risk of fire.

Rules need to be made and religiously kept, e.g. all shavings and rags to be removed from the workshop at the end of each working period. Dirty rags are notorious for catching fire through spontaneous combustion, and rags that have been used for finishing with an oil will become quite hot as the oil residue left in them oxidizes. Shavings will ignite very easily and become a raging inferno in seconds. French polish and most other finishes contain a highly volatile solvent, so only small quantities of these should be brought into the workshop; larger quantities must be stored outside. A concrete coal bunker is ideal for this purpose: all flammable substances can be stored in this bunker, thus removing the risk from the workshop.

What happens if a fire starts while you are in the workshop? First, how do you get out? Second, have you got the equipment to fight the fire? When the local fire prevention officer visited my workshop to advise me on fire precautions, he was quite impressed with the firefighting equipment that I had installed, but was not at all happy with the escape route. I had thought that with a smallish workshop the door would be the obvious choice: there would be plenty of time to get out, so it would just be a question of walking across the workshop. After a visit to the fire station where I saw a film, I now know that a room can become a ball of fire within seconds. The way to the door can be barred, so a window or a second door should be available for a quick exit at the other end of the workshop. This exit needs to be kept clear; odd lengths of timber should not be stacked against it.

There are various types of fire extinguisher available, each with a particular use – a water-filled extinguisher would be ideal on a wood fire, but would be useless on an oil or electrical fire. There are basically three distinct types of extinguisher:

CO_2 is a liquid-gas-filled cylinder; the gas smothers the fire, starving it of oxygen; as it vaporises it has a cooling effect. This is a useful general purpose extinguisher.

Powder-filled extinguishers can be used on most fires, including electrical. The problem is that when used on a minor fire the powder gets everywhere. Like the CO_2, this extinguisher works by smothering the fire.

BCF stands for bromoclorodifluoro-methane. These are the most up-to-date extinguishers reportedly the most effective, and of course the most expensive (*see* Fig 5.1).

A **fire blanket** is a useful item which can be used to smother a small fire with immediate effect. Old asbestos blankets are a health hazard and one made from the new fibres should be obtained.

HOUSEKEEPING

A tidy and clean workshop is a safe workshop.

Keep the floor clear of offcuts. It is very easy to twist or sprain an ankle by stepping on one of these – as you cut them off, kick them under the end of the bench, out of the way.

Don't let the surface of the floor become highly polished by sawdust. To fall over with a sharp tool in your hand is the last thing you want. A non-slip floor is a necessity: if you slip or fall, the instinctive thing to do is to put your hands out to save yourself – a very dangerous thing to do when there are woodcutting machines about. Hardwood dust is a health hazard; don't let it accumulate. A good vacuum cleaner with a large hose is a wise investment.

Lengths of timber haphazardly leaned against the wall have a habit of falling over. A hit on the head with a lump of four-by-two is not at all to be recommended.

Label all bottles and containers; do not let nearly empty paint tins and their like accumulate.

GENERAL HEALTH

A small first aid cabinet is one of the first things you should make (*see* Fig 5.2). While there is no need for the type of thing one sees in a commercial wood mill, the odd sticking plaster or

Fig 5.2 A first aid box; the contents will vary according to the owner's requirements.

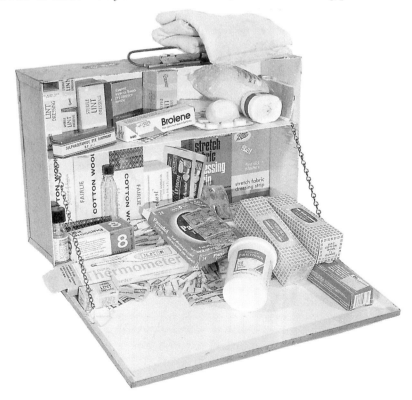

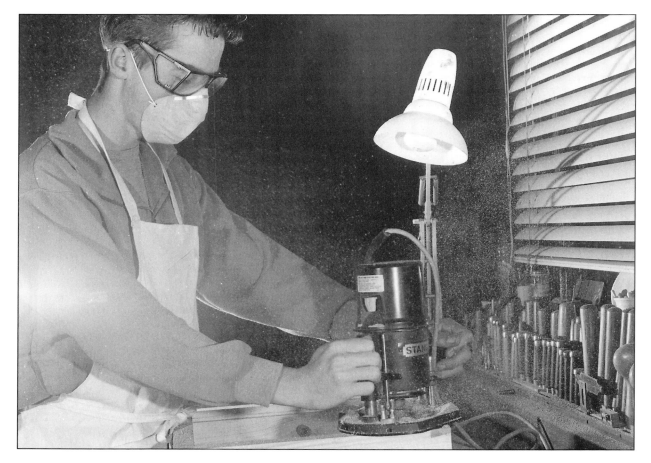

bandage will be needed. These need to be kept clean and somewhere close at hand. Small cuts and abrasions should be cleaned and covered immediately they are sustained – incidentally, most professional woodworkers keep up-to date with their anti-tetanus injections.

Protective items, e.g. ear defenders, dust masks, and eye protection, need to be to hand; they should be carefully looked after and periodically inspected for wear or damage (*see* Fig 5.3). As soon as any defect is observed, the item should be replaced.

Many modern adhesives and finishes give off pungent fumes which are injurious to your health. Work in a well-ventilated environment when using them. They can also be quite explosive, so keep naked lights away from the working area.

A noise that at the time does not seem all that loud will have an effect on the hearing when a person is exposed to it for a length of time – the high-pitched whine of a router is one of these sounds. When in doubt, wear ear defenders.

ALARMS

If the workshop is attached or within the house, a smoke alarm is a necessity. Over the past few years these have been fitted in most homes and demand has meant that volume production has brought the price down.

Burglar alarms have already been mentioned in Chapter 4. Contact the local police station for advice on what to instal. The police will be happy to send their crime prevention officer along; he is an expert and will be aware of things you might never have thought of. What is more, his advice is free, which in these days is a recommendation on its own.

Fig 5.3 Wearing a face mask and safety glasses to use a large portable router.

CHAPTER SIX
SERVICES

ELECTRICITY

It is almost impossible to imagine what a workshop without electricity would be like. Even if it is only used for lighting, it is such an improvement on any other form of artificial illumination that it can almost be considered essential.

Our house is out in the country, surrounded by woods. The electricity supply is by overhead wires. During the storms of 1987 trees fell on the power lines, and we were without electricity for over a week. The whole pattern of life changed: even the tropical fish tanks had to be kept warm by floating bottles of hot water in them. The workshop was almost at a standstill. Even after a week I would still walk up to a machine and automatically push the switch, only to realise that I would have to rip the piece of wood by hand.

The supply of electricity to the workshop means that it has to be connected to the mains, probably by way of a distribution board in the house – this is the point where the meter and main switch gear are situated. A rented garage or other building away from home will need to have its own meter and distribution board installed by the electricity supply company. Any installation on the consumer's side of the board should be done by a qualified electrician.

WIRING

A few words about the electrical installations in general may not come amiss. We all tend to take it for granted that once the installation, e.g. wires, plugs, switches, lights and machinery, is installed it can safely be forgotten. Unfortunately, like everything else, all these components age. If an existing installation is being used, perhaps with a few extra plugs, some inspection is required. If you find that the connecting wires are insulated with rubber and are sheathed with rubber or lead, the electric wiring is more than 40 years old and should be replaced; this is because the rubber insulation will have perished and become brittle, and there is a danger of fire from this poor insulation.

Cable is used for all the permanently fixed wiring in a building. It carries the electrical current from the distribution box to all the various outlets – lights, power sockets and machines. These cables should be fixed about every 12in with a cable clip; they must not be left to just hang loose. Where a cable runs at right angles to a joist it is fed through holes bored on the centre line of the joist. This puts the hole in the neutral stress layer of the joist and keeps it sufficiently low to escape any nails driven into the floor.

Cables are of different sizes for various circuits depending on how much current they have to carry. The size is stated by the cross area of the wire in square millimetres. Lighting circuits are wired in $1mm^2$ twin and earth cable and protected by a 5amp fuse. This circuit will supply a maximum of 1 200W.

A ring main, i.e. a complete loop of wire starting and ending at the distribution board, serves power points of usually 13amp sockets. The wire used is 2.5mm twin with earth, and this circuit is usually protected with a 30amp fuse. This will supply

7200W. It is a good idea to ensure that only fused plugs are used. Refer to Chapter 12, and calculate the minimum size of fuse required, and make sure that is the one fitted in the plug.

Only one plug should be inserted in a socket; adapters that allow more than one plug should never be used. Should a plug or socket get hot, turn the appliance off, and check the wire connections inside the plug. If these have become corroded, cut about 1in off the end of the wire, strip the insulation off and remake the joint, securing the new clean end with the clamping screw. If this does not cure the problem, call a qualified electrician.

Machines that draw a heavy current should have their own individual circuit. Twin and earth cable should be used; the wire will be 6mm². A fuse of 30amps will serve a machine drawing 7200W. A larger machine will require wire of 10mm² with a 45amp fuse; this will supply 10,800W, around 14hp. All the figures above have assumed single phase at 240 volts (see below).

The electrical contracting industry has set certain levels for its National Vocational Qualification, and anyone working in the industry must have these minimum qualifications. However, ensure that anyone employed to instal or service your electrical installation is an approved contractor of the National Inspection Council for Electrical Installation Contracting. This is a non-profit-making organisation to protect consumers against unsound electrical installations.

SINGLE- OR THREE-PHASE
Unless you intend installing some big machinery, only single-phase will be required (most industrial machines require a three-phase electrical supply). It is possible to use a converter to run three-phase equipment from the single-phase supply: in most cases, this is a lower-cost alternative to having the supply company connect three-phase.

Three-phase requires four wires, as opposed to the two that single-phase uses. Three-phase is in fact three single-phase supplies with a common return. The mains alternating current has a frequency of 50Hz, i.e. it changes its direction of flow 50 times per second. The point when each of the three phases changes direction is staggered so that the current flow adds together. The voltage from a three-phase supply is 415V, compared with the 240V of single-phase – this additional voltage will deliver an electric shock more severe than that from a single-phase supply. One of the advantages of three-phase over single-phase concerns the size of the motor. For equal power the three-phase motor is much smaller, and this is particularly noticeable for 3hp motors and above.

You will need to be able to tell the person doing the installation exactly what you require, most of which will come from the plans you have made (*see* Chapter 2). A decision will have to be made if electricity is taken from a house to a workshop in the garden: is the cable to be buried in the ground or suspended overhead? The distance the cable has to be laid will have some effect on this: short distances of several yards are best spanned overhead, while longer distances are best put in a pipe buried underground.

POWER POINTS
The number and position of power points needs careful consideration. There were eight in the immediate vicinity of my bench. Portable lights often account for three sockets. There are two grinders, a vacuum cleaner, and a fan heater, which only leaves

one for portable power tools. Recently I had a batch of four more installed above the bench, hung from the ceiling with a special fitting. As this is right over the centre of the bench, it is ideal for power tools. Besides these, there are two double socket units located at the extreme end of the shop.

One of the best ways to decide how many power points you require is to list all the items that will be plugged in at any one time, and then add two as spares. This may seem more than enough, but you will still find yourself unplugging one device before you can plug another in. Items that are used quite often are best left plugged in even when not in use – it is a bind if every time you pick something up to use it needs plugging in.

Manufacturers have expanded the range of cableless power tools. These have a rechargeable battery, which is fine until it becomes run down.

Unless you have spare power packs for these tools, they will be out of commission while the battery is being recharged – which of course is just when you wish to use them!

The switch mentioned in Chapter 5 that turned off the current to all the machines should also turn off all the power points as well. When leaving the workshop at the end of work the switch can be thrown: everything except the lights will then be dead. The switches installed in some portable tools tend to wear out, and electricity arcing across the contacts causes heat. A tool in this condition left connected to a live power point, is a fire hazard. All risks are removed if the circuit is isolated by a switch from the mains.

ARTIFICIAL LIGHT
Different types of work require different forms of lighting: in woodcarving the shape being carved

Fig 6.1 Movable spotlights clipped to a batten over the bench; note the bulldog clips which keep the wiring tidy and safe.

relies on shadows to show its shape and there is a need for directional lighting that will throw these shadows; setting out, however, needs shadowless lighting – there is nothing worse than trying to align a straightedge when the point it is being aligned to disappears in the shadow of the edge. These two examples suggest that more than one form of lighting is available.

Ordinary tungsten bulbs in reflectors give directional lighting; if portable, they can be moved to give the best results. Small spotlights come with an adjustable stalk and a clip that will attach them to any suitable protuberance (see Fig 6.1) – fix some strips of wood at strategic places around the bench where these lights can be clipped. In this way exactly the right amount of light can be brought to shine on the job from exactly the right direction. The bulbs for these small portable spotlights have part of their glass envelope silvered on the inside to act as a reflector. They produce a hard directional light ideal for carving and woodfinishing.

Fluorescent tubes are the best general lighting for the small workshop. The lighting can be almost shadowless if their positioning is carefully planned. When choosing fluorescent tubes, thought needs to be given to the temperature of the light they will emit. If staining and polishing is undertaken, specify Northlight Colour Matching tubes.

If there are a number of tube lights in the workshop, it is useful to have them individually switched. Ceiling pull switches are ideal for this: each light can be switched on from its position without having to walk to a wall switch, and if the cords on these ceiling switches are kept short, they will be well above head level. Having the lights switched like this makes it easy to have the light where it is required without having the whole workshop brilliantly lit when not needed, which helps keep the electricity bill down. (If you are one of the few people who do not have to worry about the bills, think of the energy you are saving.)

The type of reflector used for both bulbs and tubes has a tremendous influence on the efficiency of the light radiated – even kitchen foil behind a tube can give worthwhile results – although it is quite difficult to find a good reflector for fluorescent tube lights. A new tube installation unit often includes a diffuser that clips over the unit enclosing the tube: these might give a nice soft light, but they are useless in the workshop. I found a heavy vitreous enamelled reflector among some junk, and this has proved ideal above the bench. This type of reflector is not still available, but a fairly efficient one can be made from bent-up aluminium sheet.

There are other sorts of electric light such as sodium or mercury vapour, but these are more suitable for large buildings.

HEATING

Much of the enjoyment of owning a workshop will be lost if it is not a comfortable place to work in. Temperature is enormously influential: too hot and one becomes lethargic – any manual work is a bind; too cold and, apart from being uncomfortable, the fingers cannot manipulate the tools properly.

Apart from personal comfort there are the tools to consider: they don't feel the cold but they don't take kindly to rapid changes in the temperature. If they are subjected to a warm atmosphere after a cold spell, moisture will condense on their surface. This very soon produces rust, which must be polished off as soon as it is seen. Some liquids used in woodfinishing will be spoilt if they are allowed to freeze.

It is advisable to maintain the shop at or above a certain temperature. There are several appliances made for heating greenhouses which can be used in the workshop: tube heaters installed with a thermostat can be set at a temperature of 4°–5°C (38°–40°F), which would be ideal for a detached building away from the house. (If the workshop is within the house, the chances are that there will be some form of heating.)

This type of heating – which does not allow the shop to drop below a certain temperature – is live all the time, the thermostat only switching it on when needed. When the shop is to be used, a temperature of 20°C (68°F) is needed for the working conditions in the shop to be about right. This temperature needs maintaining within fairly narrow limits – a shop can become too warm for manual work.

If the workshop is only occupied at odd periods, e.g. in the evening or at weekends, it is necessary to be able to raise the temperature quickly. When looking at the cost of running the heating system, the first thing to decide is which fuel to use. Over the years first one and then another type of fuel has been the most cost-effective; added to this, one should read the advertisements for various types of fuel with some caution as it is difficult to compare fuels. Some can be used in a system that will give instant heat, while others take time to even warm the building. Instant heat is obviously preferable where the workshop is to be occupied only in the evenings or at weekends (see below). Most fuel suppliers provide costs for the most economical system installed in a domestic building, not a workshop, so make sure you compare like with like.

One of the best installations I have seen is heated by natural gas which has an electric fan distributing warm

air through ducts. This setup warms the workshop in which it is installed in a few minutes. It is thermostatically controlled and also has a time switch. The owner of the workshop sets the timer to switch on the heating 20 minutes before he wants to start work; he comes home from his day job, has a meal and walks into a nicely warmed workshop.

This unit was installed by the local gas board, who recommend it for small flats which are unoccupied for most of the day; there are also oil-fired installations which work on a similar principle. Check the Yellow Pages directory under the various 'Heating' headings; nearly all the advertisers will offer free advice and estimates.

Butane gas in cylinders is a very useful form of fuel. Some modern heaters which burn this gas are most

Fig 6.2 Calor gas bottles on the workshop stool: the larger is more economical, but the smaller is much easier to carry!

efficient, and one variety has a catalytic element, which means that when it is burning there is no flame to be seen. I have had one of these in my workshop for several years, where it is used as a back-up heater when the weather is so cold that the normal system cannot cope. It is most efficient and cost-effective, the one drawback being the heavy cylinder, which when empty needs loading into the van and taking to the supplier for a refill. Even with a spare cylinder, this business of lugging the heavy monster around is a nuisance (*see* Fig 6.2).

Electric storage heaters are very economical but only worth considering where the workshop is occupied most of the time. The system works on the principle of heating large blocks during the period when electricity demand is low, e.g. the early hours of the morning. They are installed via a special meter, and the electricity is charged at a low tariff. This type of installation is of absolutely no use if the workshop is occupied on a casual basis. The system runs all the time and will heat the shop even if it is unoccupied. It can of course be switched off, but one needs to switch it on at least the day before it is required. The blocks will then be fully charged, with sufficient heat to last 12 hours, even if the shop is to be occupied for only two.

There are several woodburning stoves suitable for installing in a workshop; there are even stoves designed to burn sawdust and planer chips, but you will be surprised how much you need to burn to keep the workshop warm. The average man working alone part-time, would never produce enough to warrant the purchase of one of these. However, a small combustion stove that normally runs on coke will burn wood waste; all my waste is burnt on a solid fuel boiler. There is something comforting

about a real live fire, and if the stove is installed properly it will not present a fire hazard.

Installation should be carried out carefully following the manufacturer's instructions. Some suppliers have their own installation service, and it is advisable to use this. Where a live fire is installed, common sense dictates that shavings and other flammable material should be kept clear of the appliance.

Gas, electricity and solid fuel companies are all well represented in town centres, and all offer a free advice service. Get them all in and compare what they have to offer. (Remember that you are the one who has to live with what is installed in your workshop, and that salesmen can be most persuasive.)

DUST EXTRACTION

The improvements in working conditions in wood mills during my lifetime are tremendous. All woodmachinists went deaf, it was an accepted fact; all woodworkers suffered from bronchial troubles, caused by dust, as they got older. Today, good ear defenders and efficient dust extraction units are a must by law. Noise-reducing techniques, like slotted planer beds are to be found on many new machines.

Dust is a health hazard; nasal cancer caused by hardwood dust is a threat to those of us that come into contact with it. Every workshop with woodcutting machinery needs some form of dust extraction. There are units for every application, from the single portable unit suitable for use with a router to a fully installed ducted system. If you have more than one fixed machine some form of ducting should be considered. This need not be an expensive exercise, as most of what is required can be made in the workshop. A portable unit for

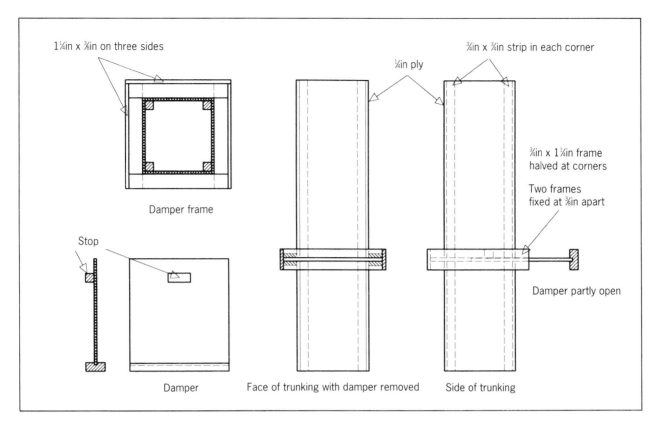

1¼in x ⅜in on three sides

Damper frame

Stop

Damper

¼in ply

Face of trunking with damper removed

⅜in x ⅜in strip in each corner

⅜in x 1¼in frame halved at corners

Two frames fixed at ⅜in apart

Damper partly open

Side of trunking

Fig 6.3 Details of plywood extractor trunking.

the single machine will be sufficient: I started with one of these, but found that it took up so much precious workshop space that I put it outside the shop and brought the intake pipe into the shop through a fanlight. Later I made plywood ducts to each machine, with dampers so only the machine in use would be served (*see* Fig 6.3). If you have a workshop without extraction and then instal a system, the sudden lack of dust is astounding.

Woodworking magazines carry advertisements from machine suppliers who offer extractors but care must be taken when choosing a suitable unit. As all of the waste goes through the fan, make sure that this is made of steel, not plastic. Several units on the market are just overgrown vacuum cleaners which draw the dust into a container, where it is separated from the air by a bag; avoid these. The true extractor *blows* the air and dust into the bag or

receiver – all the dust, shavings etc., are sucked up, pass through the fan and are then blown out.

The need for insulation and energy conservation when heating, has been discussed in previous chapters. If the extraction unit is outside the workshop, it will be sucking all your warm air out and distributing it to the atmosphere at large. Where machining requiring the extractor to run a good deal of the time is carried out, some way of recovering this warm air needs to be considered. Most extractors of the size suitable for the home woodwork shop separate the air from the dust by blowing the waste into two bags which have their open ends fitted to a common ring. The dust and waste drop into the lower bag, which is usually made of plastic, and the air escapes through the upper bag, which is made from a fabric material.

Large installations, where it would be a nuisance to keep stopping work because the bag was full and needed changing, have cyclones. These are the large conical metal contraptions that can be seen on the roof or at the back of wood mills. The cyclone works on the principle that wood, being heavier than air, will fly to the outside when the air is blown around in a circular motion inside a cylinder at high speed. The waste is thrown to the outside of the cylinder and drops down through a funnel-like attachment and the air is exhausted upwards from the centre of the top of the cyclone.

Double unit extractors are needed where several machines are to run at the same time; these have two sets of bags and a more powerful motor. For a system where only one machine is connected at any one time, a 3/4hp motor would be the appropriate size. Double units that allow three machines to be connected at the same time usually have 2hp motors. If you only use one machine at the time because you work on your own, you can connect the machines to the system via a damper; this allows the extraction to each machine to be turned on or off. Dampers are quite easy to make (see Fig 6.3).

A unit placed outside the shop will need some form of protection against the weather. Enclosing the extractor within a weathertight box means that the exhausted air can be ducted back to the workshop, thus saving the warm air. A two-way damper can be fitted into this return so that exhausted air can be directed into the shop or into the atmosphere outside. The extractor can be used in the summer to change the air in the workshop, and in the winter to return the warm air to the shop

Extractors are rated by the volume of air they pass in an hour. This is usually stated in cubic metres per hour; a small unit suitable for connecting to a portable router would be rated at 500m^3/hr, and a larger unit that could be ducted to several machines would be rated at 2,000m^3/hr. This is a useful way of comparing the efficiency of one extractor against another. When connecting a machine to the extraction by ducting, the efficiency is reduced in proportion to the length of the ducting. It is usual to have fairly large ducting near the extractor reducing in size as it reaches the machine. Extractors suitable for a small workshop with several machines would have an intake of 6in reducing to 4in at the machine end.

It is a good idea to fit some form of screen at the intake end of trunking; this stops cleaning rags, etc. being sucked up, as anything of this nature will entangle itself with the impeller and can damage the balance of the blades. A screen made from ½in mesh wire netting is about right. There is trunking made from plastic drainpipe,which is fine for short runs. The trunking installed by the firms that specialize is made from galvanised mild steel tube. I have found that plywood made into a box-like section works quite well; it is easy to construct this to fit exactly where you want it. Dampers to fit this square plywood trunking are simpler to construct than those for the tubular variety.

One thing will need continuous attention if you put the extractor outside the workshop: the bags fill up much quicker than you think they will, and when concentrating on the job in hand it is easy to forget about them. While talking about these plastic bags full of sawdust and planer chips, how will you dispose of them? If they are full of clean softwood waste they can be sold to a pet shop for litter. Hardwood waste is a different problem, and needs to be burnt. My waste goes on the central heating boiler.

CHAPTER SEVEN
REGULATIONS

There are two areas in which regulations affect buildings: planning permission and building regulations. As with all bureaucracy, there are reams of rules and regulations, too many to cover in this book. However, some guide is needed, and this is a simplified outline of the various regulations as they stand at the time of writing. If you have any doubts as to the legality of what you intend doing, consult a specialist. Most local council's planning departments are very helpful and will usually advise you.

Planning controls restrict the type and position of a building in relation to the environment. Building regulations control how a building will be constructed, and are framed to ensure safe and healthy accommodation with conservation of energy. Both controls are administered by the local authorities. Application must be made to them and permission received before any work is started.

PLANNING PERMISSION

While the regulations may seem a nuisance at first sight, just think of the situation if any old thing could be built: it would not be long before the situation became untenable. The planning laws exist to obtain the greatest possible environmental advantage with the least inconvenience, both for the individual and society as a whole. A planning application gives both the local authority and the general public the opportunity to consider the proposition, and to decide whether it is in the general interest of the locality.

Some forms of development do not require permission. These are known as permitted developments, and include the erection of boundary walls and fences under a given height, and extensions to buildings of limited size. There is also the change of use rule, such as running a business from a home listed as residential. In this case, permission would have to be obtained before starting the business.

There are two types of planning application: outline planning permission and full planning permission. Outline permission gives an owner or prospective owner approval in principle of a proposed development without the need for full working drawings. Before any building work is undertaken, full permission must be obtained. The outline permission can be dispensed with and full permission sought at the start.

Application for full planning permission will normally entail submitting four completed copies of a form, and a plan, drawn to a scale of not less than 1:2500, which shows the site, (usually shaded in red) and its relationship to adjacent properties. Further drawings of a scale not less than 1:100 need to be produced: these must show a clear picture of any new building and include any features that exist on the site, e.g. trees. The position of the proposed building within the site must be shown and the type and colour of material used for the outside walls and roof should be indicated. The proposed access to the site needs to be disclosed.

The application is considered by the planning committee and is open to inspection by the general public.

After consideration the planning committee can:

- grant permission

- refuse permission

- grant permission with certain conditions.

In the case of a refusal or the imposition of conditions, the committee must give reasons for their decision. An applicant may then modify the proposed development and re-submit the application. It is possible to appeal against a decision to the Secretary of State for the Environment.

THE BUILDING REGULATIONS 1991

Anyone wishing to erect a new building, extend or alter an existing one, or change the use of an existing one, will probably have to apply for building regulation approval.

The regulations are supported by a manual and a set of approved documents. The manual lists the type of buildings to which the regulations apply. The system of inspection and control are also described.

The approved documents give practical guidance on ways of complying with the regulations. When designing a building, you are free to use the solutions given in the documents. The documents are divided into 13 parts labelled A to N:

Part A   Structure
Part B   Fire
Part C   Site preparation and resistance to moisture
Part D   Toxic substances
Part E   Resistance to the passage of sound
Part F   Ventilation
Part G   Hygiene
Part H   Drainage and waste disposal

Part J   Heat-producing appliances
Part K   Stairways, ramps and guards
Part L   Conservation, fuel and power
Part M   Access and facilities for disabled people
Part N   Glazing – materials and protection .

APPLICATION OF THE BUILDING REGULATIONS

Certain types of building are exempt from the building regulations:

Class 1 Buildings controlled by other legislation, e.g. Explosives Acts; Nuclear Installations Act; Ancient Monuments and Archaeological Areas Act.

Class 2 Buildings not used by people, e.g. a detached building where people cannot or do not normally go.

Class 3 Glasshouses and agricultural buildings.

Class 4 Temporary buildings and mobile homes. (Temporary buildings are defined as those which are to remain erected for less than 28 days.)

Class 5 Ancillary buildings, e.g. temporary building site accommodation. Any building other than a dwelling used in connection with a mine or a quarry.

Class 6 Small detached buildings, e.g. a detached building of up to 30m^2 floor area that does not contain sleeping accommodation; a detached building of up to 30m^2 floor area designed to shelter people from the effects of nuclear, chemical or conventional weapons.

Class 7 Extensions (of up to 30m^2 floor area) e.g. the ground floor extension of a building by the addition of a greenhouse, conservatory, porch, covered yard or covered way; a carport that is open on at least two sides.

Besides these 7 classes certain authorities and organisations are exempt, including the Crown; the Department of Education and Science; statutory undertakings, such as gas, electricity and water; local authorities.

BUILDING REGULATIONS APPROVAL

When approval of the building control section of the local authority is needed, they must be notified of your intentions in one of the following methods: issue of a Building Notice; deposit full plans; private certification.

Full plans application is made by depositing in duplicate full plans of the proposed works. These consist of:

■ A statement that the plans are deposited in accordance with Regulation 11(1)(b) of the Building Regulations 1991.

■ A full specification of the work.

■ A block plan showing the surrounding area.

■ A statement of the intended use of the proposed building.

■ Drawings to a scale of not less than 1: 1250 showing the size and position of the building, the boundaries and adjoining properties.

■ The provision made for drainage.

■ Details of any cavity wall insulation.

■ Details of any unvented hot water system.

■ Any other plans that are required to show that the work will comply with the regulations.

These items will be examined to see that the proposed work will comply with the regulations. A decision has to be made within five weeks, but this can be extended to two months if you agree. The plans can be rejected for one or more of the following reasons:

■ They fail to show compliance with the regulations.

■ They contravene the regulations or show insufficient detail.

There is a similar appeal system against refusal of permission as described for planning permission. It is worth noting that the local authority has the power to relax or dispense with certain requirements.

If the plans submitted are in no way defective, the authority has no alternative but to approve them. If they are rejected the authorities must give their reasons for doing so. The approval will lapse if the work is not carried out within three years.

There are advantages to the full-deposit-of-plans method of control. Once the authorities have passed the plans, they cannot take action concerning any contravention under Section 36 of the Building Act 1984. In addition, the work is supervised by the authorities' building control officer.

The person carrying out the work must give certain notices to the local authority. Regulation 14 requires the giving of the following notices to the local authority:

■ At least two day's notice of commencement before the commencement of the work

■ At least one day's notice of: the covering up of any foundation excavation, foundation, damp-proof course, concrete or other material laid over a site; or covering up any drain or private sewer subject to the regulations.

These periods of notice commence after the day on which the notice was served. The local authority must be given notice by the person undertaking the work not more than five days after completing the following:

■ The laying of any drain or private sewer, including any haunching, surrounding or trench backfilling.

■ The erection of a building.

■ The completion of any other construction work.

The local authority will issue a 'completion certificate'; this is evidence that the requirements in the certificate have been complied with.

Building notice requires that a building notice be deposited with the local authority. Surprisingly, there is no prescribed form of building notice. The notice must be signed by the person intending to carry out the work, or by his agent. It needs to be accompanied by the following information:

■ The name and address of the person intending to carry out the work.

■ A statement that it is given according to Regulation 11(1)(a).

■ A description of the location of the proposed works and the intended use of the building.

■ If it relates to the erection or extension of a building it must be accompanied by plans to a scale of not less that 1:1250. These must show its size and the position of surrounding roads and adjoining properties, the number of storeys and details of the drainage.

■ Where any local legislation applies, it must be stated how this will be complied with.

■ Where cavity wall insulation is involved, information must be supplied about the material to be used and whether it has an agreement certificate or conforms to British Standards; also whether the installer has a BSI Certificate of Registration.

■ If there is to be a hot water system covered by Schedule 1 G3 – an unventilated system with a storage capacity of over 16 litres. Details of the system and whether the installer is approved will be needed.

The authorities are not required to approve or reject the building notice; they have no power to do so. They are, however, empowered to ask for any plans which they need to discharge their obligations under the Building Regulations 1991 Act.

A building notice remains in effect for three years, starting from the time it was first deposited with the council.

Private certification is a scheme set up to provide an opportunity for self-regulation of the building controls by the construction industry; the local authority still remains responsible for enforcing the regulations. In broad terms, Part II of the Building Act 1984 gives the person intending to carry out the work the opportunity to appoint an approved inspector. The details of the procedures and rules relating to the private certification are to be found in the Building (Approved Inspectors, etc.) Amendment Regulations 1992. The prescribed forms that must be used are also described in that document. At the time of writing the National House-Builders Council is the only approved inspector.

CHAPTER EIGHT

PREFABRICATED BUILDINGS

A VERY WIDE CHOICE

To gather information for this chapter I wrote to every manufacturer of prefabricated buildings that advertised in easily obtainable publications. Because there were so many I used a set form letter, personally addressed, explaining that I needed the information for a book, and that any illustrations suitable for publication would be appreciated. I thought that with this offer of free advertising I would be inundated with material. No such luck; every firm sent me their standard mailing, with no covering letter, just a brochure and price list. This must say something about the suppliers.

Not satisfied with just the brochures, I then visited all those manufacturers that were within a reasonable distance of my home. If you are thinking of buying a ready-made workshop, do the same: insist you see a building the same as the one you wish to buy. If this can be one that has been supplied to a customer and is erected and in use, so much the better. This measure is vital, as the quality of some of those I inspected was pathetic: some of the timber buildings had weatherboarding so thin there was almost no need for windows. This is not to say that all the buildings on offer were poorly constructed; I saw several that I would have been pleased to own, but they were expensive; in most cases I could have produced something superior by doing it myself.

The ready-made building market is very competitive and is price-dominated. The old adage that there is nothing that somebody will not make a little worse and sell cheaper is particularly apt in this case, so we end up with the fact that you get what you pay for – or, if you are not careful, you don't get what you pay for.

VARIOUS MATERIALS

Apart from the obvious – wood – there are two other forms of construction on offer. Steel frame covered with a plastic-coated steel sheeting is offered by a number of firms. Although I have not inspected any buildings made in this way, from looking at the literature and after a short telephone conversation with one supplier, I would not consider it suitable for a workshop. It seems there is no way that any form of internal lining can be added. Just having a thin sheet of steel for the walls of a workshop makes me shiver. Fittings for erecting shelving on the walls are supplied at an extra cost by several manufacturers. Then there is the question of rust, not just to the steel that the building is constructed from, but on the tools from condensation. There is also a question mark about the durability of a building constructed in this way. Some manufacturers offer a 10-year warranty, but what is 10 years in the life of a building?

Precast concrete seemed to be an ideal material for a workshop on first sight. Nearly all the firms that I contacted specialized in garages, and they all tried to sell me a garage that they claimed would make a good

workshop. As far as size went, there was no problem, they all made multiple garages and the building could be made to any length as long as it was in increments of a garage. However, each unit would have an up and over door – imagine a workshop three garages long with all the front elevation taken up by doors. The next fly in the ointment was the roof, which was constructed from sheet material in most cases guaranteed asbestos-free. The use of asbestos is illegal, so what were they saying? There was no way of insulating this roof. One firm specialized in factory units. These people had buildings that would make a very good workshop, but the smallest size was big and precluded use as a home workshop. The price of some of the garage units made me think again.

If one was looking to erect a good workshop for minimal cost, there is potential here. Of course you would have to be prepared to do some

modifications; the garage doors would need replacing with a more suitable wall, and the roof could be modified by adding a few purlins and covering it with insulating board before fixing the outer sheeting.

The best has been saved for last: of all the buildings seen, the best without doubt for our purpose was constructed from timber (*see* Fig 8.1). Although some buildings were poorly made and not to be recommended, if one made sure of what one was buying, this is the best choice. Wood lends itself so well to further work; it is easy to put an extra window in, and insulating can easily be carried out. Even banging a nail in to hang a tool on is possible; you cannot do this in steel or concrete.

A METHODICAL APPROACH

Where a large sum of money is involved, preplanning pays off many times over, so get down on paper just what you need from this building you

Fig 8.1 Prefabricated timber building by Passmores. This would make a fine workshop; it is also attractive and would not look out of place in any garden.

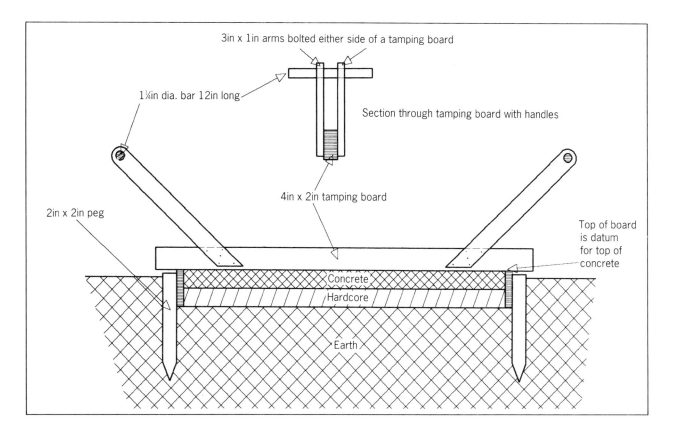

3in x 1in arms bolted either side of a tamping board

1¼in dia. bar 12in long

Section through tamping board with handles

4in x 2in tamping board

2in x 2in peg

Top of board is datum for top of concrete

Concrete

Hardcore

Earth

Fig 8.2 Laying a concrete base.

are about to buy. There is first the question of finance. Not many of us are in the fortunate position of being able to write a cheque for the amount of money that will be required, and borrowing money can be expensive. Look at as many options as possible; a talk with a friendly bank manager would probably not come amiss. The hire purchase schemes offered by some suppliers may be worth considering, but be careful.

See as many buildings as you possibly can before making up your mind, and under no circumstance order one by just looking at the glossy brochure. Visit the manufacturer's show ground at least, but remember these are show buildings – will the one you purchase be made to the same standards? Do not just fill in the manufacturer's order form; put your order in the form of a letter specifying exactly what you are ordering. When it is delivered, inspect it and make sure you are happy with it; it is no use

complaining once it is up and you are occupying it.

PERMISSION

Chapter 7 gives details of the regulations governing the erection of buildings. All reputable manufacturers supply drawings suitable for submission to the council, and some will advise on how to go about seeking permission. Use them as much as possible; they have the experience.

THE BASE

Some prefabricated buildings rely on a concrete base to form the foundation and the floor. The purchaser is responsible for this; it is never included in the price. The easiest way of forming this base is to put a board on edge around the perimeter as shown in Fig 8.2. It is important that this should be well supported on the outside with pegs driven into the ground. The top of the board should be levelled in; this will determine the top face of the concrete. The area enclosed by the boards should be excavated to a depth of 12in.

Good clean hard core is rammed into the bottom of the area to a depth of 6in; the remaining 6in is taken up by the concrete. One of the best ways of doing this concreting is to use Readymix, especially if the lorry can have direct access to where the concrete is to be placed. If the site is inaccessible, it may be best to mix the concrete yourself – tool hire companies have small electric-powered cement mixers that are well worth the cost of hire.

The mix should be in the proportion of 6 of aggregate to 1 of cement. The aggregate should be well graded ¾in ballast. Do not add too much water to the mix – only sufficient for the easy placing of the material is needed. Too much water adversely affects the ultimate strength of the mix, and if water runs out of the mix as it is placed, it will take the cement and fine particles of aggregate with it.

Starting at one end of the area surrounded by the boards, place the mix right across the full width of the base. Level the surface off roughly with a shovel, slightly above the level of the board's top edge. Take a piece of timber at least 6in x 1½in and slightly longer than the width of the base, and place this across the top of the concrete mix which has just been placed, with each end over the surrounding boards. The piece of timber, with a person at each end, is tamped up and down on top of the concrete until it is down flat and level with the top of the boards. This tamping has the effect of bringing the finer parts of the mix to the surface, leaving a good smooth finish. If the surface of the concrete is to serve as the floor of the workshop, it should be brought to a very smooth finish with a steel plasterer's trowel.

The surfaces of concrete floors need some form of after-treatment, as they tend to dust, i.e. the surface wears very quickly and the floor seems to be constantly covered in a fine dust. A liquid preparation to cure this problem should be applied as soon as the building is erected and before it is occupied. If you have been unable to get a satisfactory surface on the concrete, there are several patent floor finishes that can be applied over the surface of the concrete. These include a thick liquid that is poured on to the floor, which runs out level before hardening. Beware – 'runs out' is the operative phrase. Door openings, etc. need to have a small barrier across them, or some of the floor will end up outside the workshop. Even a cement screed on top of the concrete will tidy things up; this is much easier to get a good surface on than concrete.

One manufacturer gives advice on the construction of the base and suggests that a course of bricks should be laid with the outside dimensions to exactly the same size as the building. This will allow the cladding to oversail and the rain to drip off.

ERECTION

Nearly all the manufacturers deliver, but only a few offer an erection service. You will need assistance if you are to put the building up yourself – some of the units are heavy. There is also the question of access to the site: not all delivery men are prepared to carry the units any distance, so you are likely to arrive home one day and find the sections of the buildings blocking up your gateway. On the other hand, it is surprising what a little money and a cup of tea will do, so if you are not to be there when the delivery is made, make sure somebody else is and that they are well briefed.

CHAPTER NINE

MATERIAL STORAGE

AN INVESTMENT

All materials represent an investment of money, so it is only prudent to look after them. Some things can be spoilt if not stored in a particular way; easy access to items also saves a lot of time. It is most exasperating when one knows that an item is about but it cannot be found.

Different materials require different storage methods and conditions: timber needs a low moisture content, but the temperature within reason is not important; emulsion glues and paints will not be affected by the moisture content, but they will become useless if allowed to freeze; timber needs to be supported in a flat condition, sheet material is best stored on edge. All these requirements make a demand on space.

WHERE?

As most of the materials do not require a heated environment they can be stored away from the workshop. This means that precious workshop space need not be taken up, but it does present the problem of where to put them. A shed or some similar repository is ideal for a timber store. Of course not all craftsmen need to have a timber store, but it will be found that the price of timber comes down dramatically with the quantity purchased. This is because a good deal of the cost is transport – small amounts cost the same to deliver as large amounts.

There are advantages in building up a stock of timber: if one has a reasonable stock, the most suitable board for a job can be chosen. I need a fair selection of timber, not because I use a vast amount, but because the wood often tells me what it wants to be made into. This may seem odd, but I like to choose the grain pattern and colouring and this requires a reasonable quantity to choose from: a board might suggest a nice little table, or maybe it has a pretty swirl in the grain and I can see a pair of cupboard doors in it. So when I see a particularly fine piece of timber, I must have it! All this wood needs somewhere to live, and there is not enough room in the workshop.

THE TIMBER STORE

The hut I use as a store was originally intended for a building site, and is an ideal building. Timber needs to be stored in such a way that individual boards can be easily accessible; having to move half a lorry load to get to the required pieces is very frustrating. There is also the need to make sure that the timber is stored flat – it would be silly after paying a high price for a very good board just to stick it against the wall and to find that it had warped when one came to use it.

Because the moisture content of my timber store is that of the outside climate, the timber is not immediately suitable for making furniture, so I have to plan ahead. Timber is ripped out roughly to the dimension required and stored in the workshop for about three months before it is used; this allows it to settle down. Occasionally a piece will move to such an extent that it has to be replaced. For this reason, some spare bits are always included in the original cutting.

Just what type of woodwork is being carried out will determine the stock of timber required. When hobby

55

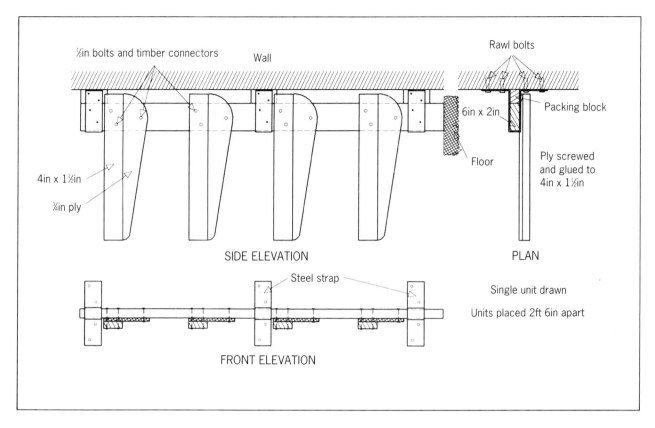

½in bolts and timber connectors
Wall
Rawl bolts

4in x 1½in

¾in ply

SIDE ELEVATION

6in x 2in

Packing block

Floor

Ply screwed
and glued to
4in x 1½in

PLAN

Steel strap

FRONT ELEVATION

Single unit drawn

Units placed 2ft 6in apart

Fig 9.1 A cantilever
timber rack.

working, most woodworkers tend to
buy only sufficient timber for the job
in hand; in this case there is no
question of storage. However, it
would be foolhardy to start work on
timber the minute it was brought into
the workshop – timber is a
hydroscopic material and needs time
to settle down to the ambient
moisture content. It needs somewhere
in which to reside for at least a month
before it is used, and this should be in
the workshop or somewhere with a
similar temperature and moisture
content.

Having decided just what will suit
your way of working, the easiest
method of storage is to place the
timber on battens on the floor. These
are bits of 2in x 1in softwood, called
sticks in the timber trade. The sticks
are placed so that their top surface is
out of wind (not twisted) with one
another; they should be about 4ft
apart. The moisture content of the
timber being stored and how long it is

likely to remain there will determine
whether sticks should be placed
between each board.

Once the first board is laid down,
sticks are placed on its surface exactly
above the stick beneath it. Each board
is placed on top of sticks in this way,
allowing a free passage of air to flow
around each board. With dry boards
that are not to be stored for any
length of time, there is no need for the
sticks. Whichever way the boards are
stacked, they should be packed so that
they are out of wind. When using
sticks, it is important that they are
placed immediately above one
another: this transmits the weight
directly downwards. If the sticks are
staggered, the weight of the boards
above bends the boards below, which
are likely to take on a permanent bow.

Where only a few boards of each
species are kept, some form of
cantilever storage is most suitable (*see*
Fig 9.1). There are several firms that
make a metal rack based on this

principle, but they are expensive. Slotted angle such as Dexion can be used, but surely a woodworker can make one out of timber. Should you undertake to construct a cantilevered rack, the joinery must be beyond reproach – the arms take a lot of punishment, and the timber will not lay flat if they become misaligned.

Having dealt with the flat boards, what about all those short odds and ends? It is not difficult to make a rack in which they can be stored. In one workshop there was a stack of 9in diameter plastic pipes against the wall. These were about 2ft 6in long and looked something like a honeycomb. All the odd ends were stored in these pipes; the ends of the timber could easily be seen and any wanted piece easily selected.

VENEERS

Veneers require very careful storage. They need to be protected from abrasion and knocks, and they must not be allowed to become too dry (contrary to the way all other wood is stored). When very dry, veneers become brittle and are easily damaged. There is only one way to store the leaves of veneer in safety: flat between two sheets of blockboard.

Parcels of veneer should be untied as soon as they are delivered and the leaves should be consecutively numbered with chalk – this prevents the inadvertent use of leaves which are not consecutive. The blockboard can be cut so that it is a little larger than the average veneer leaf used in the workshop, and several parcels can be stored between the same two boards. The veneer between the two boards is stored in a horizontal position and weights are placed on the top to keep the whole lot flat.

SHEET MATERIAL

If you have moved an 8ft x 4ft sheet of ½in ply on your own, you will appreciate its weight, so just think what the weight of a dozen sheets must amount to. The best way of storing such an amount is against a wall. Provided that the sheets are stood fairly upright, the weight on the wall is not great. Where the weight must be taken into account is when a sheet at the back is being taken out: the craftsman stands in front of the boards, leans them against his body and attempts to withdraw the back sheet. There is a danger that the sheets will be allowed to come back on him at a lowish angle: this imposes a lot of weight on him, he can be pushed over and all the ply will fall on him. There have been several accidents caused in this way, with serious damage to the craftsman's legs.

There is a simple way to stop this happening; unfortunately it requires a wall 16ft long. A rack into which the boards can be slid is constructed and is positioned against the wall, which supports it. Providing that the boards are kept in a vertical position, there is very little weight on the sides of the rack and any sheet can be withdrawn with safety from anywhere in the stack.

PAINTS AND VARNISHES

Chapter 5 advised that all flammable materials, e.g. French polish and paints, should be stored outside the workshop. Old concrete coal bunkers work well, except that access is gained via the lid on the top. A wooden box with a felt-covered lift-up lid should not be beyond the capabilities of any woodworker. WBP ply would be a suitable material, and it would not take long to make.

One possible problem is the storage of materials that could be affected by low temperatures. As these are not a fire hazard, they can remain in the workshop, but they may be a nuisance, taking up valuable space.

Some form of frost protection can be dreamed up for the storage box. It requires only a minimal amount of heat to keep the box temperature above freezing – a jar of water with a fish tank heater and thermostat, or even a low wattage lightbulb will suffice.

SCREWS

In the old days screws were supplied in stout cardboard boxes containing a gross (144). Today we have gone metric, and screws come in a flimsy box containing 200, which collapses long before the screws are all used, or are even supplied loose in a plastic bag. The nests of plastic drawers supplied in units of 12, 24 and so on are ideal. For the sort of quantities that a one-man shop uses these drawers are adequate; they will accommodate the contents of a 200 box in all the normal sizes. Once screws over 2in need to be stored, larger drawers are needed.

There is a cheap easy-to-construct form of storage made from screw-top jars similar to those that instant coffee is bought in. The jars have their lids screwed to the underside of a shelf, and each jar full of screws is attached to its lid when not in use (*see* Fig 9.2). This is a good excuse to have extra cups of coffee, as a number of jars will be required. If you adopt this system, put two screws through each lid, as one screw only allows the lid to rotate. Plastic lids are quite flimsy; their strength can be improved by putting penny washers under the screw heads (*see* Fig 9.3).

NAILS

The quantity and size of nails to be stored will depend on the type of work undertaken. It's best to store a quantity of each size in tins; if the tins are all the same size they can sit side by side on a shelf, nice and tidy, each with a label stating what it contains.

Fig 9.2 Using a coffee jar with its lid screwed to the underside of a shelf doubles the available storage space.

Here again we have a problem of changing times. Some years ago numerous things were supplied in tins with tight-fitting lids, e.g. cocoa, which could be bought in 2lb tins, but now comes in a cardboard container with a plastic lid. I will let you into a closely guarded secret: home-brew beer comes in a big tin with a plastic push-on lid ideal for storage (*see* Fig 9.4). So you see, woodworkers drink a lot of coffee and home brew – just for the containers.

PANEL PINS

Although panel pins do not take up much space, they are not easy items to pick up. The best way of dealing

Fig 9.3 Use two screws
and penny washers,
otherwise the lid will
revolve when the jar is
screwed to it.

Fig 9.4 The top shelf
supports tins from home
brew beer kits; the lower
shelf has square tins –
these are preferable, but
less plentiful.

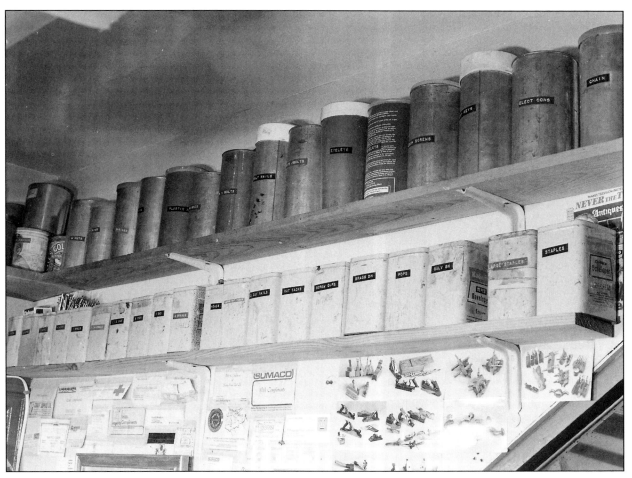

with them is to make a box with lots of partitions (*see* Fig 9.5); each size of pin has its own little space and is easy to select. The whole box lives on a shelf above the bench, in easy reach when needed. A lid on the box is required if the shop tends to be dusty, or you end up with more dust than pins.

GLUE

Not many workshops use the old-fashioned hot-melt animal glue, but for those of us engaged in the restoration of antiques or in hammer veneering, it is a must; no modern glue can replace it. Pearl glue needs storing in an airtight container that will protect it from moisture and wood dust. This is best achieved by using a large jar, the sort that sweets were once displayed in. Some catering size culinary powders come in these jars, and the local café can often be persuaded to part with one or two; if the proprietor has had to pay a deposit, offer to buy the jar. Cascamite and most powdered glues are delivered in stout tins; the industrial size can, when empty, be cleaned out and used for pearl glue.

FITTINGS

Things like small locks, barrel bolts, knobs and drawer pulls all need to have a permanent home. It is important that the craftsman is able to put his hands on anything in the workshop without having to search for it – nothing wastes time like untidiness. Drawers that are full of all

manner of items mixed together are no place to store even secondhand fittings.

There are numerous storage systems on the market; some of the cheap plastic ones are eminently suitable. A drawer or bin size that will just accommodate a selection of one item is needed. If there is a lot of spare room in a drawer, space is being wasted. Ideally, the craftsman should be as methodical and disciplined as possible, with a place for everything and everything in its place.

LITTLE ITEMS

Every workshop has numerous small items, ranging from veneer pins to scalpel blades. Tobacco tins are ideal for storage, and a small carcase can be made and the tins used like drawers in it. Square tins are useful for storage, as they stack and fit together well on a shelf (*see* Fig 9.6). It pays to keep your eyes open and scrounge any that you see.

Fig 9.6 Tobacco tins make good containers and take up little space.

Fig 9.5 Panel pins are best stored in a purpose-built box, which can be placed on the bench when using the pins.

CHAPTER TEN

THE BENCH

A VERY IMPORTANT ITEM

The bench has a great influence on the quality of work produced by the craftsman, and I believe that it is as important as any of the tools in the workshop.

A bench is a very personal thing, and needs to be tailored to suit the user. The height must be adjusted to suit the type of work being undertaken and the stature of the user. It is impossible to control the tools properly if the work is too high, while the craftsman working at a bench that is too low will soon have back problems. So what is the correct height? Only you will know this when you have arrived at it by trial and error. However, we have to start somewhere, so measure your inside leg, as though you were being measured for a pair of trousers. Add 3in to this, and that is the height of the bench top from the floor. Now cut some squares of ½in ply about 4in x 4in. By putting one or more of these under each leg, the bench height can be adjusted. If you find the bench too high, saw a bit off each leg; you can always pack it up if you overdo the sawing off.

Having got the bench to the right height, make sure the top is exactly level, something that many people neglect. If you use hand tools, it will not be long before you will be able to tell if your jack plane is sitting square on the timber being worked. Should the bench be out of level, the plane will be planing out of square when it feels level. When I am teaching a group of beginners and I tell them about this, I see the disbelief on their faces. This statement is soon proved by my planing a piece of wood perfectly square without the use of a try square. This very useful sixth sense is only acquired by practice, using the same plane. It would be impossible if the benches I have worked on were out of level.

DIFFERENT PATTERNS

There are so many different patterns of woodworking bench that it would be impossible to describe them all, but a cross section is covered here. As most benches are craftsman-made, they incorporate the needs of that craftsman. Over the years a bench is often modified to incorporate something that the owner has found a need for.

If you intend making a bench, find the best timber that you can afford to buy. The bench top is best made from a hardwood; beech tends to be a favourite. Spend time getting everything exactly right, as a bench lasts more than a lifetime and anything that is not up to standard has to be lived with. I would consider it an honour if the person that inherited my bench was proud to say, 'This bench was made by Jim Kingshott, and he used it most of his life'.

The top of the bench must be looked after. Do not drive nails and screws into the surface to hold a piece of timber being worked upon and try to avoid making saw cuts into the bench top – use a bench hook or a sticking board instead. Similarly avoid painting jobs on the bench top.

THE WELL

The bench well is that part of the bench top that is below the rest of the surface. The idea behind this is for the tools in use to be down out of the way of the job in hand. The well has a tendency to fill up with shavings and sawdust, and this is why some people do not like the feature. It is only a matter of a few moments to sweep the well out and to find little items such as pencils that become buried in the general litter.

On some benches, particularly joiner's benches, the well can take up most of the top. I like a very narrow well at the back of the bench, with a strip behind it level with the bench top; this strip need only be a couple of inches wide. As with all other features of the bench, the type of work being undertaken affects the design: where large frames are being assembled, a wide well is a desirable feature, as the tools are down out of the way. With a bench top that is level from front to back, all the tools have to be cleared off before any assembly is started on the bench top.

THE CABINETMAKER'S BENCH

Over the years one particular pattern of bench has become known as the cabinetmaker's bench. This is a bench that, like Topsy, just grew; it was probably never designed as such, but evolved through generations of use and modifications. That is how the finest woodworking tools came about, so what better recommendation could a thing have? This particular design was once known in the trade as a continental bench, and it was obviously brought here by immigrant cabinetmakers. James Krenov, for whom I have the highest regard, states that it is of Danish origin and is called a *snickarbänk*. For the general woodworker or cabinetmaker this is, in my opinion, the ultimate.

The bench has a tail vice at the right-hand end; if you are left-handed there is no reason why you should not make a left-handed bench – all that is required is to turn everything around,

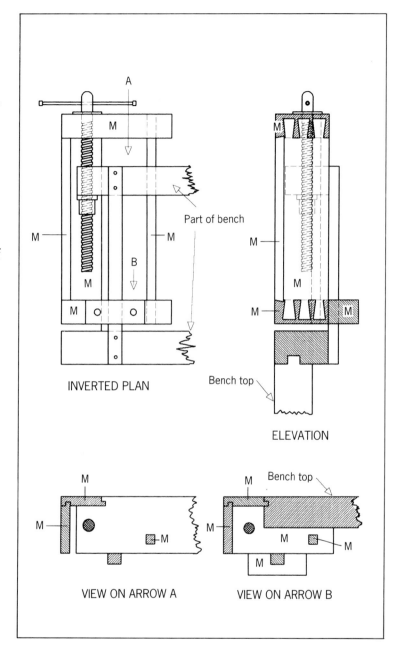

INVERTED PLAN

ELEVATION

Part of bench

Bench top

VIEW ON ARROW A

VIEW ON ARROW B

Bench top

Fig 10.1 Detail of tail vice. Moving parts are marked with an 'M'.

and the tail vice will then be on the left-hand end. A number of tool shops sell the mechanism to construct the tail vice, and there are a number of different designs. I prefer the all-wood construction with just the screw and nut made from steel (*see* Figs 10.1 and 10.2). Timber to be worked is held on the top of the bench between a dog in the tail vice and one in the bench top (*see* Fig 10.3). The vice on the left-hand front corner of the bench was

Fig 10.2 The only metal part of the tail vice is the screw. As can be seen here it is quite a chunky item.

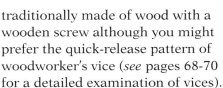

traditionally made of wood with a wooden screw although you might prefer the quick-release pattern of woodworker's vice (*see* pages 68-70 for a detailed examination of vices).

The top of the bench should be thick. Some of the proprietary benches advertised in the magazines boast a 2in thick top; my bench has a 4in top. You may wonder why: when mortising or cutting wood with a chisel that requires mallet blows, the support that this extra thickness gives is very noticeable. There is also the question of stability; the thick top stays true better than a thin one. It is probably unnecessary to stress how important a truly flat bench top is; a top that is laminated as shown in Figs 10.4 and 10.5 will be more stable than one made from wide planks.

THE JOINER'S BENCH

The cabinetmaker's bench is constructed from hardwood; most joiners' benches are made in softwood. In some joiner's shops the benches are double-length, with a craftsman working at each end. The joiner does not have a tail vice, just the normal front vice at the left-hand end of the bench (*see* Fig 10.6). The type of work the joiner is engaged on is usually of a larger size than that of the cabinetmaker, so he requires more bench space. The cabinetmaker uses his bench to make parts on, assembling the job on stools or a back bench. The joiner assembles his bigger-sized work on the bench top; for large frames, he may place two large pieces of timber across the bench and assemble on these.

Fig 10.3 Using the bench dogs and tail vice to hold timber while overhand ripping.

63

Fig 10.4 Plan of the bench and detail of the tail vice.

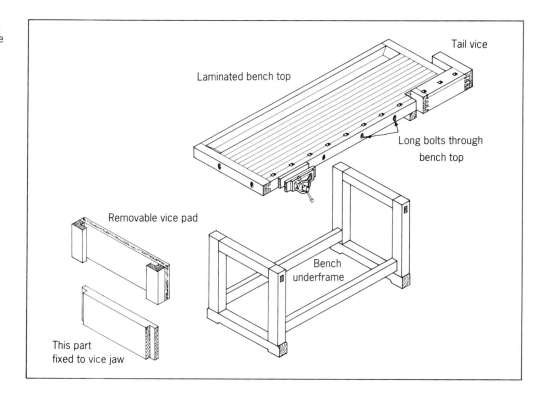

Tail vice

Laminated bench top

Long bolts through bench top

Removable vice pad

Bench underframe

This part fixed to vice jaw

Because of the weight and size, he will move the job as little as possible. A joiner's bench is normally at least 8ft long and around 2ft 6in wide. The bench usually has a single drawer in the apron board. Double benches are around 16ft long and 3ft wide.

THE STAIR BUILDER'S BENCH

Whilst this is a specialist bench, it encompasses one or two features that are worth noting, and may be applied for other uses. The bench is huge by comparison with a cabinetmaking bench, as some of the components in a staircase are long. The bench is used not only to make the different parts of the staircase on, but also for its assembly. At each end of the bench in the centre of the width, there is a post of quite a large section, sometimes as big as 9in x 3in. These posts are firmly jointed in to the underframe of the bench, and continue up to almost ceiling height.

Joining the two posts at the top and running the full length of the bench is a large beam made from stout timber, with a section as big as 9in x 4in. The whole idea of this structure is to clamp up the stair assembly. One stair string is laid on the bench top and the treads and risers are assembled into it. The other string is placed on top of the treads and risers, which are located in their respective housings in both strings. Lengths of timber slightly longer than the gap between the top string and the beam are inserted at an angle in that gap and the lengths of timber are driven with a large hammer towards an upright position thus forcing the stair assembly together. The wedges that fix the treads and risers are now fitted and glued into place. Angle blocks are glued into place where the riser fits into the tread. The whole assembly can then be released by knocking out the lengths of timber holding it down on the bench.

While it is unlikely that the average woodworker will need a bench of this design, the principle is a useful one; it could easily be adapted for holding carcases together while gluing up.

Fig 10.5 My bench, with tool storage beneath.

STORAGE

There is never sufficient room in the workshop to store all the paraphernalia that we woodworkers use so the space under the bench should be fully utilized. I keep some of my most used tools here: they are close at hand, and it only takes a second or two to have them out of the drawer and in use. When they are finished with they can be returned to their resting place, rather than cluttering up the top of the bench. There is a cupboard for the bigger items and two tiers of drawers for the little tools.

Another benefit from storing tools under the bench is stability; the weight of the tools keeps the bench firmly in place. A bench that moves about when any force is applied to work held on its surface is a dreadful prospect – imagine pushing a plane along the wood to find that the bench moves along the floor!

In some cases it may be necessary to fix a bench to the floor with angle brackets.

Depending on the type of work undertaken it may be possible to put the bench against a wall, thus saving workshop space. Some work requires that the craftsman can have access to both sides of the bench; if frames are assembled on the bench top, nothing must stand above the level of the top. If you do not assemble in this way and you do not need to work from the back of the bench, a tool rack along the back of the bench is a most useful fitment to have. All the chisels in daily use are kept in this fashion (*see* Fig 10.5); they thus never need to lie on the bench top, where their edge can become damaged. It is easy to reach out, choose the tool that is needed and return it as soon as it is finished with. After working with the tools in the same place in the rack for a number of years, I hardly need to look when one is needed; my hand goes out to exactly where it is always stored. This saves time and keeps the tools in good condition.

There is a space on the top of the cupboard under the bench, where

65

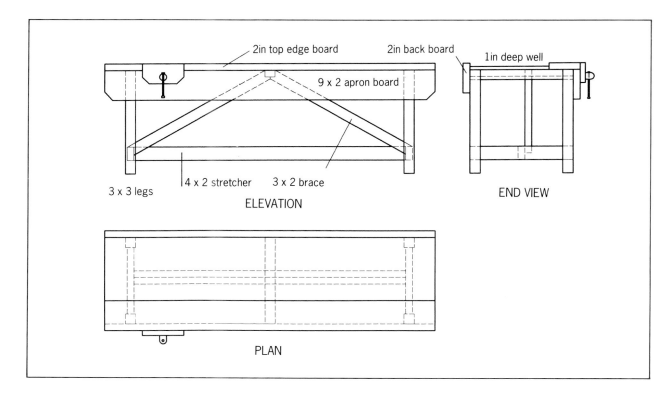

2in top edge board
2in back board
1in deep well
9 x 2 apron board
3 x 3 legs
4 x 2 stretcher
3 x 2 brace
ELEVATION
END VIEW
PLAN

bench hooks and small shooting boards can live; these too are immediately to hand. If you have to go searching for a tool or a piece of equipment, relocate it in a convenient place; it will soon be rare to have the bother of searching for the elusive item.

LOOKING AFTER THE BENCH

Having gone to all the expense and trouble of obtaining a fine bench it now needs to be cared for. A new bench takes a while to settle down and the top will move with changes in the weather. When it becomes more stable the top should be trued up. It needs to be planed up true, i.e. straight and flat with the longest hand plane you possess. There is no way that this trueing up can be done by machine or power tool, so do not attempt it.

The next point is quite controversial, as I know many craftsmen who would disagree with me: what – if anything – should you treat the bench top with? Because I

use a lot of hot melt animal glue for veneering and suchlike, I wax the top of the bench. This is not to make it shine, but to stop the glue sticking to it. It is so easy to wipe the bench off afterwards and to give it a quick wipe over with a waxy rag.

Some craftsmen give their bench top a coat of either boiled linseed or Danish oil. This oiling is often done last thing before knocking off on a Friday evening, so a thick layer of oil has all weekend to soak in. On Monday morning the bench is polished dry with a rag.

Then there is the chap who is forever slapping a coat of shellac on the top. I think this is horrible, but it is a good idea to coat the underframe in this way, as it seals the timber against moisture. From time to time when I have nothing better to do, I take a cabinet scraper and clean up the top of the bench and give it an extra special waxing. My bench top probably gets better treatment than our dining room table – but then, I spend more time working than eating.

Fig 10.6 A joiner's bench. Usual length: 8ft; height to suit stature of user; depth: 2ft 6in.

PROPRIETARY BENCHES

There are only two alternatives for woodworkers who do not have sufficient experience to make their own bench: the first is to commission a craftsman to make one to your own specification – probably the best if you have money to spend in this way – the second is to buy a readymade bench through a retailer. If you are considering buying one of these, go and see it. Make sure that it is going to be of sufficient size – because of the cost of timber, some of these benches are on the small side. I have never heard a craftsman complain about a bench being too big, but I know of several who have benches they consider too small. Unfortunately for the beginner, it is not until they have some experience that they know what is required.

THE HOLDFAST

The joiner's holdfast is a very useful tool and can be classed as part of the bench (*see* Fig 10.7). For certain types of work it could be a necessity: though there is little need for a holdfast with the dogs in the cabinetmaker's bench, it is very useful for holding flat panels when relief carving on a high carving bench.

THE BENCH STOPS AND DOGS

The end of the timber is pushed against the bench stop when its surface is planed. The bench stop is not normally fitted to a cabinetmaker's bench, as the dogs fulfil the same purpose. Most bench stops are a short length of hardwood approximately 3in x 2in, mortised through the top of the bench at the left-hand end. It is often tight in the mortise and is knocked up or down, depending on the thickness of the wood being planed. More sophisticated stops are fitted with a wingnut on a bolt through a slot in the stop. There is another pattern

where the lower end of the stop rests on a cam, which is turned around to adjust the height of the stop. Wooden stops should be fitted so that they are aligned with the face of the bench leg; this supports them when the wood is pushed against their side above the bench.

There is often a tendency for the piece of wood being planed to jump over the bench stop; this happens when the wood is slightly bowed and the concaved side is planed first. Pressure on the end of the wood furthest from the bench stop lifts the other end which is now no longer against the bench stop, and the plane pushes the wood along the bench and on to the floor. Some small panel pins driven into the face of the bench stop near its top end, with part of their length left exposed and a point filed on, will be a help in this situation. At one time it was possible to buy a metal bench stop which was fitted in to the bench top and adjusted with a screw (*see* Fig 10.8). They are only obtainable now secondhand. Metal

Fig 10.7 The bench holdfast inserted through its collar and clamping a block flat on the bench top.

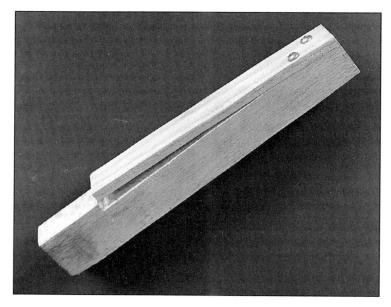

part of the world to work without a vice to hold his work. There are numerous designs and patterns of vice to be had, and here again the woodworker's own preference will play a part in the choice.

Vices have varied from the almost useless to the superb. When a wooden screw vice has been looked after, it works fine, but mechanical things do not last forever and vices, like people, wear out. At one time there was a vice that was tightened by a snail cam. This fitting looked very similar to a modern quick-release vice, but the difference appeared when it was tightened or loosened. With the handle in an upright position, the outer jaw was pushed in to grip the wood; the handle was then pushed down hard and the vice tightened on the wood.

In my opinion there is nothing to touch the large woodworking vices made by Record. Their series numbered from 52 to 53A is particularly to be recommended. Unfortunately, like so many of the better hand tools, the series has been rationalised and not all of them are still manufactured. The table on page 70 lists the series, all of which are currently available. A vice lasts for many years, and some good secondhand bargains are to be found. Spare screws and nuts can be bought to replace those that have become worn out over the years on Record vices. On quick-release vices a worn screw and nut will not allow the vice to be tightened properly. It is easy to detect this problem; the vice gets to a certain point when being tightened where it is almost gripping the job properly. There is a bang from the mechanism, and the vice jaws go slack. It is not a difficult job to replace the necessary components.

Other vice manufacturers have produced fine examples, among whom are Woden, whose models

Fig 10.8 Top: a metal bench stop by Preston. This item is no longer available new, but there is a similar one made by Eclipse.

Fig 10.9 Bottom: a bench dog made from beech. The spring is made from ash which keeps the dog firmly in position when it is being used.

stops are not to be recommended, as it is very easy to nick a plane iron on them. This also applies to the metal dogs supplied with shop bought benches: throw them away and make wooden ones.

THE VICE

Japanese woodworkers manage quite well holding the wood with their feet and body weight, but it is impossible for a woodworker from the western numbered 1, 2 and 3 are all worth fitting. Parkinson and another firm, Rededa, made similar vices. It is, however, all but impossible to get spares for these other makes, so be very careful if buying secondhand and make sure the vice screw and nut are not showing signs of wear.

The fitting of the vice to the bench requires particular care. The vice is an expensive tool, and it would be a pity to have its usefulness restricted by not being fitted properly. The face of the rear jaw is usually fitted flush with the apron board of the bench, and the top of the jaws should be about 1in below the top surface of the bench. It is customary to line the jaws with wood: this stops the vice marking the work being held in it. The fitting of these linings allows any inaccuracies in the mating of the steel vice jaws to be corrected. It is possible to make sure that the jaws close parallel by planing small amounts off one end of the lining; this is checked by putting a small piece of paper in each end of the jaws. The vice is then loosened so that one of the pieces of paper can just be pulled out, even though it is still being gripped slightly by the jaws. The other piece of paper should be gripped by exactly the same amount. Make adjustments to the wooden linings until this is achieved.

It is useful to be able to have different surfaces on the linings, e.g. a felt face would be very helpful when holding a piece of furniture under restoration, where the finish must not be damaged. False linings that fit over the fixed wooden linings are required where a piece of metal is to be held and the linings could be damaged (*see* Figs 10.12 and 10.13). The face of these false linings can be covered with different materials to suit the range of work you do.

For all normal woodwork, hardboard with the pattern side facing the job is ideal; this grips far

better than plain wood and has a certain amount of resilience. I have several sets of false linings covered with hardboard; the best set is used to hold work where the face of the job must not be marked. The next set is used for items that might damage the face of the linings. Another set is used where glue might contaminate the face; this set has been soaked in boiled linseed and waxed when dry – having knobs of hard glue on the face

Fig 10.10 Top: quick-release metalworker's vice.

Fig 10.11 Bottom: underside of quick-release vice.

69

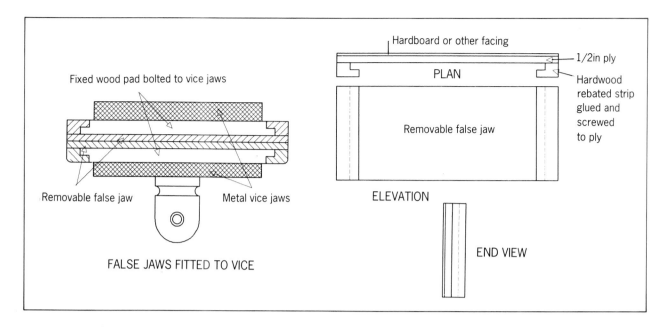

Fixed wood pad bolted to vice jaws

Hardboard or other facing

1/2in ply

Hardwood rebated strip glued and screwed to ply

PLAN

Removable false jaw

Removable false jaw

Metal vice jaws

ELEVATION

END VIEW

FALSE JAWS FITTED TO VICE

of the linings can go unnoticed until they seriously mark the face of a job. With the oiled and waxed linings, glue cannot adhere to the surface.

It is a good plan to line the jaws of the tail vice with hardboard in a similar way. There is no need for false linings here, but a periodic check of the jaws for parallel action, in a similar way to that described above, is advisable. The L-shaped part of the tail vice should not be used to clamp things in: only the jaws are used. The vice will soon suffer if you do not observe this rule.

Fig 10.12 Interchangeable false vice jaws.

Fig 10.13 Fitting a false vice jaw.

A Series of Large Woodworking Vices made by Record

No.	Width of jaw	Opening	Weight	Action
52	7in	8in	18lbs	Quick rel
52½	9in	13in	32lbs	Quick rel
53	10½in	15in	35lbs	Quick rel
52P	7in	8in	18lbs	Plain screw
52½P	9in	13in	32lbs	Plain screw
53P	10½in	15in	35lbs	Plain screw
52A	7in	8in	18lbs	Dust cover
52½A	9in	13in	32lbs	Dust cover

CHAPTER ELEVEN

APPLIANCES

WHAT IS NEEDED?

Of the numerous items needed in the workshop, most have evolved over the centuries. In addition, there are a few jigs and holding devices that are needed for machining special items or for carrying out a particular task, e.g. it is possible to cut tenons quite safely on the table saw providing a jig is used. Sawing stools, bench hooks and shooting boards are all items that the workshop must be equipped with if work is to be efficiently carried out.

For reference these items have been divided into four categories: devices for use on the bench; saw sharpening equipment; free-standing items, and jigs and holding devices for machines.

DEVICES FOR USE ON THE BENCH

THE RIGHT HOOK

One important item that it is difficult to do without is the **bench hook**. Although it is such a simple item that one is tempted to knock it up from offcuts and a few nails, it should be made properly from some solid hardwood.

There should be no metal used in the construction; there is no sound like a saw running into the tip of a screw that holds the other side of the hook on!

It is best to glue the parts together and hold them with cramps. Once the glue has set, holes are bored through the parts and dowels inserted in them. A good hook will last for years, so it is worth getting it to your liking (*see* Figs 11.1 and 11.2). A narrow second hook is very useful to support the other end of long boards; this way the

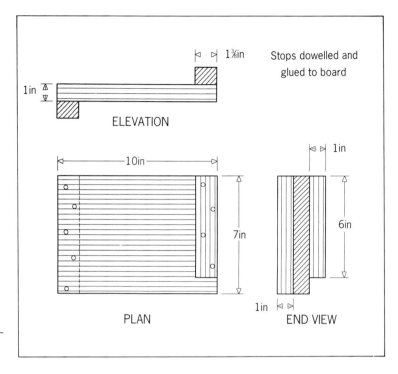

Fig 11.1 Bench hook.

board cannot wobble about. This narrow second hook needs to be the same length as the main hook but narrower in width.

The size of the bench hook is a matter of personal preference. If many wide boards are cut it is preferable to have two hooks of different length. The width of the board that the hook is made from should be at least 6in, and 9in would be ideal. The wider the hook, the easier it is to hold the work steady while it is being cut.

SHOOTING BOARDS

Shooting boards come in a variety of shapes, sizes and designs. What is needed will depend on the type of work undertaken and what other equipment is in the workshop. In *Making & Modifying Woodworking Tools* (GMC Publications 1992) I showed how to make a copy of the Stanley No. 51/52 shooting plane and board. This tool replaces most shooting boards, being adjustable to plane any angle. Even so, I need several wooden shooting boards. A short board similar to the bench hook will be very useful when shooting the ends of boards square, and this appliance would be most beneficially used with a low angle plane, for example a mitre plane (*see* Figs 11.3 and 11.4).

A long board is needed for planing the edge of thin lengths of wood square and straight (*see* Fig 11.5). One about 4ft long is suitable for most purposes. The stop on all shooting boards should be made wedge shaped (*see* Fig 11.6): this allows the end to be squared up when it becomes worn. A few shavings off the wedge side of the stop will allow the realigning of its end with the rebate on the board. When constructing a shooting board, make sure that the rebate in which the plane runs is wide enough, as the plane should be supported for the full width of its side.

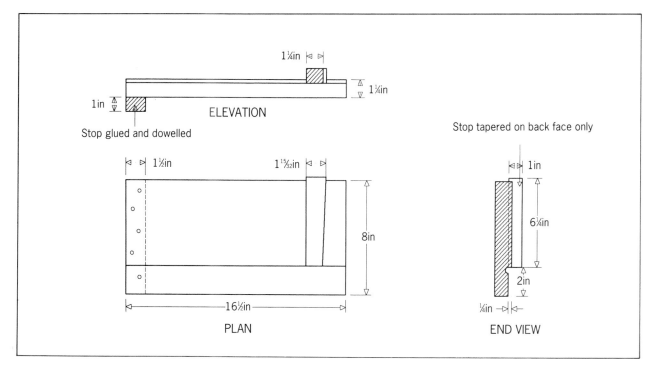

1¼in

1¼in

1in

ELEVATION

Stop glued and dowelled

Stop tapered on back face only

1½in

1¹⁵⁄₃₂in

1in

8in

6¼in

2in

16½in

¼in

PLAN

END VIEW

Fig 11.2 Left: bench hook in use.

Fig 11.4 Short shooting board in use.

Fig 11.5 Long shooting board in use.

Fig 11.3 Left: short shooting board.

IT'S NOT A MATTER OF LUCK

Mitres have to be made in every shop, mostly cut at 45° and it is worth constructing boards that can be used to shoot them true. Mitres straight from the saw do not fit as precisely as those which have been planed. Glue penetrates the pores in the wood that has been cleanly cut by the plane, but does not hold so well on the fluffy surface left by a saw.

Two mitre shooting boards will be needed, as mitres made across the wood's width and those across its thickness (known as a 'donkey's ear' in the trade *see* Fig 11.7) need different appliances (*see* Figs 11.8 and 11.9). It is very important that these items are made accurately; a shooting board that is not accurate is worse than useless.

All wooden appliances need checking from time to time for accuracy, and any errors found should be immediately corrected. lt is most annoying when in the middle of a job to find that the mitre shoot is out of kilter. So whenever there is a spare moment, all wooden appliances should be checked.

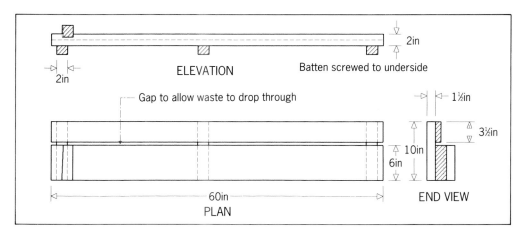

Fig 11.6 Long shooting board.

It is possible to make one appliance serve two purposes. A normal shooting board for planing edges square and straight can have a detachable mitre stop fitted by making a block of wood the required shape (*see* Fig 11.9). Put the block into place and hold it there with a cramp. Three holes are drilled through the block and into the board, making sure these are bored square to the surface. Any inaccuracy will make the mounting and detaching of the block difficult. Tight-fitting dowels are glued into the block, and allowed to protrude on the underside by about ¾in. The block can now be attached by inserting the projecting dowel ends into the holes in the board. It is a matter of seconds to lever the block off and return the board to its original use.

A TRAP

Another wooden appliance for use when planing mitres is a **mitre trap**. This is particularly useful when planing the ends of short or difficult grained timber. As the timber is clamped between the blocks, it is impossible for the grain to split off the back edge when being planed. There was a time when this item was sold in tool shops – unfortunately, like so

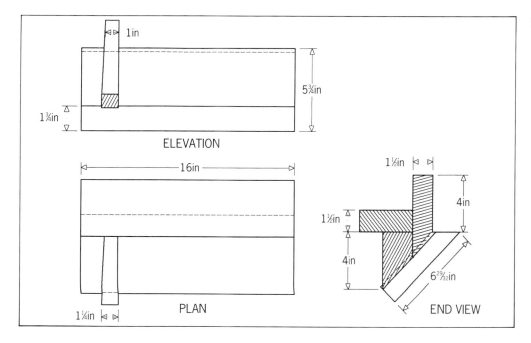

Fig 11.7 Donkey's ear.

many useful hand tools, it has disappeared from the marketplace. However, it is not beyond the capabilities of the average woodworker to make one.

Fig 11.10 shows a recently-made trap which can be used to shoot any sort of mitre that needs planing at 45°. Square ends can be planed true at 90° by inserting the wood from the

Fig 11.8 Wooden mitre shoot.

Fig 11.9 Mitre shoot.

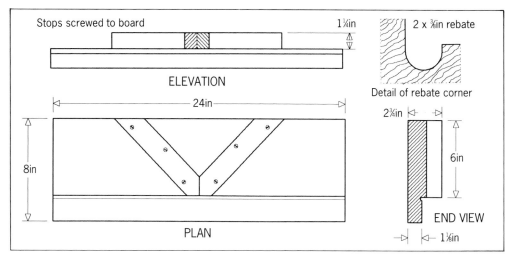

Stops screwed to board

1¼in

ELEVATION

2 x ⅜in rebate

Detail of rebate corner

24in

2¾in

8in

6in

PLAN

END VIEW

1⅛in

other end. The only tools needed to make a mitre trap, other than those normally found in the workshop, are a screw box and tap. A 1in box and tap will be needed.

Some mitre traps are made with a metal screw. There are suitable metal screws intended for tail vices, sold by some tool suppliers which are eminently suitable for use on a mitre trap. Some of the blocks of wood used to make the trap are on the large side: this means that they will have a tendency to move. It is good practice to laminate these blocks up from several layers of board, as this will produce a more stable block than one made from one piece of wood.

With the exception of the long shooting board, a close-grained stable hardwood is best for constructing the various shooting boards and related appliances. Several of my boards are made from **teak** (Tectona grandis),

which happened at the time to be freely available in the workshop. It has worn very well, and has remained true. The only fault with the boards made from this timber is that the plane does not slide on it as well as it could; however, if the rebate is polished with paraffin wax there is no problem. **Mahogany** (Swietenia macrophylla) is a favourite in the trade. This wood needs choosing very carefully: use only the straight, tight-grained boards – figured and curly grain may look pretty, but it is not

Fig 11.10 Mitre trap.

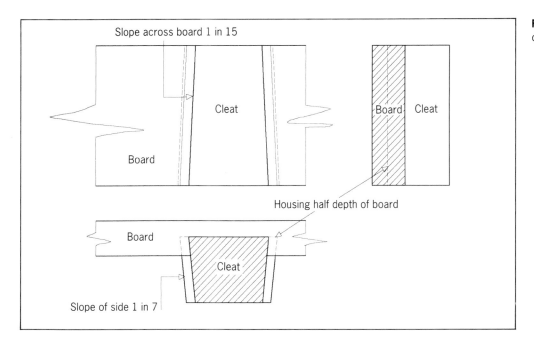

Slope across board 1 in 15

Cleat

Board

Board Cleat

Housing half depth of board

Board

Cleat

Slope of side 1 in 7

Fig 11.11 Double dovetail cleat.

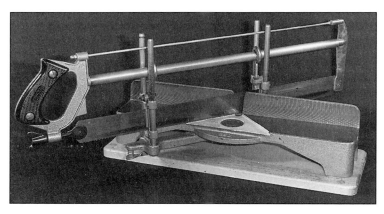

Fig 11.12 Mitre saw by Ulma; this replaces the wooden mitre block and box.

very stable. **Beech** *(Fagus sylvatica)* seems to have been used by the commercial manufacturers because of its low price compared with imported hardwood. If this timber is given sufficient time to settle down before use, it is quite suitable. Of course beech is the obvious choice if you wish to use home-grown timber. My long boards are made from pattern making quality **yellow pine** *(Pinus strobus);* while this is more expensive than any of the hardwoods mentioned, it is extremely stable and is lighter in weight, which makes the board easier to handle.

If the shooting boards are wide they will need some form of cleat on the back to help keep them flat – unless they are true quarter-sawn, there is a tendency for them to cup.

The cleats are best fitted by the double dovetail method (*see* Fig 11.11). They should not be glued or fixed in any way: driving them in until they are tight is sufficient. From time to time the cleat can be reseated by giving its broad end a tap or two with a hammer.

Shooting boards can have a hole drilled in one end so that they may be hung up when not in use. This is to be recommended, as they can then have a permanent home and you will not have to go searching for one when it is needed. Up on the wall they have a free current of air around them, and will be more likely to remain stable than if they were down amongst the shavings.

BLOCK OR BOX?
Returning to the original subject of sawing, there are two appliances for this, a **mitre box** and a **mitre block**. They both have the same purpose, but the box is used for larger sections than the block. In most modern workshops mitres are sawn on the

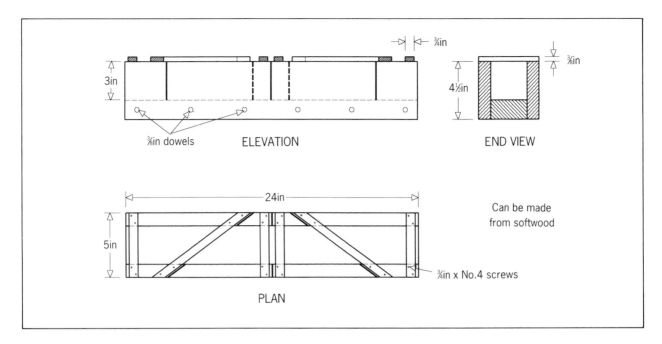

3in

⅜in dowels   ELEVATION

4½in   ⅜in

END VIEW

24in

5in

Can be made
from softwood

⅜in x No.4 screws

PLAN

Fig 11.13 Mitre box.

table saw with a jig or mitre slide. The mitre box is to be preferred to the block, as it is usually the more accurate of the two. The size of the box depends on the size of the sections of timber to be mitred: while small mouldings etc. can be mitred in a big box, large sections cannot be mitred in a small box. A small section in a large box is difficult to hold steady. Of course, if you are lucky and have one of those very useful metal mitre saws, there will be no need to make a box – there is, however, the odd occasion when wood with a section too large for the metal appliance has to be mitred, so it is useful to know how to make a mitre box.

THE BOX

The mitre box is a very simple item which consists of three short boards all the same length (about 2ft). Two of the boards are of equal size: they should be about 2in wider than the thickness of the wood to be mitred, and nominally 1in thick. The base is made from the third board, which should be about 1½in thick and slightly wider than the wood to be

mitred (see Fig 11.13). The two thinner boards are fixed to the edge of the thick board, keeping their edge flush with the underside face of the thick board. It is best to glue this assembly up at this stage. Place a temporary stretcher in the top of the box; this should keep the top of the two side boards the same distance apart at the top as they are at the bottom. When the glue has set, the assembly is marked out where the saw cuts are to be made. There should be two 45° cuts facing away from each other. A square cut (90°) is useful, so place this between the two other cuts.

A strip of wood about ¾in x ¾in in section is fixed across the top of the box alongside each cut. These strips are best left longer than needed, and cut off flush after fixing. The best method of fixing the strips is to glue and screw them. The side boards should now have their bottom edges screwed to the base board to reinforce the previously glued joint. Make sure that the screws are placed where they will not endanger the saw. It only remains for the saw cuts to be carefully made with the saw that will be used with the box to cut mitres.

THE BLOCK

The mitre block is made from two pieces of wood, the first about 12in x 6in x 1in, the second 12in x 3in x 2in. The second piece is glued flat on to the face of the first piece with the back edges of the two pieces aligning. The top surface of the 3in x 2in has 45° lines marked on it; a square line can be added if you think a 90° cut will be useful (see Fig 11.14). Make the cuts with a fine saw, being very careful to keep the cut square to the surface.

Some craftsmen glue abrasive paper on to the surface of this type of appliance to stop the wood that is being worked from slipping while it is being cut. If you do this, make sure that the abrasive paper is not where the saw teeth will come into contact with it. If you have problems holding the box, or block, steady on the surface of the bench, screw a strip of wood on to its underside and grip this in the vice.

There is yet another way of holding wood to be mitred. False linings for the vice are described in Chapter 10, and it is a simple matter to make a set of these with a strip of wood screwed to the inner lining at 45°. The piece of wood with the mitre that is to be shot square is placed against this strip and the vice is screwed up to hold it firmly. This idea can also be used where mitres are to be feathered. A block of wood cut accurately to 90° is fixed to the inside lining; it is then an easy task to drop the frame over this

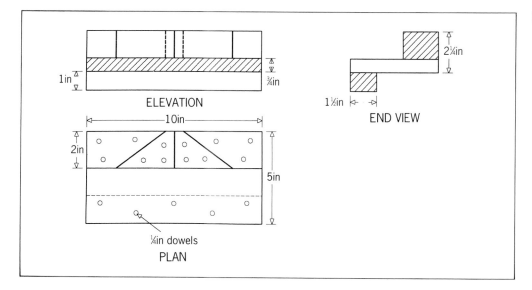

Fig 11.14 Mitre block.

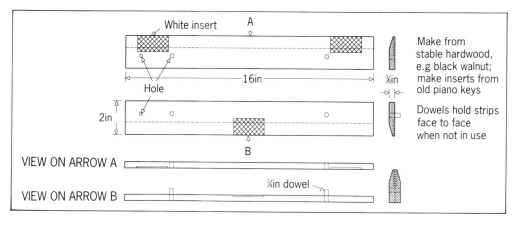

Fig 11.15 Pair of winding strips.

block and hold it squarely in the vice while making the saw cuts for the feathers.

WINDING STICKS

Two pairs of winding sticks have been with me since the first year of my apprenticeship when much of our time was spent preparing timber by hand. I still use the sticks and would be lost without them. Wood still needs to be checked for wind, and a good pair of sticks is the most effective way to do this (*see* Fig 11.15).

The term winding sticks is how I have known these useful tools, but in some places they are referred to as winding strips or winding laths. To look at them they seem so simple that one would suppose that any two strips of wood could be pressed into service, but they need to be absolutely straight and parallel. The ivory from an old piano key is let into the face of one of the sticks to make sighting through the sticks much easier: the white of the ivory stands out plain against the dark colour of the wood. Most craftsmen put two small dowels in one of the sticks that locate in two holes in the other stick; this keeps the sticks together when they are not in use. A hole in one end allows them to be hung up when not in use. Sticks are usually 12in – 18in long and 2in x ⅜in in section.

Fig 11.16 Oil wick.

AN OIL WICK

Many craftsmen stop work and rub paraffin wax on the sole of their plane to reduce the friction. The old craftsmen who worked 'on the book' (piecework) had a better method: they lost money every time they stopped, so they had a little device called an oil wick (*see* Fig 11.16). This consisted of a heavy block of wood about 4in square and 3in thick (*see* Fig 11.17). Buried in the centre of the top was an old fish paste jar, and a rolled up piece of felt stood in the jar. A very small quantity of linseed oil was applied to this wick. This device stood near the end of the wood being planed. When the plane's sole needs lubrication, it is dragged back over the wick – as this movement is part of the return stroke, no time at all is lost.

Be sparing on the linseed oil; it is most difficult to apply some finishes over oily wood, and only the smallest suggestion of oil is required to lubricate the plane. As it is so easy to apply in this way, the plane can be frequently dragged back over the

Fig 11.17 Oil wick dimensions.

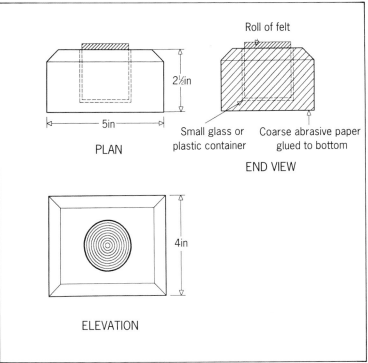

Roll of felt

2½in

5in

PLAN

Small glass or plastic container

Coarse abrasive paper glued to bottom

END VIEW

4in

ELEVATION

Fig 11.18 Squaring rod.

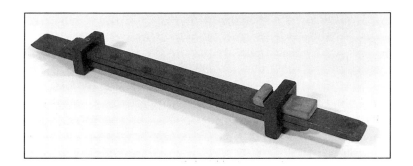

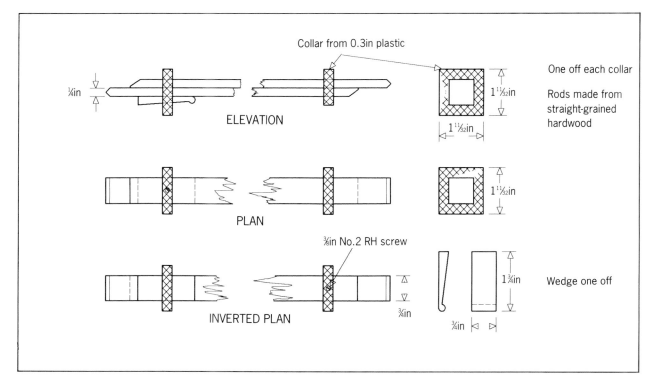

Collar from 0.3in plastic

ELEVATION

PLAN

⅜in No.2 RH screw

INVERTED PLAN

¼in

1¹¹⁄₃₂in

1¹¹⁄₃₂in

1¹¹⁄₃₂in

1¹¹⁄₃₂in

¾in

⅜in

1¾in

One off each collar

Rods made from straight-grained hardwood

Wedge one off

Fig 11.19 Squaring rod dimensions.

wick. Should the wick move about on the bench top when in use, put a small panel pin in each corner of the base. These pins should be left protruding slightly proud of the surface and filed to a point.

SQUARING RODS

All frames, carcases and similar constructions need to be checked for square. A squaring rod should be used in preference to a try square, unless they are very small. Many craftsmen just use a length of batten with a point on one end: this batten is placed diagonally across the job and the pointed end is pushed into one corner. The position of the corner diagonally opposite is marked on the rod with a pencil, and the rod is then placed across the other two corners. If there is a discrepancy, half of this is marked on the rod. The frame is then pushed until the diagonal measurement agrees with the mark on the rod. The rod is left with two pencil marks upon it. Next time the rod is used these marks need to be planed off, or they will confuse the checking of the job.

This seems a long-winded way of going about things – how much better it would be if a length of wood with a point at both ends was made the exact length of the diagonal of the frame. If you are thinking that this would be even more long-winded than the method described above, how about if the rod's length was adjustable (*see* Figs 11.18 and 11.19). The only part that needs any explanation is the collar, the small square part that holds the two parts of the rod together. A multi-laminate ply is needed for this part; mine were made from SRBF (special resin bonded fabric), a very strong man-made material. Several rods of different length will be needed, depending on the variety of work undertaken.

STRAIGHTEDGES

There is a need for a straightedge in every workshop, whatever the length. Quality metal ones are on the expensive side, and for most purposes one made from stable hardwood will be found perfectly adequate. However, do *not* use it as a guide to

cut against, or it will not be a straightedge for long.

In most workshops three straightedges are made at the same time and each is tried against the other two until they are all a perfect fit and their accuracy is assured. If you do not need three straightedges all the same length, the edges of two other pieces of wood can be used when preparing them for a job. I have two straightedges, one of 3ft, the other 6ft. The smaller one is about 3in wide x ½in thick. The other is 4in x ½in. The edge that is to be used has a wide chamfer worked on it, which reduces the edge to ¼in. The chamfer is about 1½in on the face. As with several other items already described, these have a hole in one end and are hung on the wall when not in use.

SAW SHARPENING EQUIPMENT

SAW SHARPENING BLOCK

This is to be found in all professional shops; many craftsmen make one to suit their own height (*see* Figs 11.20 and 11.21). When inserting or removing a saw, it is necessary to use a hammer to gently tap the jaws (marked A in the drawing). Some blocks are made without the metal plate; there is a tendency for the stile (marked C) to split if this is left off. Softwood is adequate for all parts except for the jaws, which are best made from hardwood. The ends of the jaws are shaped to fit over the saw's handle. This appliance is best used stood against a window ledge, as the incoming light will pitch directly on to the saw.

SAW SHARPENING CHOPS

These are used to hold a saw while it is being sharpened, and take up less room than the block (*see* Figs 11.22 and 11.23). In use they are held in the

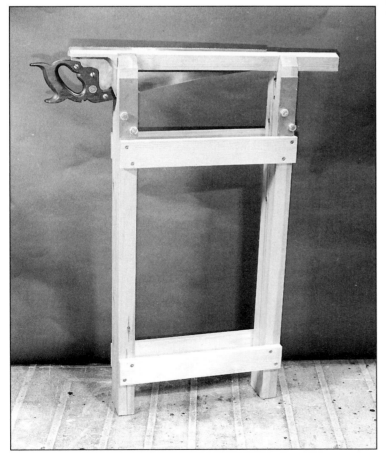

Fig 11.20 Saw sharpening block; this should be made to suit the height of the user.

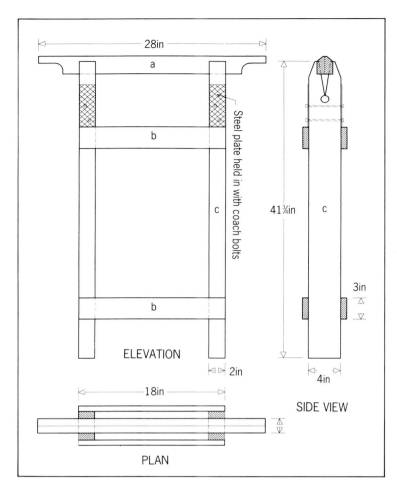

28in

a

b

Steel plate held in with coach bolts

c

c

41¾in

b

3in

ELEVATION

2in

4in

SIDE VIEW

18in

PLAN

Fig 11.22 Saw sharpening chops are used in a similar way to the block, but are held in the bench vice.

bench vice; some craftsmen line the jaws with thin cork. Hardwood is to be preferred for making this appliance. If an old valve spring from a car engine is fitted around the bolt, the jaws will be forced open as the nut is loosened. On both this and the saw sharpening block, it helps to see the saw teeth if the tops of the jaws are painted white.

Fig 11.21 Saw block; the steel plate has been omitted from plan for clarity.

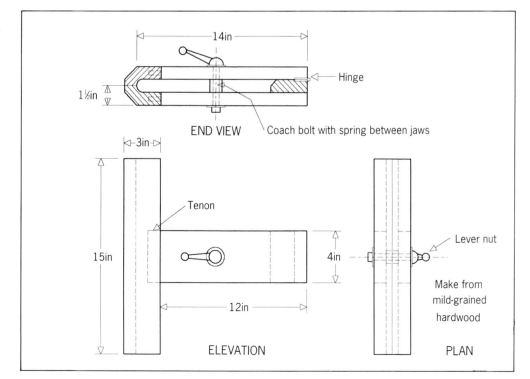

14in

Hinge

1½in

END VIEW

Coach bolt with spring between jaws

3in

Tenon

15in

4in

Lever nut

12in

Make from mild-grained hardwood

ELEVATION

PLAN

Fig 11.23 Saw sharpening chops dimensions.

FREE-STANDING ITEMS

STOOLS

You will need at least two stools for supporting lengths of timber and sheets of man-made material when sawing them. Obtaining the correct angles for the various bevelled cuts on the legs of the stool has long been a test for apprentices; although this chapter is not meant to be a treatise on craft geometry, to construct stools correctly some geometry as applied to setting out must be entered into. For the stool to be thoroughly rigid and stable when in use, the legs are splayed outwards in both length and width, and when the legs are so splayed, an ordinary elevation will neither show their true length nor the correct bevels.

Fig 11.24 shows the true length and required bevels: the height shown in the side elevation is swung into the vertical plane and projected over into the end view. The true shape of the bevels and the length of the legs can now be seen. Another way of describing this is to say that the true

shape of the plane containing the outer surface of the legs has been obtained. Yet more geometry: the legs should not be square in section but rhomboidal. The method for finding the dihedral angle has been included; in practice it will be found that square legs will work perfectly well (*see* Fig 11.25).

Fig 11.25 Stool supporting a board being ripped by hand.

Fig 11.24 Stool.

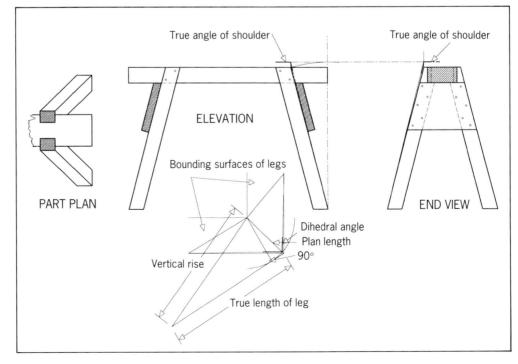

True angle of shoulder

True angle of shoulder

PART PLAN

ELEVATION

Bounding surfaces of legs

Dihedral angle
Plan length
90°

Vertical rise

True length of leg

END VIEW

83

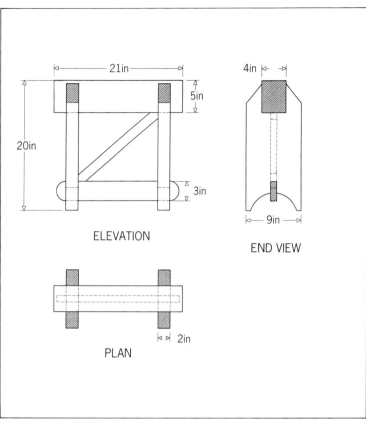

ELEVATION

END VIEW

PLAN

Fig 11.26 Mortising stool.

Fig 11.27 Mortising stool dimensions.

Fig 11.28 Some items of workshop equipment in regular use need a stand of their own to save cluttering up the bench.

The top of the stool is usually made from 4in x 2in, although if you prefer a wide top on your stools they can be made from 9in stuff. Legs are 2in x 2in, and the end rail from 6in x 1in. Softwood is quite adequate for the stool's construction, and the parts are best screwed together. A couple of coats of shellac stop the surface from becoming ingrained with dirt.

The height of the top of the stool is dependent on the stature of the user, 2ft being a rough average, though some craftsmen work on stools that are only 18in high. Cabinetmakers often have a pair of low stools on which they can stand a piece of furniture, lifting the piece to a more comfortable height.

A MORTISING STOOL
Where mortises are cut by hand, particularly large ones, a special stool can be made (*see* Fig 11.26). This is not only more stable than working on

the bench top, but you can also take the weight off your feet at the same time. The height of the stool is again variable with the user. Fig 11.27 shows how the stool can be constructed: the sizes given for the various components are arbitrary, but heavy sections will be required. The stool must be placed on a solid floor when it is being used.

TOOL STANDS

Some of the large tools that take up a lot of bench space, e.g. mitre guillotines and metal mitre boxes, are best kept on a stand; they are then ready for immediate use, and the bench surface is left clear. Unfortunately all these things take up floor space. In a small workshop this type of tool may have to be kept on a shelf and brought down on the bench when required for use.

When designing a stand for a particular tool, make sure that it will be at the correct working height. Stability can be improved if provision is made for the operator to place one of his feet on a rail. The stand's legs usually need splaying in both directions, similar to those on a sawing stool (*see* Fig 11.28). Needless to say, the tool must be secured firmly to the top of the stand. A friend of mine has a stand on which he has what he calls his sharpening station: all his oil stones and other items for sharpening are kept together and ready for immediate use.

ABRASIVE PAPER CUTTER

The standard 11in x 9in sheet of abrasive paper is too large for most purposes, and the sheet will need to be cut into four equal pieces; each piece so cut fits round a sandpaper block which is the ideal size for holding in one hand.

The cutter consists of a board with a hacksaw blade with the set ground off screwed to one edge (*see* Fig

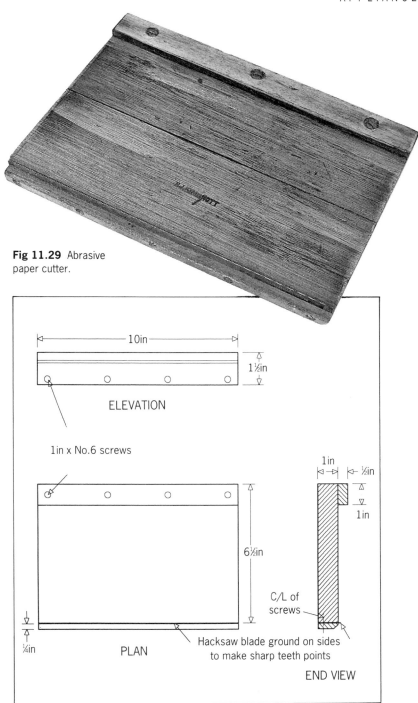

Fig 11.29 Abrasive paper cutter.

Fig 11.30 Abrasive paper cutter dimensions.

11.29). Care must be exercised when grinding the set, as the sharp points on the teeth must be maintained. A strip of wood which acts as a stop is screwed on to the face of the board and set parallel to and at half a sheet's distance from the blade. A deep cut is scored into the surface of the board, a quarter of a sheet's distance from the blade (*see* Fig 11.30).

85

To cut a sheet, place it on the board with a short side against the stop. Press the ball of the hand down on to the paper over the blade. The sharp points of the blade will perforate the sheet, which is torn by firmly holding the part on the board down and pulling the other end of the sheet down and away from the blade. The sheet is next repositioned with one end on the scored line in the board, and the process repeated.

JIGS & HOLDING DEVICES FOR MACHINES

SAFETY

There is a need for several items that can be classed as safety aids. For obvious reasons, one's hands should not come close to revolving cutters or saws, so devices are needed for holding wood being machined firmly into place, allowing it to be fed smoothly and safely into the cutters. The simplest of these items is the push stick.

There are two different types of push stick: one has a simple 'birds mouth' cut in one end, and the other has a spike made from a 4in wire nail at its end. This latter stick is only used on unwrought wood; it will not slip as easily as the one with the bird's mouth, but the spike will mark the surface of wood, so it cannot be used on work of any quality. You may require a large, thick push stick for use on wood with a big cross section and a smaller one for use on more delicate sections.

Until I started to write this book I never realised how many things I drill a hole in and hang up. The push stick is one of these: it needs to be hung near the machine where it can be easily reached when needed. There must be a rule that the stick is always returned to its place after use – if you reach for it and it is not there, you are likely to take a risk and attempt to push the wood past the saw with your hands. It is only a matter of minutes to make one. As soon as the bird's mouth becomes worn or misshapen, it should be recut.

While the push stick works well on the saw, it is of little use on the planer, where a tool can be made to

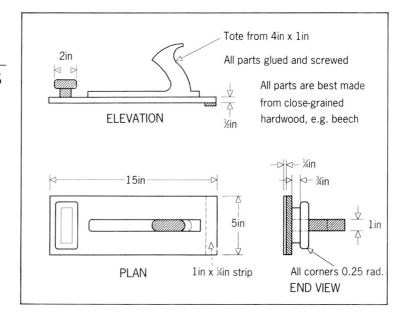

Fig 11.31 Plane push board.

hold small pieces of wood down on the table. The ends of thin boards also require holding down or they will chatter and show planer marks. The tool is made from a board 3in x 1in in section and about 18in long, and has a knob and tote (handle) fitted to one flat side. The tool looks a bit like a thin wooden jack plane without a mouth or blade. A thin strip of wood is screwed on the underside at the end under the tote. The tool is placed on the wood to be planed with the wood strip hooked over the end so that the wood can be safely held down and pushed forward (see Figs 11.31 and 11.32).

A smaller version of the above tool is often made, and is used to hold down the end of long boards. It is made from a board the same section as that above, but instead of the knob

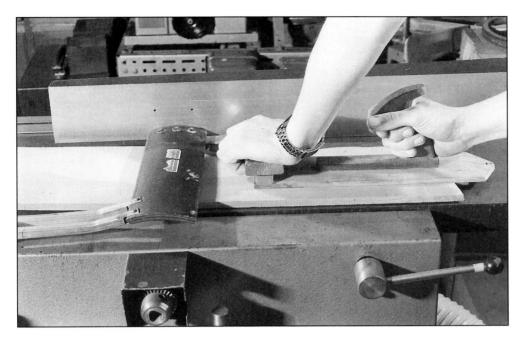

Fig 11.32 Plane push in use on a surface planer; this is a posed shot – in normal use the wristwatch would be removed.

and tote, a block of wood is screwed on. There are times when rebating or moulding on a machine when pressure in three directions is needed: downwards onto the table, sideways to keep the wood against a fence, and forward to feed the wood into the machine. A short length of 6in x 1in has a strip of ¾in x ½in fixed along one edge and one end of its flat side. A block of wood to serve as a handle is screwed to the other side. This appliance is placed on the end of the wood with the thin strips hooked over the end. Two of these tools are required, one for each hand.

V BLOCK SAW FENCE

If there is a need to rip round rod (dowelling) down the centre to produce two half round sections or to rip square section down with a

Fig 11.33 V block saw fence.

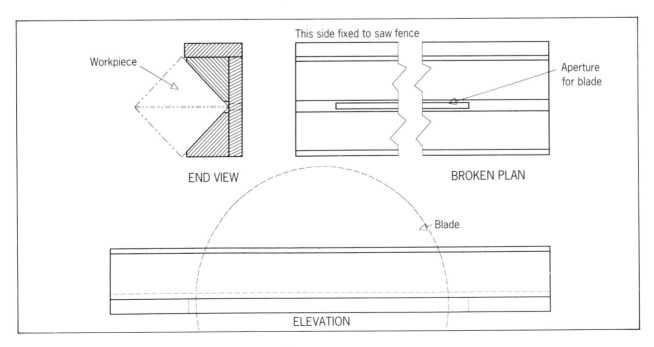

Workpiece

This side fixed to saw fence

Aperture for blade

END VIEW

BROKEN PLAN

Blade

ELEVATION

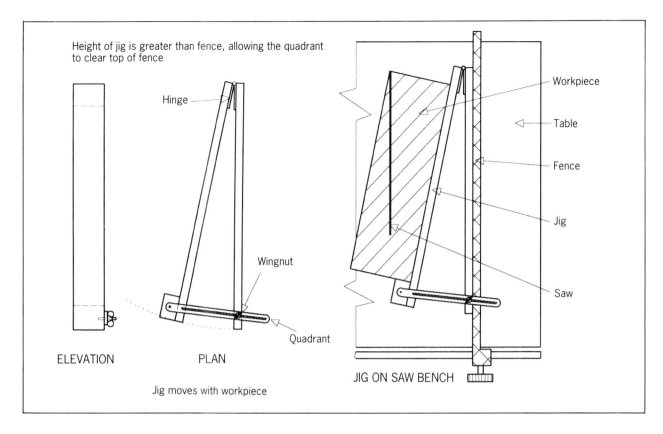

Height of jig is greater than fence, allowing the quadrant to clear top of fence

Hinge

Wingnut

Quadrant

ELEVATION

PLAN

Jig moves with workpiece

Workpiece

Table

Fence

Jig

Saw

JIG ON SAW BENCH

Fig 11.34 Tapered saw fence jig.

diagonal cut producing two three-corner pieces, a V block fence can be made. This is quite a simple apparatus which bolts on to the face of the normal saw fence (*see* Fig 11.33). There is just one feature that needs pointing out: the V block is made from two parts spaced ¼in apart. This prevents the build-up of sawdust in the bottom of the V.

From time to time there is a need to rip out a tapered piece of wood, and a special adjustable fence can be constructed for this type of work, which will enable any taper to be cut. Two pieces of 3in x 1in about 3ft long are hinged together at one end. A quadrant stay is attached to one piece at the opposite end to the hinge. A wingnut on a captive bolt in the second piece of wood runs in the slot of the quadrant. These two pieces can be opened and clamped in an open position by tightening the wingnut (*see* Fig 11.34). There may be some modifications needed to the sizes

given, depending on the machine on which the fence is to be used. When making jigs and attachments to be used on machines, there is often a need for a captive bolt. This can be made by putting a bolt in a hole in which the head is a clearance fit. The bolt is bedded in Araldite, and a little grease in the bolt threads will stop any Araldite sticking in them.

JIGS

In the surface of most machine tables there are one or two grooves running parallel with the direction of the feed. Strips of metal that are a good working fit in these grooves can be made; when these strips are fixed to the underside of a jig it can be slid back and forth parallel to the cutters. Workpieces need to be firmly secured to jigs, so that there is no possibility of them moving.

There are several types of jig clamp obtainable from larger tool shops; these can easily be screwed to a

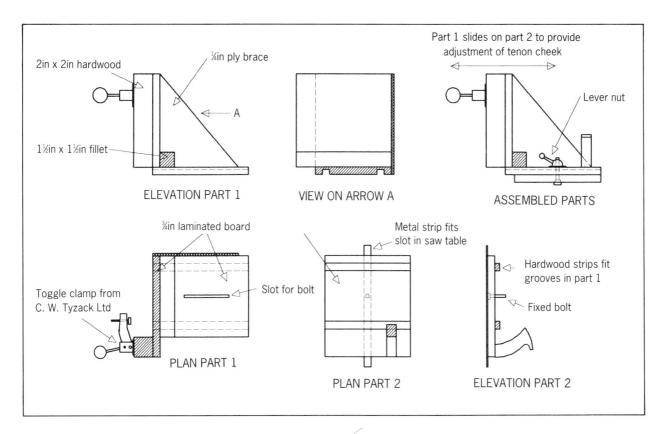

ELEVATION PART 1

VIEW ON ARROW A

ASSEMBLED PARTS

PLAN PART 1

PLAN PART 2

ELEVATION PART 2

2in x 2in hardwood

¼in ply brace

A

1½in x 1½in fillet

Part 1 slides on part 2 to provide adjustment of tenon cheek

Lever nut

¾in laminated board

Slot for bolt

Toggle clamp from C. W. Tyzack Ltd

Metal strip fits slot in saw table

Hardwood strips fit grooves in part 1

Fixed bolt

wooden structure and enable work to be quickly clamped into a jig and released with the flick of a lever.

A JIG FOR CUTTING THE CHEEKS OF TENONS

Tenons are sometimes run in on a circular saw without any jig or special attachment; it makes the blood run cold. This is courting disaster and the daft thing is that the process can be carried out very accurately and in complete safety with a special jig. Fig 11.35 shows this jig in detail, you may have to modify the design to suit your own purpose. It is worth giving this device some thought and constructing a good one, taking time to get it about right. In most shops much time is spent cutting tenons, and the time spent making this jig will be repaid many times over.

If your table saw is not fitted with a cross slide, make one that runs in the grooves in the machine table described above. It may be worth

making two, one set permanently at 90° and the other at 45°. If you need to cut a lot of different angles, an adjustable one can be made. Basically, the slide is just a flat piece of stable board; ¾in ply is ideal. The strip of metal screwed to its underside runs in the slot in the machine's table. A fence is fixed at the required angle on the top surface of the board, or this may be pivoted with a quadrant and wingnut to make it adjustable.

This idea of building fences on top of a board that is running back and forth parallel to the blade can be developed in a number of ways. If a large block splayed at 45° is fixed on its surface with a stop screwed at one end, mitres can be cut across the thickness of a wide board. It is even possible to make a comb-jointing jig for use with a drunken or wobble saw. A piece of plastic laminate glued on to the face will act as a bearing for most of these jigs that slide on the surface of the machine table.

Fig 11.35 Tenon cheek cutting jig for use on table saw.

CHAPTER TWELVE

WOODCUTTING MACHINERY

WHAT DO YOU NEED?

While it is useful to have machinery in the workshop, it is not essential. For centuries woodworkers managed with only hand tools. In the commercial workshop where time is money and the business must be competitive, machinery is of paramount importance, but where a person is working for their own pleasure as a hobby, there is a lot to be said for the 100 per cent hand shop. All woodcutting machinery is noisy and dusty. That said, I would hate to have to do without my basic machines, though my enjoyment of woodworking is mainly derived through the hand tools.

Just what the workshop will be used for will determine what machinery is needed; the occupant's way of working will also be a determining factor. There are machines manufactured for large-scale production, these are intended to be installed in a factory not the home workshop. Some of these machines are CNC (computer numerically controlled) and can produce elaborate three-dimensionally shaped items such as cabriole legs. There is also a need in industry for machines that will work a double day shift (16 hours) day in day out, with little maintenance, whereas the small workshop may only require a machine to run for short periods. The machines made are targeted at each market: the machines made for continual use in industry are of very heavy construction, with large bearings, in heavy cast frames, and some machines aimed at the amateur end of the market are made from pressed metal with welded sections.

The small machines on the market are not all they seem at first sight. The increasing interest in machine woodworking as a hobby has opened up a vast market, and many manufacturers try to capture a larger share of the market by making their product cheaper. Once cost engineering comes in, quality goes out. Inspect what you intend to buy very carefully – try to see the machine where it is installed and in daily use, preferably where it has been in use for some time. If you are inexperienced, get somebody who knows the ropes to come with you. Most woodworkers are only too pleased to help a fellow craftsman.

Just what should you look for when buying a machine? The heavier the machine the more accurate the work it produces, all other things being equal. Weight does not always mean quality, although it must be said that all quality machines are heavy. There is a lot to recommend cast machine tables. Look very carefully to see how the surface of the table has been finished: a finely ground surface is required. Beware of the surface with parallel ridges spaced about ¼in apart; this has been finished on a shaper and will not be as flat as a ground surface. The flatness of machine tables should not be taken for granted; castings take a while to settle down, and they may have moved after being machined – a pair of winding strips and a good straightedge will soon show up any inaccuracies. Inspect the surface of fences to make sure these are also flat and straight. When considering surface planers, the length of the table is as important as the width of the cutter. The overhand planer is called a jointer in the USA, which describes very well what we are asking of it.

One of the most important things is the motive force. Electric motors are so often taken for granted, but just like all mechanical things there are well-made ones and some that are not so well made. Motors are usually rated in horsepower; just what *is* a horsepower? First, we have two different horses: the imperial horsepower is equal to 1.01 metric horsepower, so I suppose you could say that the English horse is stronger than the horse on the continent of Europe. Anyway the imperial horsepower is equal to:

- 746 watts
- 0.707 btu/sec
- 550 foot pounds per sec
- 746 joules/sec
- 178 calories (int)/sec
- 76 kg m/sec
- 1.01 metric horsepower

This information is included, not to baffle you with science, but because the power of motors is quoted in different ways on the plate fixed to the machine. With a bit of simple arithmetic you can convert any units to imperial horsepower. The power required for each type and size of machine is one of those questions like "How long is a piece of string?" Some guidance is needed, but this must be applied with common sense, e.g. a tilt arbour saw bench can be used for a number of difference processes. It can be used to rip timber to the full depth of its capacity. The power to do even this simple process is dependent on the gauge of the saw, which has to remove wood from the kerf to the full width of the set on its teeth. A saw twice as thick as another will require nearly twice the power to cut at the same speed. The powers quoted are for normal work with cuts of average size.

Circular saws

- 6in diameter ½ – ¾hp
- 10in diameter 1½ – 2hp
- 12in diameter 2 – 2½hp

Band saws

- 12in diameter wheels ½hp
- 18in diameter wheels ¾hp
- 24in diameter wheels 1½hp

Jigsaws

- Small machine ½hp

Planers

- 4in cutters ½ – ¾hp
- 6in cutters ¾ – 1hp
- 10in cutters 1½hp
- 12in cutters 2hp

Lathes

- 4in height of centre above bed ½hp
- 6in height of centre above bed ¾hp
- 8in height of centre above bed 1hp
- 12in height of centre above bed 1½hp

Disc sanders

- 10in diameter ¾hp
- 16in diameter 1hp
- 24in diameter 3hp
- 30in diameter 4hp

Bobbin sanders

- Small spindle type ½hp
- 6in diameter ¾hp
- 10in diameter 1½hp

Mortising machines

- Hollow chisels up to ½in ½hp
- Hollow chisels up to 1in ¾hp

Spindlemoulders

- 1 – 4hp dependent on size of cutters

Pillar drills

- For boring holes up to 1in diameter ½hp

Overhead router

- ¼ – 3hp dependent on size of cutters

POWER TRANSMISSION

The power generated by the motor must be transferred to the machine. Even when the motor is enclosed within the framework of the machine, there is still some form of transmission involved. In most modern machines this is by v-belt; where considerable power is involved, multiple belts are used. The arc of contact of a v-belt with the pulleys should never be less than 120°, or slippage is likely to occur. Belt dressing is often applied to flat belts, but should never be put on vee belts, as the principle of surface contact is totally different. The v-belt pulls into the pulley and works on a wedge-like principle, while flat belting relies totally on the friction between the surface of the belt and that of the pulley, and often needs some dressing to increase this friction. If dressing is applied to a v-belt, it tends to build up in lumps and can cause vibrations through variable tension of the belt. Where it is impossible to get the

required 120° of contact, it may be expedient to instal a layshaft. Obviously, the larger the pulleys the more of their surface is in contact with the belt; this transfers more power before slippage is a problem. Belts should not be overtightened to try and transfer power without slippage, as belts that are too tight impose heavy loads on bearings.

PULLEY CALCULATIONS

When calculating the size of pulleys required, remember two things: first, keep the pulleys as large as possible within reason; second, when the motor pulley is smaller than the machine pulley, the machine will run slower than the motor, and vice versa. Where v-belts are concerned, the outer diameter of the pulley is not the true driving diameter, but it is near enough for most practical purposes. Should you need to work more accurately, you will need to find the pitch circle diameter (PCD) of any pulley to be used. This is found in the following way: outside diameter of the pulley, minus the thickness of the belt, plus ⅟₁₆in. As an example: 8in outside diameter pulley, and ⅜in thick belt.

$$8\text{in} - \tfrac{3}{8}\text{in} + \tfrac{1}{16}\text{in} = 7\tfrac{11}{16}\text{in PCD}$$

The arithmetic involved in finding the required pulley size is very simple, as it is basically just a ratio. For instance take a motor running at 1425rpm (this is quite a common speed). We want to drive a 10in circular saw. The peripheral speed of the saw is 9,500ft per minute. First we need to know the rpm of the saw.

$$\frac{\text{Peripheral speed}}{\text{Diameter of saw} \times 3.1416} =$$

$$\frac{9.500 \times 12 \text{ (to change feet to inches)}}{10 \times 3.1416} =$$

$$\frac{114000}{31.416} = \text{Say 3600rpm}$$

Fig 12.1 Right: circular saw. The plastic strips fitted to the window to enable large pieces of wood to be fed in can be clearly seen (see Appendix A).

Fig 12.2 Right: the principles of rise and fall and the tilt arbour on a circular saw.

The ratio of pulley size is $\frac{3600}{1425} = @2.5$

This is about 2.5:1, so if we have a 3in pulley on the saw we need a 7.5in pulley on the motor.

CIRCULAR SAWS

The general term 'circular saw' can be applied to any one of a number of different types of machine – the type under discussion here is that which is most adaptable to general woodwork in a small shop (*see* Fig 12.1). The saw is mounted on a spindle under the table, and the blade is made to rise and fall so that the amount protruding above the table can be adjusted. The motor and saw spindle are mounted in a subframe within the main frame of the machine and move up and down within the machine to provide rise and fall. On tilting arbour machines this frame is made to tilt as well as to move up and down,which means that the saw can be tilted to cut at other angles than 90° (*see* Fig 12.2).

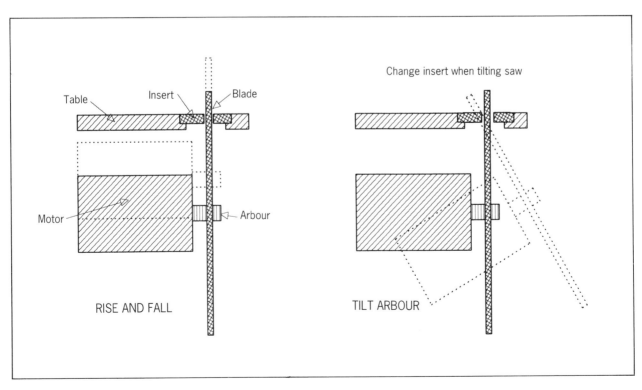

Table

Insert

Blade

Motor

Arbour

RISE AND FALL

Change insert when tilting saw

TILT ARBOUR

For the small workshop a 10in saw is about the minimum size that will cope with most of the work. However, no matter how big the saw, there is always an occasion when a larger one will be needed. You might think from this that the largest size of saw would be the best, but this is not so. There are many processes that it is possible to carry out with this machine that require smallish diameter blades. Remember that the optimum peripheral speed of the blade is dependent on its diameter, so the rpm of the arbour approximately determines the optimum diameter of the blade. The size of circular sawing machines is stated by the diameter of the blade. Because of the peripheral speed of the blade, it is not possible to put a small blade in a machine that is designed for a large blade.

There are a number of different designs, all with their individual uses – e.g. there is one that has two arbours with a saw mounted on each. On one arbour there is a blade designed for crosscutting, on the other a blade for ripping. The two arbours work on a pivot system so that either of the blades can be brought quickly into use. If you intend to use the machine for grooving and similar processes, the blade should be easily changed. Some machines require a side panel to be removed to obtain access to the blade, and this is time-consuming.

THE IDEAL CIRCULAR SAW

A small circular saw which would be ideal for general woodworking would have the following features:

■ 10in blade capacity.

■ The arbour should have plenty of room for wide grooving cutters or a Whitehill cutter block.

■ There should be rise, fall and tilt facilities on the arbour.

■ A rise and fall table is acceptable on very large saws, but on the smaller size the arbour should move – not the table.

■ The top guard should be fitted to a post at the back right-hand corner of the machine; guards that bolt to the top of the riving knife are a nuisance.

■ There should be grooves in the table on either side of the saw to allow the use of jigs (see Chapter 11).

■ A wooden insert should be fitted around the blade. Some machines have an aluminium insert; see if it can be replaced with wood. Different inserts will be needed for different tasks, and an aluminium one cannot be made to fit individual saws or cutters properly.

■ Adjustment of the arbour should be by hand wheels that can be locked once the saw is positioned.

■ There should be some form of stop when the arbour is set for the saw to cut at 90° to the table. The best fences are secured both at the front and the back of the bench. The fence should have a single clamp lever and a micro adjustment.

■ There should be some form of calibration for setting both the width of cut and the cant of saw. Most saws come with a protractor slide.

■ The frame of the saw bench should be completely closed under the table with means of attaching dust extraction.

Many first-time woodworkers think that once they have purchased the machine the expense is over. Unfortunately, this is not true – tooling costs quite a lot of money. A small table saw will need several blades; the blades classed as 'general-purpose' are not very efficient. Today most craftsmen use TCT (tungsten

Fig 12.3 Surface planer showing bridge and back guards. The back guard covers the cutters behind the fence that are not in use.

carbide-tipped) saw blades. Each tooth has a piece of this very hard metal brazed to its tip, so the saw stays sharp much longer than a normal steel one. For cutting man-made sheet material they are almost essential.

THE PLANER

As with the circular saw, no matter what size of planer you instal, there will be times when it will not be big enough. However, 10in is the optimum size for the small workshop; this is the length of the blades, so a 10in machine can comfortably plane 9in wide boards. In most small workshops this machine serves a dual purpose, being used as both an overhand, and underhand planer, i.e.

it is a surface planer and a thicknesser. The same cutter block is used for both processes.

There is a second bed under the surfacing table that is adjustable in its distance from the underside of the cutter block. Power-driven rollers feed the wood between this bed and the cutters. There is an attachment that can be installed above the table of small surface planers to act as a thicknesser (*see* Fig 12.3) – while this may look a bit Heath Robinson, it is very effective. Although there is no power feed, if the surfaces of the appliance are kept clean it doesn't take much energy to push the wood through. While this machine may look very innocent, the cutters need guarding at all times, so be careful.

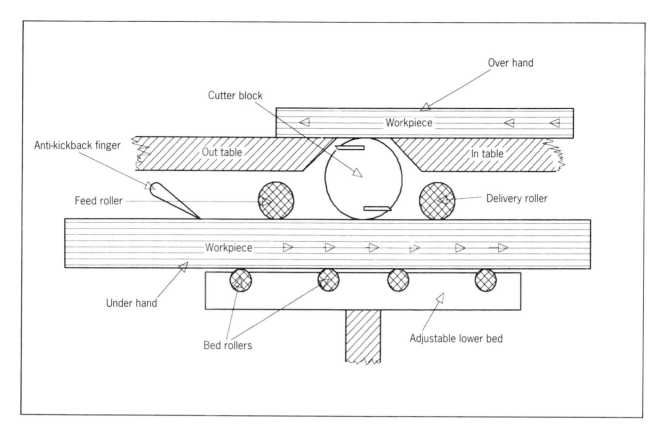

Fig 12.4 Schematic
section through, over
and under hand planer.

If you have the room and the money, separate thicknessing machines are available. These save the small amount of time needed to change the surface planer to thicknesser. Their main use is where timber is constantly being prepared: one worker can plane the faces true while another thicknesses the wood. Thicknessers are sometimes referred to as panel planers because they usually have a wider cut than the surface planer. It is difficult to hold thin wide boards on a surface planer, but they will go through the thicknesser with no trouble.

The fence on the planer needs to be as long as possible. There should be stops so it can be set quickly at 90° and 45°. Some machines have both tables freely adjustable by handscrew or cam and lever, but it is really only necessary to have this feature on the feed table – once the out table is adjusted to the height of the cutter arc, it needs no further attention.

Machines designed for smaller workshops have slot mortising attachments. Thicknessers and planers used for thicknessing must be fitted with an anti-kickback device (*see* Fig 12.4). If the infeed roller is a solid serrated bar, only one piece of wood should be fed in at a time. Segmented feed rollers are only fitted on expensive machines.

BANDSAWS

The bandsaw gets its name from the fact that the cutting blade is a continuous band of steel. The machine is divided into two groups: wide-bladed saws and narrow-bladed saws. Wide-bladed saws are 3in – 14in and are used for converting treetrunks into planks or resawing bulks of timber to usable size. The narrow-bladed bandsaw is a simple machine to operate, and is used mainly for cutting curves and irregular shapes. It is also a useful machine for straight cutting operations (*see* Fig 12.5).

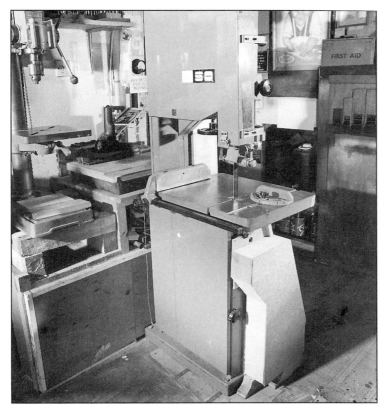

Fig 12.5 Bandsaw.

guides and thrust bearing should be fitted above and below the table.

For some unknown reason bandsaw tables seem to vary in height: small machines need to be put on a stand to bring them to a comfortable working height, and even some sizeable machines need some packing up from the floor.

Most bandsaw blades lead to one side or the other, i.e. they don't cut straight. It is almost impossible to keep a bandsaw in a condition where it will not lead to the left or right, so the sliding mitre fence supplied with some bandsaws is pointless. The wider the blade, the more likelihood there is of the saw cutting straight.

The upper wheel on all bandsaws is tilted with a tilting mechanism, so that the blade can be made to track on the right part of the wheels. A brush which runs in contact with the lower wheel should be fitted to keep the tyre free of sawdust. When working wood with a lot of resin in it, the sawdust can stick to the tyre and become impacted into lumps. This makes the saw tension erratic and causes vibrations.

Your blade requirement will depend on the amount of work you do on the bandsaw. A variety of blades may be needed, with various widths and different tooth configurations. There are blades made for cutting metal, but the speed they run at is somewhat lower than that required for wood. The speed of a woodcutting bandsaw is usually 5,000 to 7,250 feet per minute (lineal); 6,500rpm is looked on as the best in practice. If much work is done on the bandsaw it will be found economical to buy blades in bulk; boxes of 100ft length are obtainable. *See* Chapter 14 for more details on bandsaw blades.

Because of the flywheel effect of the wheels on a bandsaw, the machine will run for some time after the motor is turned off; the machines fitted with

The size of the machine is given as the diameter of the wheels: 14in – 24in is most common for narrow bandsaws. The throat of the machine – the distance between the saw and the machine frame – should be as big as possible. There are a number of smaller machines, but their use is somewhat limited; some of them have three wheels so that the throat clearance can be increased. The maximum depth of cut is important: I use my bandsaw for deep cutting 9in boards. The bandsaw has a narrow kerf, which has two benefits for straight cutting: it wastes less wood and uses less power than the circular saw.

The guides that run either side of the blade come in all shapes and sizes. The plastic ones seem to wear out at an alarming rate; some 14in bandsaws have little rollers which are ideal but this is unusual. The thrust bearing at the back of the blade should be a roller with ball bearings. A full set of

Fig 12.6 Small spindle moulder.

a brake are to be recommended. A few machines are fitted with tension gauges: these are indicators which point to a scale of blade widths as the saw tension is adjusted. This is useful for the beginner, but with a bit of experience it is quite simple to test the tension by flexing the blade between thumb and finger.

Most bandsaws have a small wooden insert in the table where the blade goes through it, and this is also to be recommended. The table has to have a cut running from the front to the saw position so that the blade can be put on and taken off the machine. To keep the two sides of this cut level, there is usually a small tapered plug; this is better than the plate that bolts under the table on some machines.

THE SPINDLE MOULDER
The spindle moulder is used mainly for rebating, grooving and moulding on the edge of timber; it is also possible to cut complicated shapes out using jigs and templates. A spindle hand is a highly skilled and well-paid craftsman, but the spindle is one of the most dangerous machines found in the workshop, and therefore should be used with caution.

The operating principles of the spindle moulder are very simple: as its name suggests, it is a vertical spindle protruding through a machine table (*see* Fig 12.6). There are various ways of attaching cutters to the spindle; also there are several different sorts of fence that can be attached to the surface of the table. The amount that the spindle protrudes through the table is adjustable.

Once the capabilities of the machine are understood, the spindle moulder can prove to be very useful. If you are not conversant with the machine, some form of basic instruction should be sought. To start with, take only light cuts; you will progressively learn just what the machine can do.

The spindle requires a number of different cutters, and there are numerous different designs of cutter block. One of the advantages of this machine is that cutters can be ground to any profile, making it possible to cut any moulding. The speed that the spindle revolves at is 5,000 – 10,000rpm, and some machines have a single set speed, usually 6,000rpm. The speed used depends on the size of the cutters. Some machines have variable speed, others have different sizes of pulley; the belt is moved to get the required speed.

There are numerous guards and devices for holding the work against the cutters. A leaflet issued by the Health & Safety Executive states, 'No single type of guard or other safety device can deal adequately with the variety of work which can be done on the spindle moulder. Each job must be considered individually and the most effective protection provided for the particular circumstances.'

A separate power feed which enables the operator to keep clear of the cutting head can be purchased. There are several standard spindle diameters, but some manufacturers have made spindles of nonstandard dimension; this means that only tooling made by that manufacturer can be used. The most common size of spindle is 30mm.

THE PILLAR DRILL

This machine is also known as a drill press. On first sight it might not appear of much use to a woodworker, but with the proper tooling it can be a useful adjunct to any workshop (*see* Fig 12.7). Basically it is a vertical spindle (called a quill) with a morse taper in its lower end; the top of the quill has a series of stepped pulleys driven by a motor via a V-belt. A Jacobs pattern chuck is usually attached to the morse taper. The quill assembly is made to rise and fall

Fig 12.7 Pillar drill fitted with telescopic guard.

vertically by a rack-and-pinion mechanism connected to a lever on the side of the machine. This mechanism is attached to the top of a column. A table is attached to the same column below.

Work to be drilled is placed on the table and the quill assembly, with a suitable tool in the chuck, is lowered by the rack and pinion, drilling the hole. That may seem a rigmarole just to bore a hole, but the hole will be dead square to the surface, or at any other predetermined angle; the depth of the hole can be accurately set and maintained, and numerous holes all at the same angle and depth can be drilled. There is also a hollow chisel mortising attachment that can be used with the machine. Even if you do not have the mortising attachment it is possible to bore most of the waste from a mortise with this machine before finishing off with a chisel.

A suitable machine for a small woodwork shop would have a ½hp motor and pulleys giving five speeds; these would typically be 380, 700, 110, 1750 and 2800rpm. Some machines are fitted with a mechanical gearbox beside the pulleys which would halve the speeds and give a 10-speed machine. With the appropriate tool a machine as described is quite capable of boring a 2in diameter hole in hardwood. With a fly cutter it will cut large holes in sheet material.

When choosing a pillar drill, one on which the table can be raised or lowered by rack and pinion should be sought; those where the table has to be lifted into position and then locked with a lever take a lot of muscle power. The machine comes with different pillar lengths; those with long pillars are made to stand on the floor, and short pillar machines need to be bench-mounted.

THE ROUTER

This is often termed the overhead router, to differentiate it from the portable router. The term *routing* in my dictionary is defined: 'To poke, search or rummage. To turn over or dig up with the snout, as swine' – a very graphic description of this machine in use.

The router consists of a routing head suspended on a frame over the worktable. The head is connected to a treadle which, when depressed by the operator's foot, lowers the head down to a predetermined level. Cutters, held in the chuck of the routing head revolve at 12,000 – 24,000rpm.

The cutters enter the workpiece held in or on a jig on the worktable. The operator moves the workpiece so that contact is maintained between the shaped jig or template and a steel pin in the worktable; this pin projects above the surface of the worktable and is in direct alignment with the cutter. The pin is interchangeable, and a diameter of pin the same as that of the cutter is usually used. The jig and workpiece are moved around so that the cutter makes a cut completely around the periphery of the job.

The work that the router is capable of can be divided into three main groups: shaping and edge-moulding flat material, recessing into the face of material and perforating material, i.e. cutting out internal shapes. The operations that a router can do are only limited by the ingenuity of the operator. It is possible to obtain or make a frame in which a portable router can be mounted so that it is converted into an overhead router.

MORTISING

Many branches of woodwork require mortises to be made; if there is a constant demand, some form of mechanisation will be worth considering. As mentioned above, it is possible to have an attachment on the pillar drill for chisel mortising, or a slot mortising attachment on the surface planer. This latter attachment is an offshoot of the universal woodworker. I have a hollow chisel mortising jig that fits on the Myford lathe (*see* Fig 12.8), and this has served me well for over 20 years, having been used more for mortising than turning.

A hollow chisel mortising machine is very simple to use – apart from changing the chisel, its operation is unskilled. The only instruction needed is to take it easy: there is no need to lean on the handle to force the cutter into the work; allow the twist bit inside the chisel to cut away and clear the waste wood. (There are several types of machine used in industry, such as the chain mortiser, the Maka system and the Alternax machine. These are all unsuitable for the small workshop.)

Fig 12.8 Myford ML8 lathe fitted with bandsaw and mortising attachments.

Slot mortising is sometimes done with an oscillating bit mortiser, often called a slotter or jigger. The cutting bit is a double-fluted end-cutting tool; this revolves fast and is plunged into the work, which is oscillated back and forth the length of the mortise. Each time the tool travels the length of the mortise, it penetrates a little deeper. This is a very fast way of cutting a mortise.

The mortise made with this device has round ends; the mortise can be squared up by hand with a chisel, or the edges of the tenon can be rounded to fit the mortise. The tool used for slot mortising should not be confused with a plunge cutter for a router: the router cutter also cuts on its sides and a slot mortiser cuts only with its end, which is of larger diameter than the rest of the tool. The recommended speed for a plunge router is 8,500rpm although this is not critical. The power requirement is 1000 – 1500W

THE LATHE

The lathe can be said to be more a tool than a machine, as if one does much turning one gets accustomed to a particular machine. Because woodturning has become such a popular hobby, there are more companies making lathes than any other woodworking machine; these machines have had various gimmicks added to them in an attempt to outdo the competition. The hobbyist woodturner is inundated with gadgets and tools, all of which the supplier would have us believe are essential. If you have the chance go and watch a professional turner, one who has served an apprenticeship in the trade. You will see that he uses a basic lathe and about three different tools.

The lathe you choose will reflect the type of work you wish to produce (*see* Fig 12.8) There are lathes which are just for turning bowls, there are small lathes suitable for making lace bobbins and similar delicate items, and there are the massive brutes on which one could turn the columns for a four-poster bed. Don't forget there will be tools to buy as well.

The best advice that I can give is to go for a well-engineered and manufactured machine, and do not be persuaded by the size of some of the welded sheet metal jobs that are offered at extremely low prices. The quality of the work that can be produced is dependent on machine stability, which, as already mentioned, has a lot to do with weight.

THE RADIAL ARM SAW

The radial arm saw consists of a worktable with a pillar attached to the back of it, rising a couple of feet above it. To the top of this pillar is attached an arm projecting out over the worktable; this arm can be swung around to any angle. Under the arm there is a track on which runs an assembly containing a motor. The spindle of the motor protrudes at one end and forms a machine arbour. The motor can be pivoted to any angle, and runs back and forth on the track under the arm.

A saw fixed to the arbour can be made to crosscut any angle from a true 90° to a compound angle. If the motor is turned so that the arbour is at 90° to the workfence at the back of the table, long lengths of wood can be ripped. By replacing the saw with a moulding or rebating cutter, complicated sections can be worked. There is even an attachment that enables surface planing to be carried out. This machine could be ideal for the very small workshop where space is limited, as nearly all the processes which can be carried out by the machines above can be done by the radial arm saw – how accurately is a matter of opinion.

COMBINATION OR UNIVERSAL WOODWORKING MACHINES

These vary from the sublime to the ridiculous. Those that consist of separate units that stand together to save space are fine machines; they look like a planer and circular saw that have been joined back to back. The saw table usually doubles as a spindle moulder. The better designed machines have a separate motor for

Fig 12.9 Scroll saw.

each part of the machine, so using one is almost the same as using separate machines. However, there are also machines where belts have to be changed and motors moved to re-tension the belt. In others, various bits and bobs have to be bolted on or taken off to perform different operations. Many universal machines are bought under the misapprehension that they will save space, but this is not always so. If possible, instal separate machines, if necessary replanning the space available as suggested in Chapter 2.

OTHER MACHINES

The machines described here are those commonly found in the small workshop. There are many more, some with very special applications: scroll saws (*see* Fig 12.9), disc, bobbin and stroke sanders, dovetailing and combing machines all have a place in the small workshop where there is a special need. For more information on the machines described or machines with special applications, refer to the bibliography on page 179.

CHAPTER THIRTEEN

POWERED HAND TOOLS

WHAT'S IN A NAME?

Just what is a powered hand tool? This title has come about in the last few years, and before that they were known as portable electric tools, a much more explanatory name as most of my hand tools are powered – by me.

Some basic powered tools can save much time in the workshop, and the good craftsman knows their abilities and their limitations. If you are considering the purchase of a tool, make two lists, one for and one against. Do not forget to compare its capabilities with that of your hand tools. There is one further consideration: powered hand tools have small high-revving motors, invariably fitted with a commutator and brushes. The wear on these parts is quite high, so portable power tools need regular inspection and maintenance.

The quality of these tools varies a tremendous amount. If you are able to afford those described as professional quality, you will find the extra expense well worthwhile. Some of the lower value tools have a small card in their box stating that they are not guaranteed for professional use. If you need a tool for very occasional use and it will never be subjected to hard work, this can be a cost-saving reason for purchasing one from the bottom end of the market. As in all things, you get what you pay for.

WHICH TOOLS TO PURCHASE

Again, this depends on the type of work produced in the workshop; however, there are some tools that are more or less standard. One item that needs to be taken notice of when

buying a tool is the power of the motor (*see* Chapter 12). Most electric power tools have the power stated in watts. Some machines have electronic controlled speed, which is very useful: the machine reads the speed and as it drops under load the circuit supplies more power, thus stabilising the speed.

Always check the service back-up. A number of foreign imports do not have any recognised after-sales service. As with any mechanical item, the tool can break down and need spare parts with servicing. These tools are sold over the counter in retail shops, not by the manufacturer as happens with many woodworking machines. The chap selling the tool has very little interest in what happens once he has sold it, so if possible check with somebody who has experience with the make of tool you propose buying.

Cordless power tools rely on rechargeable ni-cad (nickel-cadmium) cells for their power. For most tasks within the workshop you are better off with mains power although a few tools e.g. electric screwdrivers, are more manageable in their cordless form. Make sure you have a spare power supply fully charged and ready to use otherwise you may find that the tool is unusable just when you need it most.

PORTABLE ROUTER

What did we do before the invention of this tool? It is without doubt the most useful of all the powered tools. There are innumerable tasks that can be done with a router, and whole books have been written describing the different uses the tool may be put

Fig 13.1 Miniature portable router with power supply.

Fig 13.2 Elu Trend MOF96 router; a very popular tool.

My bench. Note the storage underneath, the metal cabinet for abrasive papers, and the tools in the rack at the back of the bench (see pages 62-3 and 65-6).

A 15kg (33.1lb) bottle of calor gas is quite heavy (see pages 43-44).

A large square is needed, particularly when marking out sheet material (see page 140).

A textured face Fletton brick (see pages 14-15).

The tool storage unit.

The head of a T-bar cramp (see page 158).

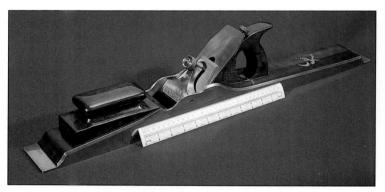
A very fine 30in jointer (see pages 133-4).

Bronze chariot and thumb planes (see pages 136-7).

The inside of the lid of my tool chest, showing the marquetry.

My tool chest. Note the rope handles and the plain painted appearance.
Only the inside is embellished (see pages 157 and 174).

Tobacco tins make good storage containers for small items (see page 60).

The afternoon sun floods into the workshop.

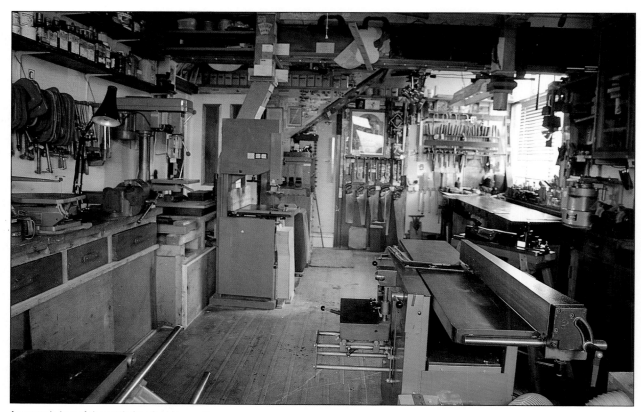

A general view of the workshop looking south.

to (*see* Bibliography). This machine comes in sizes from little miniature versions for model makers (*see* Fig 13.1) up to large high-powered machines used by joiners. Nearly every manufacturer in the field makes at least one size of router and some firms have specialized and made only routers.

The first decision when considering buying a router is the power. Although the more power the better is still true, the more power the larger the size and the heavier the tool is also the case. As the tool has to be manipulated, the big heavy ones are only suitable for work on largish sections of timber: the joinery trade tends to use some of these high-powered machines, which are around 3hp. My biggest machine is 2hp and is very seldom used, while the Elu MOF96, 600W router is used in preference to any of my others (*see* Fig 13.2).

Nearly all routers on the market today are plunge routers. The motor and chuck slide up and down two columns that are attached to the base of the machine. There is a spring that keeps the motor assembly at the top of the columns. Because of this position, the cutter is above the base when not in the working position. When the tool is in the cutting position the motor is depressed against the spring and descends down the columns into the working position. The moment pressure is released from the motor it ascends the columns, thus withdrawing the cutter from the workpiece. This makes the tool very versatile compared with the fixed head router, which is going out of fashion. A cut can easily be started or finished in the centre of a flat panel, and in addition the cutter is safely above the base, out of harm's way when not working.

The cutter is held in a collet (chuck) on the end of the spindle which carries the rotor of the motor. For the smaller machines this collet takes ¼in diameter cutter shanks. A number of larger machines have interchangeable collets which take a maximum cutter size of ½in shank. Collets are easily spoilt by overtightening.

There are a number of useful attachments for the router: the trammel bar enables the router to work a true arc of a circle and can be used to cut some intricate patterns. It would also be ideal for working the arch mouldings on longcase clocks and similar pieces of furniture. It is possible to mount the router under a small machine table; it is then like a small spindle moulder. There are a number of devices for guiding the cutter, which include roller bearings that fit above or below the cutter. A fence is usually supplied with the tool; if not one will be needed. There are jigs and guides designed to cut lapped dovetails, and while these are not very elegant they make a very strong joint.

There are one or two extra safety tips that should be mentioned with particular regard to the router (*see* also Chapter 5). The cutter revolves at a very high speed, typically 24,000rpm; this means that the wood is not cut into shavings but into a fine dust, so always wear a dust mask, Because of this high speed small fragments of wood are thrown out at high speed; eye protection is therefore a necessity, particularly as people tend to have their face very close to the machine when observing the cutters. The high-speed motor emits a high-pitched whine that is injurious to the hearing; wear ear defenders. Always unplug the machine when changing or adjusting the cutter.

ELECTRIC DRILL

This was the first electric-powered tool to be invented and many attachments were made for it. It was used as a power source for numerous items from a small lathe to a paint stirrer, with the proliferation of modern power tools many of these attachments have disappeared.

The tool is most useful when put to its primary use, that of drilling holes. The electric drill comes in a very wide range of powers (*see* Fig 13.3). There is little need for the high-powered versions in woodworking; one with a power of 400watts will be found adequate. Some of the newer machines are fitted with electronic speed controls, which will vary the speed in a stepless range from a few rpm to the full speed of the motor. The normal way of speed change is a two-speed gearbox, with typical speeds of 2100rpm and 1075rpm. A large capacity chuck is desirable, ½in being the optimum.

ORBITAL SANDER

The orbital sander has become a very popular tool in recent years (*see* Fig 13.4). There are two sizes in common use, the half sheet and quarter sheet, which are made to use that part of a standard sheet of abrasive paper (11in x 9in). The paper is attached to a pad that is made to oscillate in small circles. The tool should not be used in fine finishing, as part of the motion is across the grain.

The latest machines are being made with vacuum dust collection built into them: there is a small separate plate the size of the base of the machine, with spikes on it. The paper is pushed on to this plate and the spikes perforate it. The perforated paper is put on to the machine and the holes made to line up with vacuum holes in the machine. The dust is blown into a small cloth bag similar to that on a domestic vacuum cleaner. The quarter-sheet size of sander is also known as a palm sander.

Another tool that looks very similar to the orbital sander is the finishing sander. The main difference is the motion of the paper; on this latter machine it moves back and forth in a straight line. This motion is more difficult to obtain mechanically and this makes the machine more expensive. Unfortunately, most shops do not stock it because of its similarity to the orbital machine.

Fig 13.3 Electric drills – good ones will keep working well for years.

Fig 13.4 An early model orbital sander; most models are now fitted with a vacuum dust collection system.

JIGSAW

This tool is also known as the sabre saw; it is a motor-driven short saw with the saw fixed at its upper end to a reciprocating drive. The saw travels up and down in short strokes, cutting only on the up stroke because the sole of the machine rests on the surface of the work. The upward cut pulls the sole on to the work. If the saw were to cut on the downward stroke, the tool would be forced away from the work and would become unstable. Nearly all the machines made today have an adjustable pendulum action controlled by the small bearing roller at the back of the blade moving back and forth. The reason for the pendulum action is to bring only part of the blade into contact with the cut at any time, this allows a much faster cutting rate as the sawdust can freely escape and does not rely on the saw gullet for removal from the cut.

The jigsaw will cut all sorts of material and will make bevelled and curved cuts. There is a wide variety of blades, all with special uses. Different materials and thicknesses require different amounts of pendulum swing; most tools have a plate with a table of pendulum settings printed on it. Nearly all the worthwhile tools have an electric speed control for different speeds for some materials (*see* Fig 13.5). I find the metal-cutting capabilities of the jigsaw are also very useful.

There are so many different blades that one is at a loss which to use. The following is a starting point, but I would recommend that you experiment.

- Heavy cuts in 2in timber:
  6 teeth per inch

- General cutting in timber:
  7 – 10 teeth per inch

- Smooth cuts in timber:
  12 teeth per inch

- Plywood and hardboard:
  12 teeth per inch

- Cardboard:
  Knife

- Leather:
  Knife

- Metal:
  Special metal cutting blade

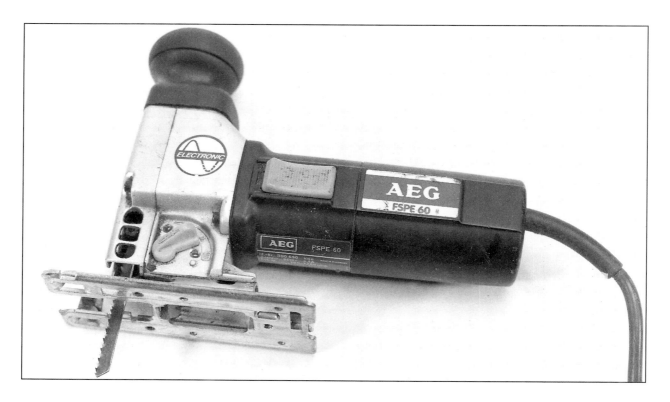

Fig 13.5 This jigsaw is fitted with electronic speed control.

The normal power is 500W. There are several different designs: some have a pistol grip, others are grasped around the body of the motor and still others are made to be held with two hands. Try holding the machine in the shop before buying it and if possible, try one or two different machines, with different handle configurations. When buying the machine, get in a supply of as many different blades as possible, but not too many of one sort.

PORTABLE POWER SAW
These tools are sometimes called cut-off saws and are also known by their trade names, e.g. 'Skillsaw'. In the workshop where there is a good saw bench the requirement for this tool will be small. However, one of the smaller versions will be found useful for cutting sheet material where it is difficult to get it on the saw bench (*see* Fig 13.6). There are tools from sizes with a 6in blade up to large machines capable of taking a 10in blade; it is also possible to get special blades for cutting non-ferrous metals.

It is possible to get a bench which this tool can be fitted under, turning it into a table saw; this may be ideal on the building site, but is not really recommended in the workshop where work of reasonable quality is being produced. I have a small 710W version of this tool; it will only take a 6in blade and is fitted with an extremely fine toothed one. It is often used to pre-cut large sheets of material before bringing them into the workshop.

ELECTRIC POLISHER
Where there is much wax polishing to be carried out this tool will save a lot of time. The machine is quite a simple appliance, consisting of a motor (typically 550W) with a right angle drive on it (*see* Fig 13.7) The polishing is carried out by a lamb's wool mop on an 8in diameter rubber disc. (There is a need for several spare mops, as these frequently require washing.) In the interests of safety, the machine is made to be operated with both hands.

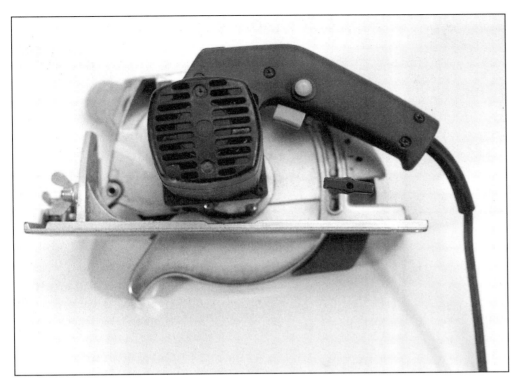

Fig 13.7 Electric polisher.

The machine is only used to give the final burnish to the work – it is not suitable for applying or removing polish – and I have yet to see the wax finish that cannot be improved with this tool. It is possible to fit large abrasive paper discs and use the machine as a rotary sander, but the main market is the car finishing trade.

ROTARY ORBITAL SANDER

This tool is very similar to the orbital sander except that the abrasive pad revolves as well as orbiting in small circles (*see* Fig 13.8). The abrasive paper has Velcro on its back and adheres by this to the machine base. This base is made of rubber, and there are three grades of hardness: the very hard is used on flat surfaces, and the softer ones on shaped surfaces. There is a polishing pad that will replace the abrasive paper but it leaves a lot to be desired. The machine is fitted with a vacuum dust collecting system. It removes wood at a much faster rate than the plain orbital sander; the motor is rated at 180W. In use, the

Fig 13.8 Top: rotary orbital sander.

Fig 13.9 Bottom: belt sander with vacuum dust collection.

the width of the belt, 4in being the most common. One of the rollers is adjustable, to make the belt run true across the pressure plate. These machines are fitted with vacuum dust collection, and most machines have two speeds. When using the machine for the first time, be careful. The belt sander is a bit like a tank – the belt is like a track, the abrasive grips the surface of the wood and if you are not careful the tool will be off down the job at a fair rate of knots. Power is usually in the region of 1000W.

machine requires very little pressure, and cuts much faster under light pressure than under heavy. One immediate problem is the round base, which makes it impossible to work into a corner.

THE BELT SANDER

On this tool there is a continuous belt of abrasive material coated on a cloth backing; this belt is driven by two rollers, and runs over a pressure plate mounted between them (*see* Fig 13.9). The machine runs on the surface of the job to be sanded and the pressure plate keeps the abrasive material in contact with the job. The machine needs to be kept in constant movement or it digs a hole in the workpiece. Machine size is stated by

POWER SCREWDRIVER

Most electric screwdrivers appear to be bought by wives as presents for their DIY husbands; this appliance also appeals to the gadget collector. If the number of screws to be used per day amounts to three figured numbers, then perhaps it would be worth considering purchasing an electric screwdriver, in which case a cordless tool should be chosen. The screwdriver bit that engages the screw head is interchangeable, so make sure that your purchase includes types and sizes to fit the screws that you intend using. This is one of the reasons why it can be quicker to use the old-fashioned screwdriver, and the electric version works to a Murphy law which states: 'Whatever screw you intend to drive, the wrong bit will be fitted.' There is a strong temptation to make do with the bit that is in the tool, to the detriment of the screw head. It is actually much quicker to take the correct size of screwdriver from the rack at the back of the bench, where after use it is returned, ready for immediate use when it is next required. The power screwdriver is mainly supplied as cordless, because the lead would make the tool very unwieldy to use. Make sure that you have spare power packs charged and ready to use if you have one of these tools in the workshop.

POWER PLANERS

In the workshop with a planing machine there is little use for a portable planer, but it is useful when working away from the workshop. The tool is very much like a small planing machine turned upside down with a pair of handles attached. Most of the tools on sale have reversible cutters which are sharpened along both edges. When the first edge becomes blunt the cutter is turned over and the second edge used. The size of the tool is given by the length of the cutter, a common size being 3in. Some models can be used to cut rebates; all can form chamfers. It is a difficult tool to hold square on a narrow edge, and practice is needed to become proficient in its use.

THE BISCUIT JOINTER

The biscuit here is a small elliptical piece of compressed beech; the tool is a small-diameter thick gauge circular saw which is driven at right angles to the motor through a gear train. In use the machine is placed on the joining surfaces of the pieces of wood to be joined and a plunge cut is made by the blade. This cut is segmental in depth and the width is that of the blade's thickness. A similar cut is made in the second piece of wood. A biscuit is then placed in the pre-glued cuts and the joint assembled; the moisture from the glue causes the biscuit to expand, and the joint is held fast, even before the glue sets.

The tool has a fence so that the cut in both joining surfaces can be placed in the same position. The saw blade is interchangeable so that biscuits of different thicknesses can be used, the thickness being determined by that of the wood to be joined. The tool can also be used to cut grooves. Joints can be made in any two mating surfaces, whether they be long grain or end grain. The motor is usually rated at around 600W.

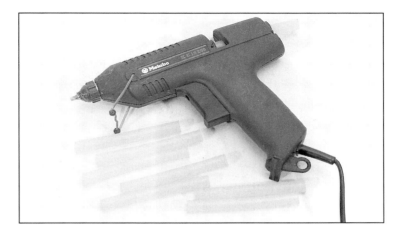

GLUE GUN

This tool may be useful where quick assembly is required as the open time for the joint is very short (*see* Fig 13.10). This can be helped if the wood is heated, but that is not a recommended practice. The tool is also useful for mounting work on a lathe faceplate. If a wooden disc is attached to the faceplate, and both this and the workpiece warmed, they can be stuck together with the gun. As soon as the job cools the glue is set, and the work can proceed. A hot air gun is used on the back of the faceplate disc to release the work (*see* Fig 13.11). There are no screw holes or other blemishes from the mounting.

Fig 13.10 Glue gun with glue sticks.

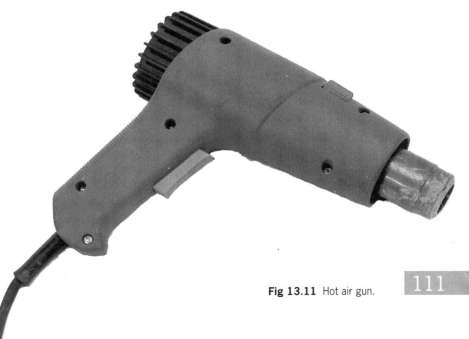

Fig 13.11 Hot air gun.

111

CHAPTER FOURTEEN
TOOLING FOR MACHINES

A MOST IMPORTANT ITEM

A workshop can be equipped with the finest machines that money can buy, but it will mean nothing without adequate tooling – all the blades and cutters that fit in the machines, some of which can be surprisingly expensive. When fitting out a workshop one could very easily just include the cost of the machines and forget all about the tooling. So, what is required? The list could be broken down into two parts, essential and useful but not indispensable.

SAW

The saw bench will obviously need a saw blade. Most saw benches are sold with a blade installed, and unless it is a fairly expensive machine the blade will probably be a steel general-purpose one, which will get you started, but the machine is going to be very limited in what can be done on it.

The first addition could be a pair of wobble washers; these are washers which, when placed on the arbour either side of the saw, make the blade wobble from side to side as it cuts. By retracting the saw until only a small part of it protrudes through the table, a groove can be worked. By rotating the washers in relationship to one another, the amount of wobble can be controlled, and thus the width of the groove can be adjusted.

After a short while the blade will lose the nice sharp edge it had when it was new, and will need resharpening. Heat very quickly builds up because of the speed that the cutting edge of any woodworking machine is running at. This heat is controlled by the tool being fed into fresh cool wood. If the wood is fed very slowly the tool will become overheated, and can even be spoilt in this way. If you see scorched wood, something is wrong – a blunt tool cannot cut fast enough to keep itself cool. Back at the blunt saw blade, the periphery of the blade that is in contact with the wood heats up and expands. The centre of the saw, which is not in contact with the wood and is bolted to a cold arbour, does not expand and the periphery of the saw has to expand somehow and takes on a wavy configuration. The poor blade can no longer cut straight, and the saw cut starts wandering. The wood starts to pinch between the saw and the fence, and we have all the makings of a serious accident. Always use sharp tools – this is as important with machines as it is with hand tools.

Most craftsmen using the smaller size of saw bench, i.e. up to and including 12in, use TCT (tungsten carbide-tipped) blades. These are expensive to start with but the time saved in sharpening conventional steel blades soon repays the investment. When the TCT blade requires sharpening it is best entrusted to a reputable saw doctor. Many tool shops offer a sharpening service, and there are saw sharpening and repairing firms listed in the Yellow Pages. It is not possible to get tungsten carbide as sharp as good silver steel, but the difference is minimal and not sufficient to dispose with the TCT saw's edge-holding capabilities.

The next decision is how many teeth to have on the saw and what gauge saw to buy; this is very difficult without knowing just what the saw is going to be expected to cut. Fig 14.1 shows a selection of the blades that I

Fig 14.1 Circular saw blades. From left to right: TCT ripsaw; multi-purpose silver steel; TCT crosscut and man-made board saw.

use in my workshop. The more teeth the saw has, the smoother the surface of the cut wood. With ply and similar sheet material the surface break-out is less with a fine-toothed saw. When it comes to ripping solid wood, there is need for a deep gullet to carry the sawdust away, so large teeth are the requirement here.

If the arbour speed is reasonably high, say 3,500rpm or above, a Whitehill moulding block with an overall diameter of at least 6in, can be used. This will still give a fairly low cutting speed of about 5,500ft/min. With care this can be used for running all sorts of interesting edge moulds.

A dado head is a tool that has a number of uses in the small workshop; it consists of two saw blades with special tooth configurations. These two blades are spaced apart the width of a groove or rebate to be cut, and the space between them is taken up by a number of chippers, cutters with two cutting teeth spaced at 180° to one another. The cutting edge of the chippers is swage set. The dado set

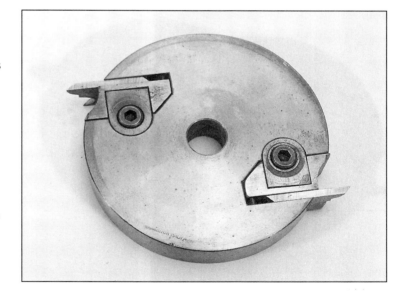

(*see* Fig 14.3) contains a number of chippers of different thicknesses, and in this way a tool can be made up to cut a groove of any width. The dado head is an effective tool for cutting both across and with the grain.

SURFACE PLANE AND THICKNESSER

The blades for a planer are known in the trade as knives. There are three distinct types of conventional knives.

Fig 14.2 Whitehill pattern cutter block.

113

Fig 14.3 Dado set. The two saw blades are set apart with chippers of different thicknesses, so a groove of any width can be cut.

First, the ones at the bottom of the price range: these will be made from straightforward high carbon tool steel, and do not maintain their edge for very long. Next up the list are those made from high-speed steel: these maintain their edge for considerably more time than the plain steel variety. Last and most expensive are the tungsten carbide edged knives: these hold a reasonable edge for a very long time, but cost a great deal.

A new machine will, as a rule, have one set of knives installed; these are invariably plain tool steel. When they need grinding you will need to remove them, and unless you instal your own grinding facilities they will have to be sent away, leaving you without any blades. So a second set must be purchased before the first set need grinding.

In my case, I have two sets of plain steel blades which came with the machine. There are a further two sets of high-speed blades which I use most of the time, and I have one set of tungsten carbide knives which are used when there is a lot of abrasive wood, e.g. teak, to machine.

Some modern machines are fitted with disposable cutters. It seems a great waste to take them out and throw them away. Added to this, there must always be at least one new set spare.

SPINDLE MOULDER

This machine is very versatile, but only as far as its tooling will allow it to be. The machines used in commerce have interchangeable spindles. Most of the lower priced machines sold on the small machine market have fixed spindles, but for most purposes this is no disadvantage.

The French head is probably the simplest of several alternatives: the spindle has a slot through it and cutters are inserted through the slot. There is a bolt tapped into the central axis of the spindle that clamps the cutter into place. Most French lead cutters are just a flat bar of tool steel with the moulding profile ground on each end. Some cutters are notched at the centre to make them more secure when fitted to the spindle: while this is good safety practice, it makes the grinding of the cutters a precision job, as both ends must be an exact measurement from the notch – if there is any inaccuracy in this, one end of the cutter does all the work.

When a cutter is revolving at speeds of 6000rpm or more. the inertia caused by centrifugal forces accentuates any out-of-balance in the cutter. An out-of-balanced cutter causes vibration and imposes heavy loads on the machine's bearings. (It can be likened to the effect of an out-of-balance wheel on the steering of a car.) If a single-ended cutter is used in a French head, a blind cutter must be inserted to balance it.

Slotted collars can be used to hold a pair of cutters. The cutting angle of the cutters is much more efficient than the French head (see Fig14.4). Some collars are fitted with little machine screws that engage in a slot in the cutter; these make adjustment much easier than with plain cutters.

There is little purpose in using the French head or a pair of collars for rebating or grooving, as a rebating block is far quicker to fit and set up. This is a disk of steel about 1½in thick and 4in in diameter, with two cutters in its circumference and spur cutters in each edge (see Fig 14.5). This drops straight over the spindle and is locked into position with collars and the top spindle nut.

Grooves are best worked with a disc cutter (see Fig 14.6). A steel disk a little under ¼in thick and 6in or so in diameter with cutters at 180° to one another inserted in its outer circumference. The cutters are made in different widths so that grooves of any width may be worked.

A square block can be fitted to the spindle. This is a very versatile tool in that it can a have a different cutter fitted to each of its four sides. The block is a square section of steel, and there is a dovetail-shaped groove running from top to bottom in each

Fig 14.4 Pair of collars with cutters. The cutters are ground to the reverse profile of the mould, and are clamped between the collars of the spindle nut of the spindle moulder. This pair of cutters works a small ovolo.

Fig 14.5 Rebating cutter. The small tungsten spur cutter on the side of the block leaves a clean cut on the side of the rebate.

Fig 14.6 The cutters can be changed on this disc cutter for use on a spindle moulder.

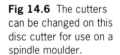
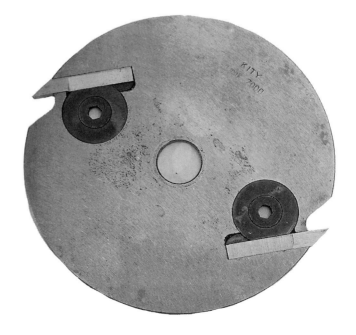

115

side. The centre of the block has a hole through it that fits over the spindle. Cutters are bolted on to the block with special bolts; these bolts have dovetail-shaped heads that fit the grooves in the block.

The standard Whitehill cutter (*see* Fig 14.2) can be used on a spindle moulder and is a most efficient tool and there is yet another form of cutter, the solid profile cutter. These are self-contained tools, each being a complete cutter and head in its own right. There are no loose parts, and because the cutter is symmetrical there is no problem with balance. They are very quick and easy to fit, but expensive to buy in the first place. They also need to be ground on specialized machinery as they mostly have TCT fitted.

It is possible to fit small circular saws on a spindle: some craftsmen run the cheeks of their tenons in using this set-up with a sliding table.

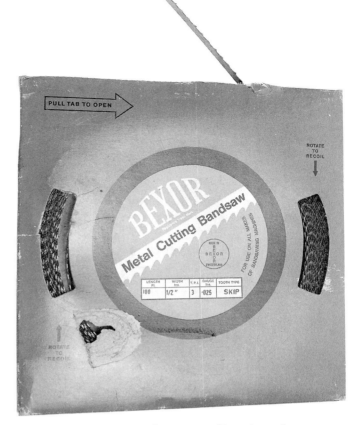

Fig 14.7 Bandsaw blade bought in bulk.

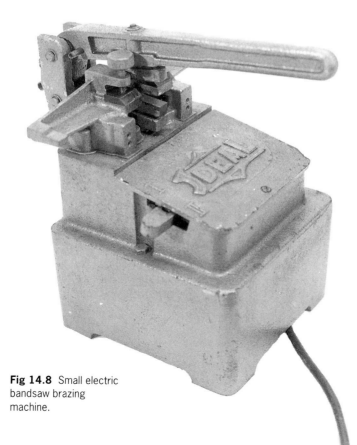

Fig 14.8 Small electric bandsaw brazing machine.

Another type of head used on some small machines has a collet very similar to that fitted to a router. The machines of this type cannot be classed with the normal spindle moulders, being more akin to the router.

BANDSAW

The bandsaw can be used for a number of different operations. One blade will not be suitable for them all, so it is important that the blade fitted to the bandsaw is the most suited to the type of work undertaken. It takes quite a while to change a saw blade and set it up to track properly, so any blade fitted should cover the widest variety of the work carried out in the shop.

The width of the blade determines the size of curve that the machine will cut: a narrow blade will cut a much tighter curve than a wide one. There is a variation because the amount of set on the saw also affects the cutting circle of the saw. The widest saw blade that will suit should be chosen, because more tension can be applied to a wide blade – the more the blade is tensioned, the truer it runs (this is most apparent on a straight cut). Most shops that have only one machine fit a ⅜in wide blade

Tooth configuration affects the cutting efficiency of the blade, however, each manufacturer seems to have a different term for the same tooth configuration. The pitch depends on the thickness of wood to be cut; there should be a minimum of two teeth in contact with the wood at any one time, so a saw with 5 points to the inch will be used for wood of ½in and above. The teeth will be set so that the kerf is wider than the gauge of the saw.

Bandsaws over 1½in wide are often swage set. This entails the top of the tooth being flattened and made wider than the gauge. The tooth then cuts a wider kerf than the blade thickness. There is a form of setting that is termed skip tooth where the first tooth is set right, the next tooth is not set at all, the third tooth is set left, the next tooth is not set, etc.

The final choice is one of hardness of blade. In recent years there has been a tendency to use blades that have inductance hardened tooth tips. There are even blades that are primarily intended for metal cutting that can be used with good effect on wood. The cost of sharpening a narrow bandsaw blade is almost the same as the cost of a new blade; the extra life obtained from the hard point that cannot be sharpened is therefore a bonus. Fig 14.7 shows a metal cutting blade which can be bought in 100ft lengths and used as a general purpose woodworking blade.

Once made up for the machine, a bandsaw blade is quite unwieldy.

A small electric brazing machine (see Fig 14.8) or a butt weld machine will be needed to join the blade. Those who use the butt weld say that it is easier to use than the brazing machine because of the preparation needed to prepare the ends for brazing; however, the brazing machine will repair blades as well as making new ones.

Fig 14.9 Section of bandsaw showing splayed joint.

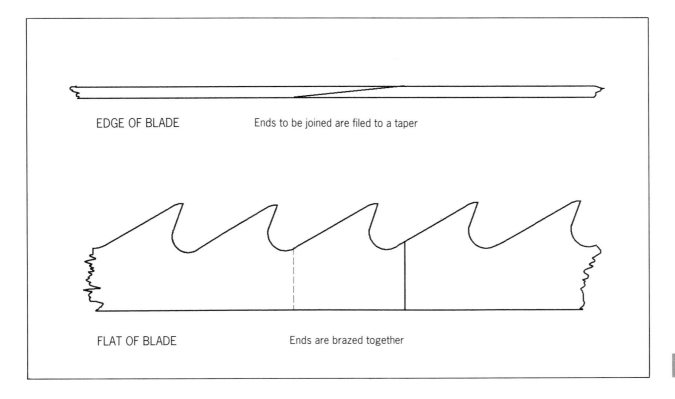

EDGE OF BLADE — Ends to be joined are filed to a taper

FLAT OF BLADE — Ends are brazed together

Fig 14.10 Router cutters in a storage case.

ROUTER

No matter how many cutters one has for the router, there is always another one that would be useful (*see* Fig 14.10) the best plan is to buy the cutters as they are needed. There are one or two that will obviously be required; these will be sufficient to start with. Try to settle on one size of cutter shank as it is a nuisance to have to keep changing the collet for different sizes. For most purposes the 0.188in size will be found adequate. Most shops stock more cutters in this size than in any other.

Most cutter manufacturers issue free sheets of illustrations of their cutters. It would be impossible to show all the cutters available as there are literally hundreds. The most used cutters are the straight fluted variety: these are used for grooving, rebating trimming and cutting out shapes, and can be used for plunge cutting if they have cutting edges at the bottom of the cutter. The most useful are described as 'two flute, bottom cut'.

Complicated mouldings can be made by combining cuts from different simple-shaped cutters. Guiding the cutter in the path where the cut is to be made affects the choice of cutter. When working the edge of a piece of wood, a cutter with a guide pin can be used. The pin is a permanent fixture on most cutters, and means that the cutter can only be used on the edge. A fence can be attached to a portable router so that any cutter will work parallel to the edge. Some cutters have a small tapped hole at their bottom end where a bearing can be bolted on with an Allen screw. This bearing runs against the edge of the wood and thus guides the cutter. The mould cut can be

Fig 14.11 Guide bushes for the portable router; these are bolted on to the bottom face of the router, with the cutter protruding through the centre hole. The outer surface of the bush follows the contours of a template, cutting a predetermined shape.

Fig 14.12 Set of twist drills in a stand.

varied by using different sized bearings.

Bushes can be attached to the base plate of some portable routers. This is a small attachment that resembles an inverted top hat. The bush is fixed to the base plate with countersunk bolts through what would be the brim of the hat (*see* Fig 14.11). The cutter runs through the centre of the bush, and the outside of the bush bears against the template. As the router is moved around with the bush touching the template, the cutter cuts the required shape.

Overhead routers, while using the same type of cutter, do not require the guiding systems required by the portable router, the interchangeable guide pin in the worktable being used for most purposes. A fence can be attached for straight line routing.

BORING AND DRILLING MACHINES

In every workshop there are times when holes have to be drilled in metal. This may only be for screw holes in a fitting, but when they are needed it will be a bind if the correct size of drill is not to hand. A set of high-speed twist drills, stored in a block or box so that the required drill can easily be found, will always be needed (*see* Fig 14.12). These drills can also be used for drilling holes in wood; up to ½in in diameter is probably the most economic tooling for wood. Once this maximum size is reached, twist drills start to become expensive and not very efficient for woodworking.

Deep holes need a machine auger bit (*see* Fig 14.13). These bits are made in a variety of sizes and lengths. Should the bit have a screw thread cut on its point, file it off, as the thread will pull the bit into the workpiece at an alarming rate. The machine's rack and pinion feed should be used to advance the bit into the work, not a thread on its point. For shallow holes requiring a flat bottom, Forstner bits are required. These are very useful – and expensive – tools which can be used to remove the waste from housings and any recessed areas. The Forstner bit is made in sizes from ¼in to 2in diameter.

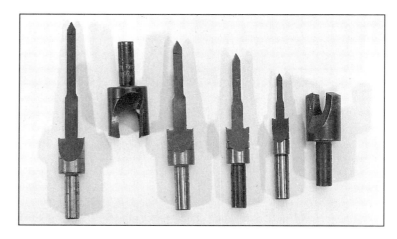

Screw sinks are ideal tools if screw holes have to be frequently drilled. This tool is made to fit an individual size of screw (*see* Fig 14.14). The hole made can either be finished for countersunk screws, or for sunk screws that will be pelleted. There are cutters that will cut pellets to fit exactly the hole made by the screwsink.

There are twist drills made specially for drilling wood. These are similar to those used for metal, but with a brad point at their end. This makes them much easier to position accurately, especially when starting a drill at an angle to the face of the job.

Fig 14.14 Screw sinks. Each size of screw has a separate tool, so the hole made fits the screws. When the tool is drilled to the first depth notch a countersunk hole is made; the second notch produces a recessed screw hole, and the third a counterbored hole. The plug cutters produce a pellet that fits the counterbore perfectly.

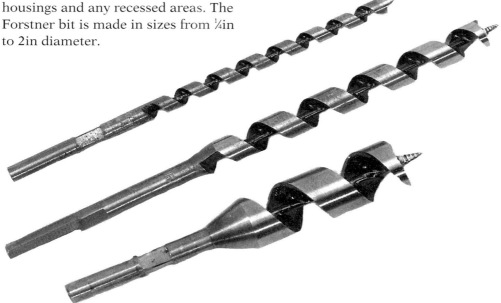

Fig 14.13 Machine auger bits; most of the thread has been filed away from the screw.

CHAPTER FIFTEEN

SHARPENING EQUIPMENT

PRE-EMINENT THINGS

A workshop which lacked the equipment for sharpening tools would soon come to a standstill. There are various methods of sharpening, and each craftsman has his own likes and dislikes – there have been more arguments in the workshop over sharpening than any other subject. Sharpening can be divided broadly into two separate operations: grinding by machine and honing by hand.

GRINDING

The subject can again be divided into two groups: wet grinding and dry grinding. Because the characteristics of carbon steel are affected by heat, it is important that tools are not subjected to it. The energy expended at the grinding surface of a tool as it is ground is considerable, and some form of cooling is of paramount importance if the tool is not to be spoilt.

When grinding on a dry wheel, dipping the tool frequently into cold water will cool it. Even so, one has to be extremely careful – at the tool's tip where the metal is thin there is little material to absorb the heat and it only takes a second to destroy the temper of the tool in this region. Wet grinding keeps a constant flow of a cooling agent – usually water – over the grinding surface. But there is still a need for caution: too much pressure from an impatient operator can still cause heat to build up.

DRY GRINDING

The process of grinding on a dry wheel is usually carried out on a bench grinder. This consists of an electric motor with the motor spindle extended at each end to form an arbour. A grinding wheel is mounted on each arbour. The composition of the wheel, and its surface speed are important.

The word Carborundum, applied to grinding wheels, is a trade name applied to one of two basic materials supplied by the Carborundum Company of Manchester. This artificial abrasive material is made from a mixture of sand, coke, sawdust and salt. The mixture is heated in a resistance electric furnace. The resulting crystalline substance is silicon carbide. The product from the furnace is crushed, washed with alkalis and acids to get rid of impurities, and finally graded by size and made into grinding wheels.

The other abrasive made is sold under the trade name of Aloxite. This is produced by heating bauxite in an arc electric furnace to form aluminium oxide, which is a hard crystalline substance. This, as Carborundum, is ground, graded and made into wheels. Carborundum is much harder than Aloxite. However, Aloxite is tough and will withstand heavy loading where Carborundum would break down.

There are two main methods of bonding the abrasive material into a wheel. The first is a vitrification process, where the abrasive is mixed with suitable clay. The mixture is moulded in a hydraulic press, and fired in a kiln. Sodium silicate is used for the other method, and is mixed and fired in a similar way so that a bond of porcelain or glass is formed. Silicate wheels have a mild cutting action, and must not be subjected to heavy loads.

Fig 15.1 A grinding station with a Sharpenset (the jig is for grinding planer knives) and a dry grinder. Note the goggles and case hung above the grinders.

Classification of Grit Size

The crushed grit is passed through a series of sieves arranged in a stack with the coarsest at the top and the finest at the bottom. The grit that passes through a screen but is retained on the next screen below is classified by the number of meshes per inch of the screen through which it has passed. The table below lists the standard sizes of grit used for grinding wheels.

Very Fine		150	180	200	290
Fine	70	80	90	100	120
Medium		30	36	46	60
Coarse	12	14	16	20	24

Grade of wheel

Grade is often referred to as the hardness of the wheel. This is quite so, though it does not refer to the hardness of the grit, but to the tenacity with which the grains are retained in the wheel by the bonding material. As the grains on the surface of the wheel lose their cutting ability they break away and expose a new cutting surface. This way the stone does not take on a glazed surface and lose its cut. Letters of the alphabet are

Very Hard	V W X Y Z
Hard	U
Medium to Hard	M N O P Q R S T
Soft to Medium	E F G H I J K L
Very Soft	A B C D

used to denote the grade of wheel, D being very soft and W extremely hard. The following table is a guide to the hardness represented by different letters. Both vitrified and silicate wheels are represented in the same way.

All new wheels have a label on their side. The code on the label identifies the characteristics of the wheel, e.g.:

A 60 – G – 180
A is the abrasive material (Aloxite)
60 is the size of the grit
G is the grade
180 is the bond

Other manufacturers use similar systems. For instance, Norton has the following system:

The letter 'A' stands for Alundum, a trade name for aluminium oxide, 'C' for Crystolon (silicon carbide), 'ZE' or 'ZS' for zirconia alumina (zirconia). Zirconia is made from the mineral zircon, found in igneous, sedimentary and metamorphic rocks. There is sometimes a number in front of this letter that indicates special characteristics the abrasive may have.

The grit size and the grade are identical to Carborundum's system. However, there is another number included next which indicates the structure of the wheel. This indicates how tight together the grains of abrasive are packed. The last letters indicate the bond, 'V', standing for vitrified and 'B' for resinoid bond.

Wheel mounting

Nearly all wheels have a lead bush at their centre. It is essential that the hole size in the bush is the same as the diameter of the spindle of the grinding machine. The wheel should have a paper washer on both sides to stop the flanges that clamp the wheel in position bearing directly on to the wheel's abrasive surface. The pair of flanges, one fixed and one sliding, are

tightened either side of the wheel with a nut. Where a machine has two wheels, the nut on the left has a left-hand thread, while the nut on the right has a right-hand thread. The flanges are relieved at their centre, so that only their outer surface bears on the wheel. When a wheel is mounted, the surface should be dressed to ensure that it is running true.

The speed of most bench grinders fitted with a 6in diameter wheel is around 3000rpm; this gives a surface speed of 4700ft/min. Should a wheel break up in use, there will be pieces of abrasive material thrown all over the place, so great care should be taken to ensure that wheels are fitted and trued correctly. If a wheel is supported loosely and tapped gently it should emit a clear ringing sound; a cracked wheel emits a dull sound. If you suspect a wheel of being damaged in any way, for safety's sake it should not be used.

Wheels are designed either to grind on their edge, or their side; no wheel is made for both. There is particular danger of the wheel breaking when grinding on the side of a wheel that is intended to work on its edge.

No wheel should be subjected to extremely heavy loads. Do not grind nonferrous metal – this clogs up the surface of the stone and can cause it to fracture. Stones made to work dry should not be made wet. Under no circumstance put oil on a grinding wheel: oil mixes with the grinding dust and clogs up the pores of the stone.

A small machine with two 6in wheels, one coarse and one fine, will be quite adequate for the average workshop. A spark guard to stop the small red-hot pieces of metal from flying everywhere should be fitted; this guard is not a replacement for eye protection, which should be worn whenever the grinder is being used.

Fig 15.2 A small, inexpensive wet grinding machine, ideal for the small workshop.

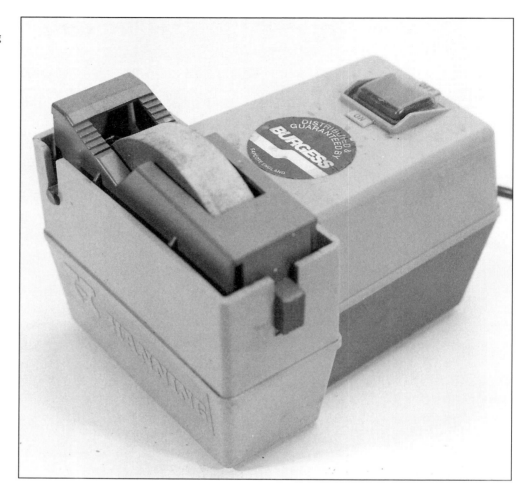

WET GRINDING

Wet grinding is preferable to dry grinding for woodworking tools, as many tools are spoilt by heat when dry grinding. The cooling liquid used varies with different machines; it can be plain water, a special thin oil or a mixture of soluble oil and water. The cooling liquid that the machine is designed to use should be used. Do not experiment with other liquids, or you may ruin the wheel.

The simplest form of cooling is where part of the stone runs in the cooling agent (*see* Fig.15.2). A certain amount of the liquid clings to the surface of the stone and runs up over the surface of the tool being ground. If the stone runs at a fast speed it throws the liquid off and becomes ineffective. A better method is where the agent is pumped on to the wheel just in front of the tool, and a better method still is the system where the coolant is sprayed directly on to the tool.

There are wet grinding machines that are designed to grind on the side of the wheel: this gives a flat-ground surface, as opposed to the hollow surface given by the edge of the wheel. There is a grinding machine made that has a sump at its centre, filled with oil, which percolates through the stone under centrifugal force. However, when the machine is at a standstill for some time, gravity makes the oil seep down through the stone. This machine is very good in a large workshop where it is often being used, but would not be advised in a one-man shop.

A machine with a large flat wheel that can best be described as

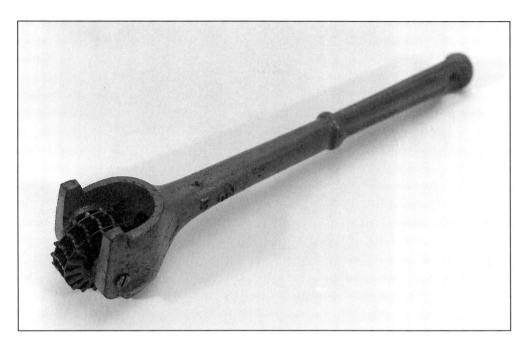

Fig 15.3 Despite the resemblance to a medieval weapon, this is a star tool for trueing grindstones.

resembling a gramophone record is to be found in many commercial workshops. There is a spray bar which delivers a curtain of oil across the radius of the wheel. Also fitted is a special tool holder that holds both plane irons and chisels. The grinding angle is very easily adjusted. This machine is very effective; the only thing that can be said against it is that it takes up rather a lot of space.

A machine sold under the trade name of Sharpenset was originally marketed for butchers to sharpen their knives on, but woodworkers discovered it and now the manufacturers market it vigorously to woodworkers (*see* Fig 15.1). As it takes up a very small amount of space, the machine is ideal for the small workshop. There are a number of attachments for grinding various tools, from planer knives to twist drills. The machine has a cup-shaped wheel 4in in diameter. The grinding is done on the lip of the cup,which is only ¾in wide. At first sight these dimensions seem small but in 15 years of use my machine has ground everything that I have asked of it. A pump keeps a copious supply of water

flowing over the grinding area. There are various grades of stone made for the machine – even one for grinding tungsten carbide.

Dressing the wheel
From time to time the wheel will have to be dressed to true its surface. Three different tools will do this task. First and cheapest is a very coarse and loosely bonded man-made stone known in the trade as a 'devil stone'. Various sizes are manufactured, the most useful for our purpose being ½in square bar about 6in long. This is sold as a dressing stick. Second is a tool that consists of a number of star wheels loosely mounted in the end of a metal handle (*see* Fig 15.3). This is held against the wheel as it revolves, and the star wheels chip minute pieces from the surface of the wheel, making it true. Finally there is a diamond dressing stick. This is a handle with a diamond impregnated end which is pressed against the wheel as it revolves and cuts the old surface away. While this tool is very effective, it is also quite expensive. For the small workshop the star wheel is probably the best.

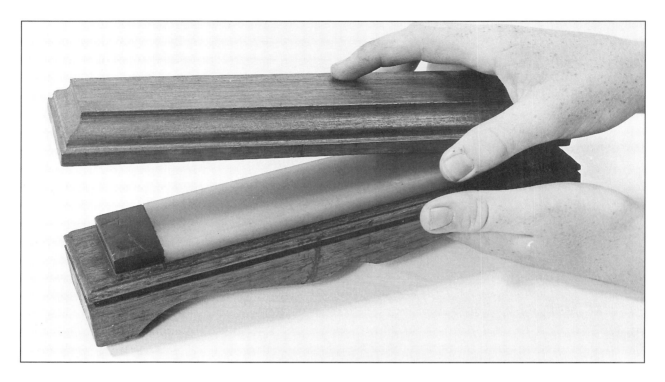

Fig 15.4 Oilstone in box. The pieces of wood at either end of the stone allow the full length of the stone to be used when sharpening with a honing guide.

There is much dust as the surface of a dry wheel is dressed. This dust is very abrasive; under no circumstances breathe it in. A face mask should be worn, and of course eye protection consisting of goggles that will keep · the dust out. Ordinary safety spectacles are of little use in this situation.

Dry grinders in commercial premises have to be fitted with dust extraction by law. This is because in use they create abrasive dust particles, some of which are so small they are easily airborne. It is a good idea to do the same if you can. However, do not connect the grinder to the same extraction as the woodworking machines. Fine wood dust is an explosive substance and grinders create sparks . . . . A suitable separate extractor can be made from an old domestic vacuum cleaner. There is a tube attachment point in the wheel guard on most machines.

OILSTONES

Man had stone tools long before he used metal, so it is no wonder that he abraded metal with stone to shape and bring it to a sharp cutting edge. John De Trevisa wrote in 1398 'Ben diverse maner of whetstones, and some neden water and some neden oyle for-to whette.' Very little has changed. There are man-made artificial stones which in the coarse grades are better than natural stones. Craftsmen still argue about what to put on the stone. Some old craftsmen have a mixture, the ingredients of which they keep a closely guarded secret. No doubt over the centuries man has experimented with all sorts of rock and stone.

For general bench tools we need a stone about 8in long, 2in wide and 1in thick. The surfaces need to be flat. The stone should not wear fast, but it should cut fast. There have been natural stones from quarries in Britain that have been used for sharpening. These include: Scotch Dalmore Blue, Charnley Forest, Rag, Tam O'Shanter, Welsh slate, and Water of Ayr.

Two sought after imported stones are the Arkansas, and the Turkey. The

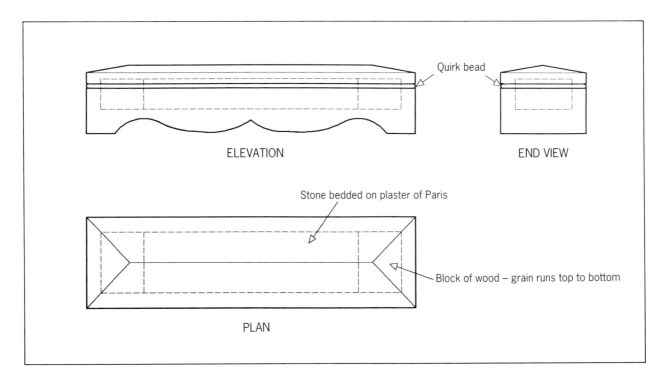

ELEVATION

END VIEW

Quirk bead

Stone bedded on plaster of Paris

Block of wood – grain runs top to bottom

PLAN

latter, which was quarried in Asia Minor and finished in Marseilles, has become scarce. Either the vein of stone ran out or the drop in demand made it no longer a commercial proposition.

The Arkansas is a hard stone quarried in the Ouchita Mountains in North America. Washita, a corruption of Ouchita, is softer stone from the same quarries. Both these stones are composed of the mineral novaculite. The Arkansas stone comes in a variety of hardness: the black stone is the hardest and finest grade, next comes the hard white. Some stones are pied, with streaks of both white and black in them, but this does not seem to impair their working characteristics. The softer stones are a dirty white bordering on grey.

There is a softish grey stone called a Belgium stone. While being on the soft side, these are very fine if one uses water with a little washing-up liquid in it on them. They are fine for sharpening knives, mainly because they wear fast and it is difficult to keep the surface true.

MAN-MADE STONES
These are stones made from the materials described above for grinding wheels. The Norton Crystolon is much favoured by site carpenters, and there is a stone made from this material known as a combination stone. One side is a medium grit, the other is from fine grit. This is ideal for the man who has to carry his tools about, but is of little practical use in the workshop, where it is quicker to have several separate stones. Stones made from aluminium oxide can also be obtained as combination stones: with these man-made materials it is important to keep the pores of the stone open by using a thin oil and wiping the stone clean after use. This can become a mucky operation, and needs to be kept away from any important piece of work.

All stones need to be stored carefully when not in use by making a box for each stone (*see* Fig 15.5) Stone boxes are traditionally chopped out of a solid piece of wood; the box is a block of wood in the surface of which the stone is housed . A similar block

Fig 15.5 Oilstone box.

forms the lid. Many craftsmen put a brad into each corner of the underside of the box; with their heads cut off and filed to a point the brads grip the surface of the bench and stop the box from sliding about when in use. However the brads rough up the surface of the bench where the stone is used, and this roughness can damage the surface of a workpiece. It is better to keep stones on a separate stand, where they are immediately available for use. Stones on the bench can transfer dirty oil to the work in hand and sawdust can soon clog up the surface of a stone.

If all the sharpening equipment is together in one place, it is then only a question of walking a couple of paces from the bench to use everything that is laid out ready.

DIAMOND SHARPENING SYSTEMS

In recent years several firms have produced a flat steel surface impregnated with diamond dust (*see* Fig 15.7). These systems work well and cut very quickly. While they are a bit fierce to give a very fine edge, they could easily replace the medium and coarse stones. One thing they offer which is unobtainable elsewhere is perfect flatness. This method of sharpening has not been around long enough to be able to ascertain their life; I have used them for two years for coarse sharpening and flattening the back of blades, and to date they show no sign of wear.

JAPANESE WATER STONES

For my money the Japanese water stone is the best sharpening medium obtainable. It differs in several ways to that which we in the West are used to; there are natural stones and man-made stones in this system; the material comprising the stone is totally different, and the way the stones cut is also different. A fine

128

Fig 15.6 Left: slipstones for sharpening gouges and other shaped tools are needed in every workshop. Murphy's law states that however many you have, you will not find the one to fit the tools to be sharpened.

Fig 15.8 Japanese water stone being removed from its trough.

Fig 15.9 Water stone box.

Fig 15.7 Left: diamond sharpening systems. The one on the left is a stainless steel plate with a surface coating of diamond dust; the one on the right uses a diamond-coated, perforated steel plate mounted in plastic.

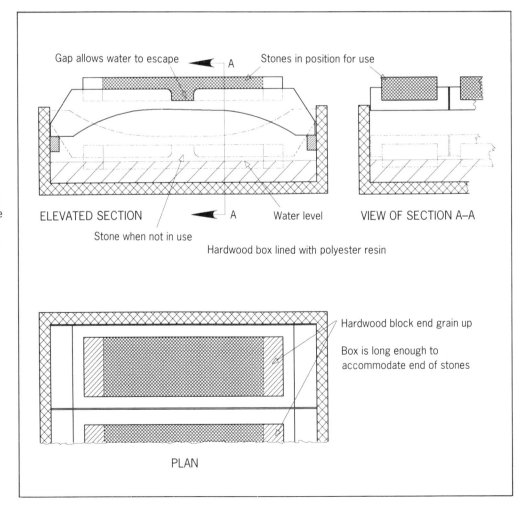

Gap allows water to escape   Stones in position for use

ELEVATED SECTION

Stone when not in use   Water level

Hardwood box lined with polyester resin

VIEW OF SECTION A–A

Hardwood block end grain up

Box is long enough to accommodate end of stones

PLAN

129

slurry builds up on the surface of the stone as it is used; this slurry also acts as an abrasive as well as the surface of the stone. The stone is soft and continually exposes a new working surface, so even a very fine grade stone cuts at a fast rate. The size of the grit the stones are made from can be much finer than any man-made stone here in the West. The finest stone, with a grit size of 8000, is referred to by the Japanese as a polishing stone.

The stones are kept constantly in water. The best method is a trough in which they are placed upside down – this allows the slurry and any other debris on the surface to drop off and descend to the bottom of the trough (*see* Figs 15.8 and 15.9). The stone when next needed has a pristine surface. Because the surface of these stones is soft, care needs to be taken or lumps can easily be dug out of it. A set of stones with 800, 2000, 4000 and either 6000 or 8000 grit will quickly impart the finest edge possible. The slurry that settles in the bottom of the trough can be used on a steel plate to flatten the face of chisels, etc.

HONING GUIDES

Here we come to a very controversial piece of equipment. Some workers argue that any craftsman worth his salt should be able to sharpen his tools without the aid of this appliance: in my opinion if the tool is sharpened better with it than without it, it has a place in the workshop. There are two guides on the market which are worth serious consideration. One is made by Eclipse and is suitable for most blades, even small combination plane blades (*see* Fig 15.10); the other is made by Footprint, and is a copy of a Canadian tool (*see* Fig 15.11). This is a very well thought-out device, it is possible to vary the honing angle by one degree, with the turn of a small brass knob, enabling a small micro bevel to be put on the blade. Some years ago I designed and manufactured a guide for honing plane blades; this has a wide nylon roller the full-width of the tool. There are attachments for setting up the angle super-accurately to 20°, 25° and 30°. All these guides and my own design are shown in Figs 15.12 and 15.13.

Fig 15.10 Left: the underside of the Eclipse honing guide; the narrow roller can wear a stone hollow in the centre.

Fig 15.11 Right: the Footprint honing guide; the small knob adjusts the bevel up or down by 1°.

Fig 15.12 The author's own design for a honing guide for plane irons.

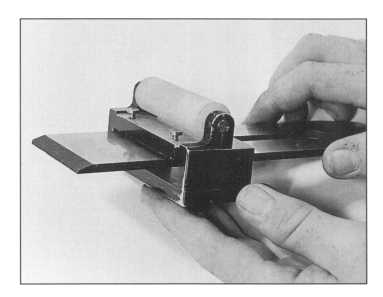

Fig 15.13 The honing guide.

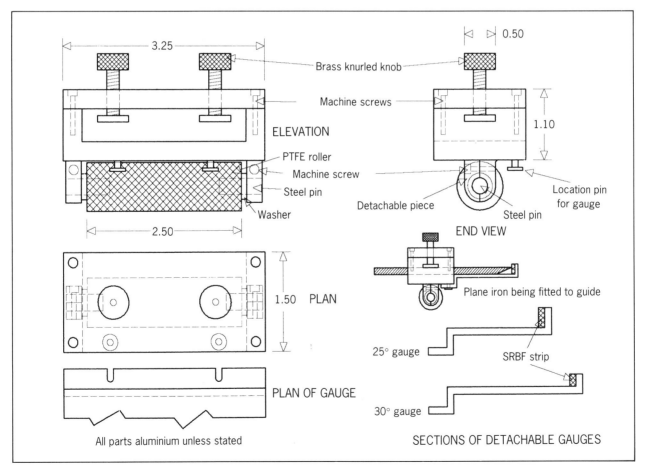

0.50

3.25

Brass knurled knob

Machine screws

ELEVATION

1.10

PTFE roller

Machine screw

Steel pin

Washer

2.50

Detachable piece

Steel pin

Location pin for gauge

END VIEW

1.50 PLAN

Plane iron being fitted to guide

PLAN OF GAUGE

25° gauge

SRBF strip

30° gauge

All parts aluminium unless stated

SECTIONS OF DETACHABLE GAUGES

MACHINE HONING

Honing tools by machine really comes down to using a motor-driven wheel, which can be a hard buffing wheel dressed with a fine abrasive material, a leather-covered wheel with a stropping compound on it, or even a rubber wheel impregnated with abrasive material.

131

CHAPTER SIXTEEN

HAND TOOLS

ONLY THE BEST

I have long had a theory that the quality of work produced by a craftsman is proportional to the quality and condition of his tools. There is also a psychological aspect; with fine tools, one is prompted to produce the finest work. The old adage 'only a poor workman blames his tools', is in my opinion completely wrong. The very best work and I emphasize **the very best**, can only be produced with the very best tools.

Hand tools are very expensive, and it is better to have a few top quality tools than a workshop full of mediocre ones. If you can't afford the best, you can make them. I have had to resort to this, and my book *Making & Modifying Woodworking Tools* tells how to do it. What is intended to be made in the workshop will have a bearing on what is required, so this chapter looks at most of the hand tools that a woodworker might need. Not all of them will be needed by one individual craftsman. It might be best, if you are inexperienced, to start with a basic kit; one is listed in Appendix B, and other tools can be added as they are needed.

BUYING TOOLS

As a young apprentice I learnt a lot about tools just listening to the conversation between the craftsman and the ironmonger. In those days ironmongering was considered a trade, and people were apprenticed to it.

The craftsman would ask to see some ½in firmer chisels, or whatever tool was required. At least half a dozen different ones would be produced. They would be thoroughly inspected. Some would be rejected with a cursory glance, others would be checked with a straightedge. Handles would be compared, maybe even more chisels would be brought from the stock room.

In one local town we have quite a large tool emporium (the same place where I bought tools as an apprentice 50 years ago) where today there is no counter and tools are displayed in cases, one of each tool. When you see what you want, you tell the assistant who brings one, which is pre-packed, from the store room. There is no chance to inspect it – why should you want to, it is the same as that which is on display.

There are many firms offering mail order on tools, but here again one does not see what one is buying until it arrives. You might think that in these days of mass production there would be little difference from one item to the next; this is not so. In recent years I have been responsible for buying tool kits for apprentices. Out of 10 items supplied (all the same and from the same manufacturer), as many as three would be rejected as below standard. These tools were not from the low end of the market but supposedly the best available. So what does one do to ensure that the tool is up to the standard required?

Buying at one of the national exhibitions is quite a good policy. Arrive when it opens on the first day – the exhibitors are all fresh and bushy-tailed; they are keen. Towards the end of the exhibition they are worn out and have had enough awkward customers without dealing with another one. Being there as it opens means it will not be crowded. Take a metal straightedge and a small try square with you; these will be needed to check the tool you are thinking of buying. If you cannot find a tool of the quality you require, do not take second best; there is always another day.

If you are going to buy many tools, as one would when starting from scratch, it is worth letting the proprietor of the local tool shop know this. It is possible to get on friendly terms, and make him understand what you are looking for. He may even give a discount if he thinks your business worth it.

Often the best tools are those which were made some years ago and have found their way on to the secondhand market. It has always been the custom in the cabinet trade that when a craftsman dies his tools are auctioned at a union branch meeting, the proceeds of the sale going to his widow. This is not a way to get cheap tools, as anybody bidding below the going rate is looked down upon. This process has meant that the quality tools stay in the trade.

There are still many good tools that find their way to car boot sales and secondhand stalls at markets. Here, as with new tools, one has to be careful. There are more things to look for than with a new tool, e.g. rust. Now, a little surface rust can be a good thing: it makes the tool look worth less than its true value. Surface rust can be polished off with a little emery, and the tool is bright and shining again. However, beware of rust that has pitted the surface; this has ruined the tool. A saw or any cutting tool that has become pitted can never take on a sharp edge.

BENCH PLANES
These are the flat-soled planes traditionally used on the bench for preparing and smoothing the workpiece. Those used in the

preparation of timber are the jack, jenny, trying, fore, and jointer. The requirement here will depend on what machinery is installed. If material is prepared from the sawn state by hand, a wooden jack will be a valued item. The wooden-soled plane has far less friction than the all-metal plane. A wooden jack will remove shavings as thick as a soldier's belt. Using two planes, first wooden and then a metal one, it is surprising how quickly a surface can be planed true. To describe every plane and its individual characteristics, together with its uses, will require another book, so the main characteristics of the planes used in the preparation of timber are listed below.

First, here is a brief description of the manufacturers mentioned in the list: Stewart Spiers made planes in Ayr, Scotland (c.1840-1920). Thomas Norris & Son made planes in London (c.1860-1940). Richard Melhuish & Sons made planes in London (c.1828). Alex Mathieson & Sons made planes in Glasgow, Scotland (c.1792-1954); however during the latter part of their existence they were a dormant part of Record Ridgeway. Stanley refers to all the Stanley planes manufactured by the Stanley Rule and Level Co. from 1857, Stanley Works from 1920 and Stanley Works Great Britain from 1938. Preston were renamed Record when C. & J. Hampton purchased them in the early 1930s. Of these companies, only Stanley and Record remain in business. Record's plane numbering system is similar to Stanley's except it has an 0 in front, i.e. Stanley No. 5 is identical to Record's No. 05.

Jointer, jointing or joynter 20in – 30in long, with a blade as wide as 2⅝in
Wooden ones were used in days gone by, but are not to be recommended. Firms such as Stewart Spiers of Ayr

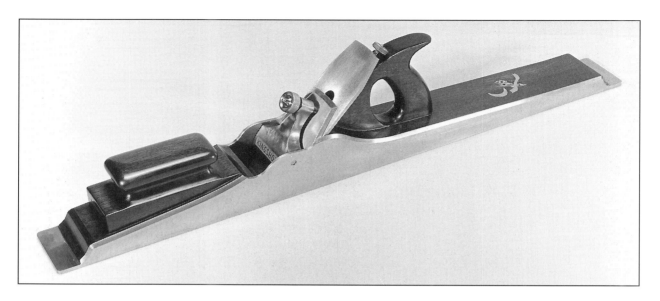

Fig 16.1 30in jointing plane, made to the author's own design.

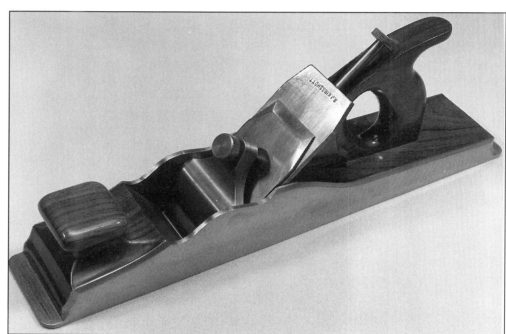

Fig 16.2 Panel plane.

Fig 16.3 The jenny plane is a cross between a wooden and a metal jack plane: the wooden sole reduces friction, while the metal part includes fine adjustment and ease of blade extraction.

and Thomas Norris made 30in jointers in metal to order. There are Bailey pattern jointers i.e. Stanley No. 7 which is 22in long, with a 2⅜in cutter, and the No. 8 which is 24in long with a 2⅝in blade. Norris made jointers down to 20½in (these are very useful bench planes).

**Trying, panel or fore
16in – 20in long**
Here again, secondhand wooden ones are to be found, but are not to be recommended. Those made by Norris, Spiers and their contemporaries were prime tools in the cabinetmaking trade (*see* Fig 16.2). Bailey pattern fore planes are made by Stanley and Record, Nos. 6 and 06 respectively.

**Jack and Jenny
14in – 16in long**
This is where a wooden plane can be of some use. Wooden versions are usually 16in long. There is a type called a technical plane, which is 14in long and has the depth of the body reduced behind the blade, dropping the height of the tote. These planes were made for use in school woodwork classes. The reduced height allowed the student who was not of adult height to control the plane. Incidentally, when choosing a wooden plane, get one where the medullary rays are perpendicular to the sole. A plane cut from the timber in this way remains more accurate than one cut any other way.

Bailey pattern jacks are made: No. 5 is 14in long with a 2in wide blade. No. 5½ is 15in long and has a 2⅜in cutter. The jenny is an interesting plane: it has a wooden sole with the Bailey pattern metal adjustments on its top surface, giving the advantages of both types of plane (*see* Fig 16.3).

Norris-type jack planes are available on the secondhand market, and are superior to any other pattern. It would not be fair to use a plane of

this calibre to remove the rough surface of sawn timber: far better to save its accuracy for the final few shavings.

Fig 16.4 This old steel-cased, coffin-shaped smoother still works well after generations of use.

**Smoothing Plane
5in – 10in long**
This category includes so many different patterns of plane that only principal ones are mentioned here. The early British manufacturers all made metal versions, both parallel-sided and coffin-shaped (*see* Fig 16.4). Some have no handles while others have both knob and tote – the latter is to be preferred in the larger sizes. There are some fine wooden versions with steel soles. Bailey pattern smoothers are made by Record and Stanley; some of the smaller sizes have been discontinued.

■ No. 2 is 7in long and has a 1⅝in cutter

■ No. 3 is 9¼in long and has a 1¾in cutter

■ No. 4 is 9¾in long and has a 2in cutter

■ No. 4½ is 10in long and has a 2⅜in cutter

Planes that have a C after their number have a corrugated sole to reduce friction. While most smoothers have a blade pitched at 45°, a plane with a steeper pitched iron is useful on difficult grained wood. The old cabinetmakers often had a plane with a pitch of 50°, known as York pitch. Some of the early English smoothers have a pitch of 47½°.

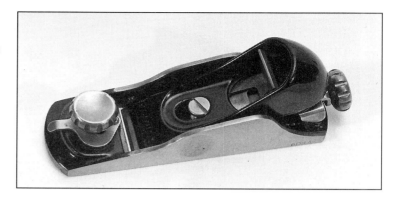

Badger and coachmaker's rebate planes

Where there are a number of large rebates to be worked or cleaned up, as in joinery, a largeish rebate plane is required. There is a very useful wooden plane, similar to a jack but with the iron protruding from one side; this is the badger. The better versions have the iron on the skew. Stanley and Record make coachmaker's rebate planes (sometimes referred to as carriagemaker's). These are similar to the normal Bailey pattern bench plane, except for the iron which protrudes from both sides of the plane. The plane therefore cuts a shaving the full width of the sole. No. 10 is 14in long with a 2⅛in cutter, while No. 10½ is 9¼in long with a 2⅛in cutter. These planes all have double irons pitched at 45°.

BLOCK PLANES

It is said that this plane was originally made for butchers to clean their chopping blocks with. Whatever the case, the versions made by Record and Stanley are sophisticated tools: they are small metal planes designed to be used with one hand for trimming small work. They are single ironed, with the cutters bevel upwards; this means that there is no gap behind the iron as there is when the cutter is fitted bevel down. The angle of the blade is 12°– 18°, the lower angle being particularly suited to trimming end grain. Unfortunately,

except for the Nos. 9½ and 60½, block planes have all been discontinued. No. 9½ is 6in long with a 1⅝in cutter pitched at 21°; No. 60½, is 6in long with a 1⅜in cutter pitched at 12° (see Fig 16.5). Both of these planes have adjustable mouths. There are also many cheap block planes aimed at the DIY buyer.

CHARIOT PLANE

A few wooden chariot planes were made, usually from exotic hardwood. The types made by the early metal plane makers are very useful little tools, those made from bronze or gun metal being particularly desirable. These planes vary in design; the very best are fitted with some form of

Fig 16.5 Top: 60½A low angle block plane; this is an ideal plane to use on end grain.

Fig 16.6 Bottom: shoulder planes.

Fig 16.7 Providing they are in reasonable condition, old tools are capable of producing fine work. This sash fillister was made around 1820, and still works well.

mechanical blade adjustment. The chariot plane is 3in – 4in long. The blade is usually fitted very near the front of the plane – as there is very little metal in front of the mouth, it is possible to plane right up to an obstruction.

THUMB PLANE

The *Dictionary of Tools* states that this is a general term for miniature planes, including smoothing, rabbet, hollows and rounds, side rabbet and side rounds, straight-soled and compassed, etc. In the trade it is usually used to refer to a small metal plane similar to a block plane. They can be 1in – 5in long, so literally any small plane can be termed a thumb plane.

SHOULDER PLANE

This tool is sometimes referred to as a shouldering plane. It derives its name from one of its uses, that of easing or cleaning up the shoulder on a tenon. However, this is only one of its uses. The metal version is a most useful tool: it can be used both with and across the grain when working complicated mouldings; cleaning up small rebates is also an easy task (*see* Fig 16.6). Preston made a number of

these planes in different sizes. Record continued to make them for a few years, but now only No. 073 is manufactured. When a late manufactured 073 is compared with the original Preston, one can see what price engineering has done to the hand tools manufactured today. A small company by the name of Clifton has started making copies of the original Preston planes; while the finish is not in the same class as the originals, they are still very useful tools.

- 073 is 8½in long with a 1¼in cutter
- 072 is 8in long with a 1in cutter
- 420 is 8in long with a ¾in cutter
- 410 is 5½in long with ⅝in cutter
- 400 is 3¼in long with a ⁷⁄₁₆in cutter

Most of the early British plane makers made shoulder planes. There is a particularly useful one made by Norris in gun metal, with a skew mouth and cutter adjustment mechanism.

PLOUGHS, FILLISTERS AND COMBINATION PLANES

The requirement for any of these will depend on the machinery installed in the workshop. The modern portable electric router will do nearly everything that these planes will do – not only much faster, but with more noise and a lot of dust. For those not in a rush, who want to enjoy working wood, there is much pleasure to be derived from working with these hand tools. The old wooden ploughs and fillisters are works of art in themselves (*see* Fig 16.7). Some of the ploughs made for cabinetmakers are made from exotic hardwood with ebony and ivory inlay and brass fittings.

There are a number of metal ploughs and combination planes (*see* Fig 16.8). As these are complex and

137

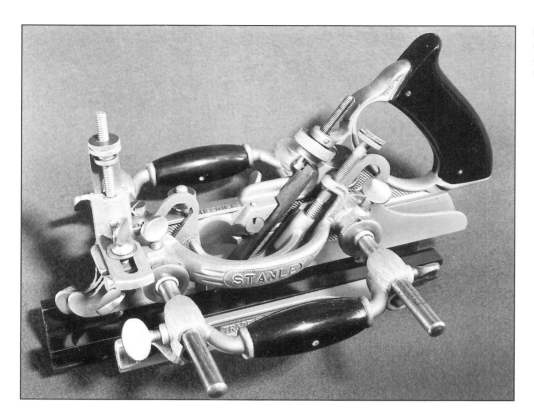

Fig 16.8 Stanley 55 combination plane; it was advertised as 'a wood mill in a box'.

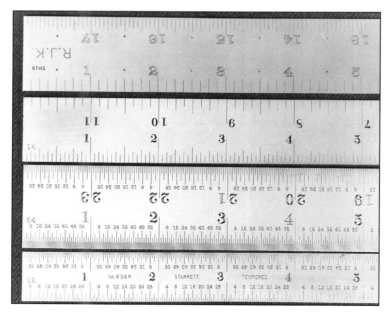

Fig 16.9 Steel rule ends. The divisions are the same graduations for the length of the rule.

difficult to make, the manufacturers have redesigned them; this may have kept the price down, but it has in no way improved the tools. Try to obtain secondhand items made before the end of 1945. Modern cutters obtainable as replacements will fit most of the early tools.

OTHER PLANES

There are hundreds of types of plane not included above which have very special uses. Violin planes have an obvious use. Side rebates, which come in a number of different patterns have several uses, from widening grooves to working parts of awkward mouldings. Bullnose rebate planes are of use where stopped rebates are encountered. There are planes made for working chamfers. Then there are moulding planes, for the countless different mouldings there are. Patternmaker's core planes, handrailing planes, butt planes, piano maker's block planes and all those special planes the cooper uses. Many of these planes were never manufactured commercially, but were made by the craftsman for a specific use.

MEASURING AND MARKING TOOLS

Rules

The rule is the woodworker's main measuring tool. While a tape or a folding wooden rule are fine for approximate measurements they are not sufficiently accurate for setting out, and steel rules are needed here. The type finished with satin chrome is to be preferred as the graduations and figures stand out (*see* Fig 19.9). Whether you decide to work in metric or imperial, settle on one or the other; don't go in for rules that have both on them. You need all four edges of a rule depending on where it is being used, and to find the edge you are using has the wrong graduations on it will not help the job along. Nor should you use an engineer's rule; these have inches and tenths of an inch etc. which woodworkers do not use. Worse still is the rule that has both tenths and eighths on it – these look so similar that sooner or later the wrong ones will be used.

Rules of different lengths are made in increments of 6in up to 2ft and then in increments of 1ft; what is required will entirely depend on the type of work undertaken. A good selection for cabinetmaking is: 6in, 12in, 18in, 2ft, 3ft, 6ft. These are all graduated in ⅛, ¹⁄₁₆, ¹⁄₃₂, ¹⁄₆₄ of an inch, the whole length of an edge having

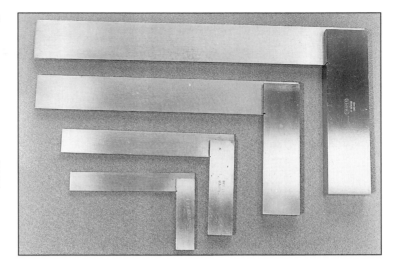

Fig 16.10 Engineer's squares.

the same graduation so that the four fractions occupy all four edges of the rule. It is worth having one metric half-metre rule for the odd occasion when you need to use a French measurement. Rules are precision instruments and should be treated as such; make a case for them to live in when they are not in use.

Try squares

The inaccuracy of some of the try squares on the market today is awful, as a square that is not true is worse than useless. The way to test a square for accuracy is to mark a line with it on a board that has a straight edge, using the stock of the square against the straight edge. When the mark has been made turn the square over, keeping the stock against the edge. The amount that the line differs from the new position of the square's blade is twice the amount the square is out.

Engineer's squares guaranteed to BSS939 are a better buy than the wooden stocked woodworker's square (*see* Fig 16.10). My engineer's square with a 12in blade is less than 0.001in out in 12in. Try squares are also made with an 'L' shaped blade, the foot of the 'L' being inside the wooden stock. This type of square is superior to the type that has a straight blade held in the stock with five rivets.

139

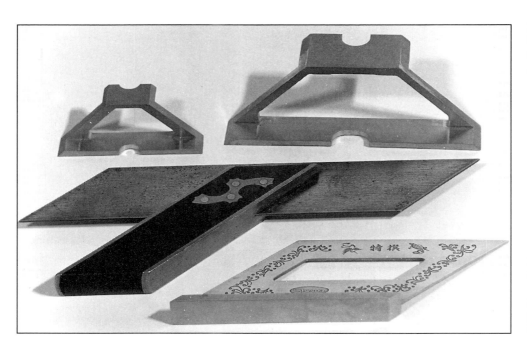

Fig 16.11 Top: mitre templates; middle: mitre square; bottom: Japanese mitre template.

Fig 16.12 Mortise gauge.

Fig 16.13 Cutting gauge made by the author.

Large squares

There will be a need in most workshops for some means of marking square lines on sheet material: some form of large square will be needed. Some craftsmen make large wooden squares, others use a metal framing square. The framing square is also known as a roofing square or a steel square. It has tables printed on its faces from which all the bevel cuts required in roofing can be obtained. This is of course a site carpenter's tool, but it can be very useful in the workshop. Some tool shops sell a blacksmith's square; this is a flat metal square; graduated in inches both on the stock and blade. The stock is usually 16in and the blade 24in long.

Mitre squares and templates

In many workshops there will be a need to cut 45° mitres and scribe mouldings. A mitre square is similar to a try square except for the blade, which is set at 45° instead of 90°. Mitre templates that can be used for scribing mouldings and paring mitres come in a variety of shapes and sizes (*see* Fig 16.11).

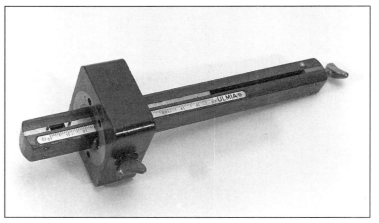

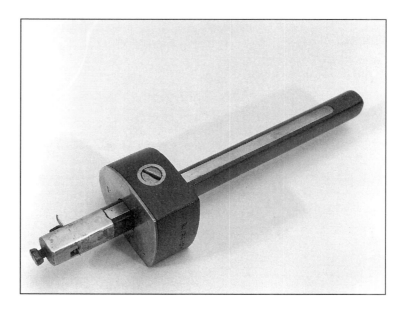

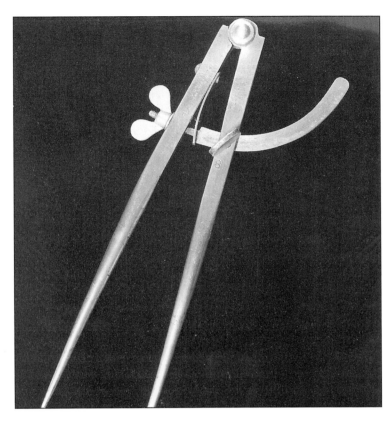

Fig 16.14 Compasses with fine adjustment.

Marking gauge

It is easy to underrate the importance of a tool when it looks so simple; it is only when we come to doing without it that we realise just how important it is. The basic all wood gauge that we are all familiar with, whilst being an effective tool, leaves a bit to be desired. Several firms have made metal marking gauges, which can be an improvement on the wooden version. There are some which are made in Germany which have double or even quadruple graduated stems; the attachment which allows them to be used on circular work is very effective.

Mortise gauges

This is a tool where some manufactures have excelled themselves (*see* Fig 16.12). There are some beautiful specimens made from ebony and brass to be picked up secondhand, but because they are so attractive to look at, collectors also

like them. Some of the new models are equally efficient tools. Make sure that the pin spacing is adjustable by a screw – the ones with the second pin on a slide should be avoided. If buying secondhand make sure that the pins are not worn out and that if they are they can easily be replaced, as this is impossible on some casings.

Cutting gauges

Not all craftsmen will require a cutting gauge. They are not in very great demand, so the manufacturers make only a simple type with the blade held in with a wedge. If you do much complicated veneering with a need to cut narrow strips, the blade will need frequent sharpening. This is difficult with the wedge-held blade. Getting the blade to protrude the exact amount required is difficult, so the pattern where the blade is held by a screw is preferable. Here again it is either buy secondhand or make your own (*see* Fig 16.13).

Trammels and compasses

Some means of scribing circles is required in nearly every workshop. The compasses normally used are better described as dividers, as they have a point on both of their legs which makes them useful not only for marking circles but for transferring dimensions. The best type of tool for our use is the winged variety with a means of locking the legs secure once the dimension is set (*see* Fig 16.14). The types that rely on a friction joint between the legs are useless – the leg being used to scribe the line follows the grain and alters the setting.

For large diameter circles, a pair of trammels will be required. The design with some form of fine adjustment is to be preferred (*see* Fig 16.15). If they are designed to run on a wooden beam this is all to the good, as it is then an easy task to make your own set of beams.

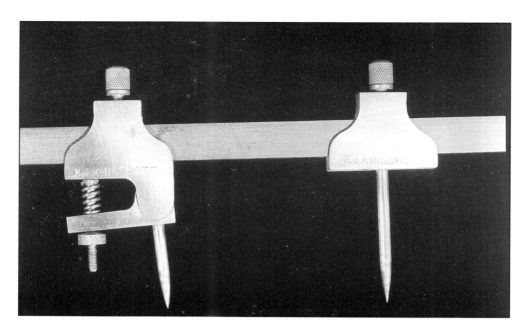

Fig 16.15 Trammels; note the adjustment mechanism on the left-hand head.

Marking awl and knives

Where accuracy in setting out is required a fine cut line is made with a knife. The design of the knife will have a marked effect on its ability to be used in a number of situations; e.g. it is impossible to transfer the size and shape of fine dovetails with a thick blade, or a blade with the cutting edge at the wrong angle. Over the years I have made my own marking knives and have found that the best material is the wide blades used on hacksaw machines, which are ground to the shape shown in Fig 16.16.

The marking awl is used for pricking down a dimension point or marking through a hole onto another piece of wood. The awl needs to have a very slender tapered point, or it will not be able to mark close up to an edge.

SAWS

Here, as with planes, there are so many with such varying levels of quality that the only general comment is that a proper taper-ground blade mounted in a good handle is a completely different tool to the cheap throwaway item.

Fig 16.16 Marking knife made from an old machine hacksaw blade.

Fig 16.17 Disston tenon saw.

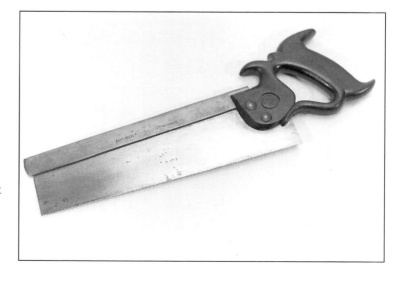

Rip Saws

These have almost disappeared from the shelves of the tool shops. The old craftsmen who had to reduce their bulk timber to working dimensions relied on this tool a good deal, but with the amount of machinery available even in the humblest of shops today – usually at least a bandsaw – there is little need for it. If you feel you need some physical exercise, perhaps you should use one. The rip has a 30in blade with 3½in points per inch which is why the old woodworkers were so muscular; not only did they have to push this saw but there was also all that work with the jack plane.

The half rip is a more practical tool for use in today's workshop. This is an ideal tool for running in tenon cheeks on wide lock rails, etc. The half rip has 4½ teeth to the inch on a standard 26in blade. Most modern saws are skewback, a shape invented by Henry Disston, which gives them a longer life.

Handsaw

The handsaw is a general-purpose saw which is used for crosscutting and ripping. The blade needs to be 26in with around 6 or 7 points to the inch.

The teeth are raked so that they will cut across the grain without tearing the grain too much and still rip with some efficiency. Good taper-ground saws need far less set than the cheap thick-bladed variety.

Panel saw

This is fine enough to cut without leaving a rag on the back of the work. Most panel saws have a 20in or 22in long blade; the longer version is to be preferred in the workshop. The teeth are pitched at 10 points to the inch. For some work the panel saw will double as a tenon saw.

Backed saws

A saw blade needs to be thick to remain rigid enough to cut without bending when it is pushed. However, if the saw is not used to make deep cuts some form of stiffening can be applied to its top edge. If the top edge is beaten so that the metal is stretched, it has to take on a wavy configuration because the rest of the saw has remained at its original size, and the metal cannot move out to its new length. If a thick piece of metal is folded over the top edge so that the waves are flattened, the rest of the

Fig 16.18 Dovetail saw in use.

143

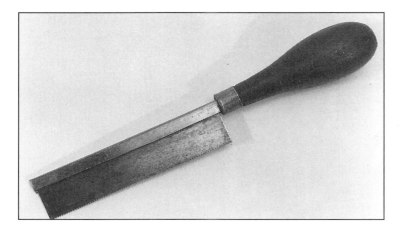

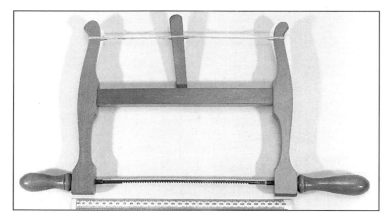

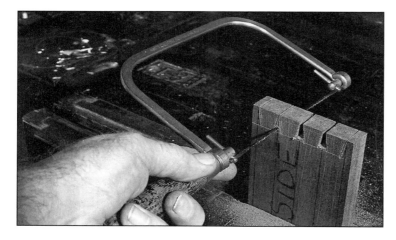

Tenon saws are usually 12in or 14in long with 10 or 12 points to the inch. The teeth are usually sharpened for crosscutting. Where many tenons are cut by hand the craftsman may use two saws, a large one sharpened to rip down the grain and a smaller one sharpened for crosscutting. Tenon saws have closed handles (*see* Fig 16.17).

Dovetail saws have blades 6in – 10in long. The teeth are spaced at 15 to 22 points to the inch. The tooth configuration is a debatable subject; some prefer them to be filed for crosscutting, but others state that they should be filed for ripping, because dovetails are cut down the length of the grain. This is fine if the saw is only used for dovetails, but it precludes its use for any operation requiring crosscutting. The handle can be either open or closed (*see* Fig 16.18).

Bead saws are also known as gent's saws, or jeweller's saws. The blade is 3in – 6in long, with the teeth at 24 to 30 points to the inch (*see* Fig 16.19). The very cheap versions of this saw are not worth consideration. The handle is of the turned pad variety. Jeweller's saws are very thin, have extremely small teeth and are not set; in use they are smeared with tallow to lubricate them and stop them binding in the cut.

Other saws
In the workshop where there is no machinery there will be a need for several other saws. The bow saw is useful for curved cuts. The narrow blade is held in tension in a wooden frame and tension is usually applied by a twisted cord (*see* Fig 16.20). This tool is also known as a sweep saw or turning saw using a short length of narrow bandsaw blade with a small hole drilled at each end.

Fig 16.19 Top: very small gent's or bead saw.

Fig 16.20 Middle: the bow saw is often made by the craftsman; it is a very useful tool for those without a bandsaw.

Fig 16.21 Bottom: coping saw in use.

blade will be in tension; this keeps a thin blade straight, and stops it bending when it is pushed to make a cut. The tensioning of a backsaw blade is a skilled operation – cheap backsaws are not tensioned, and the blade is thick.

There are three distinct classes of backsaw:

Compass saws are narrow-bladed handsaws used for sawing out shaped components; there is a version known as a nest of saws, where several interchangeable blades fit one handle. The coping or scribing saw is a small metal frame with narrow blade about 6in long, which is held in tension by turning the handle (*see* Fig 16.21). This saw is of recent invention, about 1920; it is a very low priced tool, and is worth a place in any workshop.

HAMMERS, PINCERS, MALLETS and PUNCHES
Hammers

There are many different kinds of hammer made for different trades. The two types commonly found in the woodworking trade are the cross-peen and the claw hammer. The cross-peen can be obtained in several patterns; the main ones being Warrington and London (*see* Figs 16.22 and 16.22a). Cabinetmakers have three: a pin hammer at 3½oz; a bench hammer for setting planes and driving oval brads at 8oz, and a framing hammer of 12 – 20oz. This last tool is used to drive framing together, with a softening block of wood used between the work and the face of the hammer. An upholsterer's magnetic hammer is useful for furniture restoration.

Pincers

The two patterns of pincer are the Tower (*see* Fig 16.23) and the Lancashire (*see* Figs 16.23 and 16.23a); each is as good as the other.

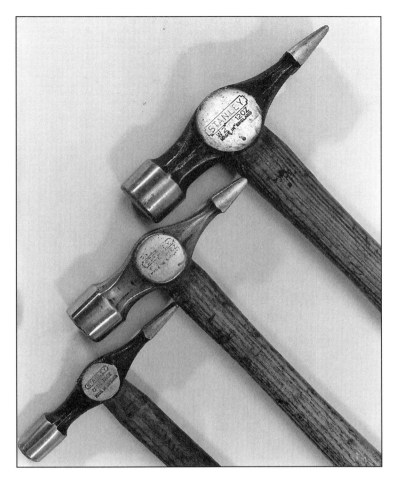

Fig 16.22 Warrington hammers.

Fig 16.22a A London pattern hammer.

Fig 16.23 Tower pattern pincers.

Fig 16.23a Lancashire pattern pincers.

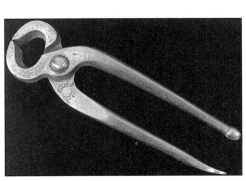

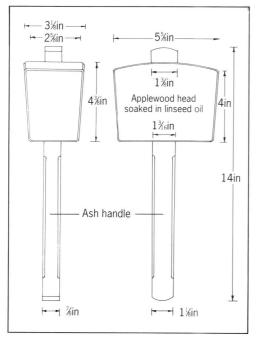

Pincers are classified by their length, a 6in or 7in pair being the norm for workshop use. As with all tools, the quality is important: cheap pincers will have soft jaws that will soon become spoilt and need replacement, but a good pair will last a craftsman all of his life. Where repairs and restoration are the main function of the workshop, there will be a frequent need to extract difficult nails, screws and pins. An assortment of tools modified especially for this purpose are needed. Electrician's side cutters can have their jaws reground so they can grip heads that are slightly below the surface. The nail puller, a tool many people are not aware of, can usefully be employed here.

Mallets

The mallets sold in tool shops have straight-grained beech heads, will only last a short while, and are not really a good buy. Fig 16.24 shows a simply constructed mallet, which even a beginner should be able to make successfully. However, you will need a mallet to make a mallet – buy a dead blow mallet (see below) and use this to drive the chisel when chopping the mortis in the head; boring most of the waste wood away will ease the task.

The head is best made from apple – beech can be used, but is a poor second best – and the handle from ash. When you have finished making the tool, soak the head in linseed oil for a few days; this will give it extra weight. One mallet that has been with me a long while has the head made from a twisty bit of elm. It is so heavy that other craftsmen have said that it is a lazy man's tool, because it only has to be picked up – it comes down on its own.

The dead blow mallet, made for the engineering profession, is a metal headed tool with interchangeable plastic frames. The head is hollow and contains loose lead shot. This tool is most useful for driving frames together or knocking things apart, as the soft plastic face does not mark the timber and the dead blow is most effective (see Fig 16.25).

Nail sets or punches

There are several designs of nail punch (see Fig 16.26); the best ones

Fig 16.24 Left: mallet.

Fig 16.25 Right: dead blow mallet.

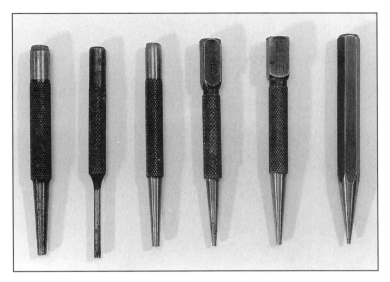

Fig 16.26 Nail
punches.

SCREWDRIVERS

This tool is more mistreated than any other. For some reason the poor old screwdriver is used as a lever, a paint stirrer and any other task where there is not a tool handy with which to do it. How often do we see screws that have had their heads ruined by a poor tool?

For most workshops there will be a minimum requirement of four screwdrivers for driving wood screws only. Too big a tool for the size of screw will ruin the slot, so the blade of the screwdriver should be the exact width of the head of the screw, enabling it to impart the maximum torque with the minimum of damage. The thickness of the blade should fit snugly into the screw's slot, reaching right to the bottom. A screwdriver used on large screws, e.g. 12s and upwards, needs to be big enough to use with two hands.

There are two types of driver, the London and the Cabinet: the London pattern has a flat blade while the cabinet has a round blade (*see* Fig 16.27). There is little to choose

have a recess in their point which stops them slipping off the nail. It is worth having two or three sizes, as a small punch is soon spoilt if it is used on large nails. When the top of the punch becomes burred over where it is struck with the hammer it should be discarded. The burred pieces of metal are likely to break off when struck, and fly off with considerable force, possibly causing serious damage, particularly to the eyes.

Fig 16.27 Cabinet
screwdrivers with
elliptical handles.

Fig 16.28 Cranked or right angle screwdrivers around a ratchet tool with interchangeable bits.

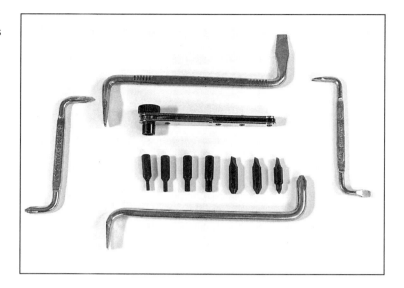

Fig 16.29 New and old chisels; note the difference at the root of the tang.

Spiral and ratchet screwdrivers can save time, but not much. However a cranked or right-angled screwdriver is often required where there is insufficient room for a normal tool and a very useful ratchet version of this tool is marketed by Drapers (*see* Fig 16.28).

CHISELS AND GOUGES

Chisels are used from the heavy chopping out of material to the delicate paring of finished work, and there are chisels made to suit every kind of work. The chisel is one of the tools that wear out: the average professional craftsman will get through a couple of sets of firmer chisels in a life-time, so the odds for finding a good set of second-hand chisels are pretty long. Fig 16.29 shows an old and a modern chisel – the difference can be seen when you compare the way the metal was beaten into shape and forged by hand. Modern steel is much tougher than the carbon steel the old tools were made from: this means that the tool holds its edge much longer, but unfortunately the edge is not as sharp to start with. If you see old hand-forged secondhand chisels and they have some wear left in them, snap them up.

between them in effectiveness. The handle is where most new screwdrivers fail – trying to apply a twisting motion to a round handle soon has the hand slipping. A handle should be elliptical in section, or even flat.

Today there are numerous patent heads on screws, which all require a special tool: there are super screws, Phillips screws, cross-point screws, and now one with a square hole in its head. Settle on slotted screws for the workshop: they are still the best, and you only need one set of drivers.

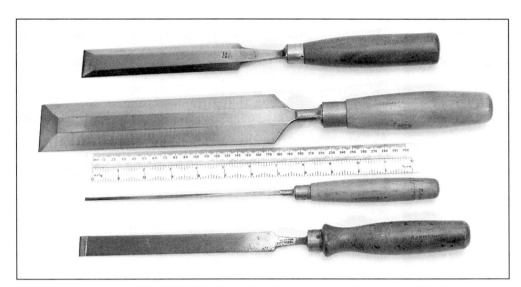

Fig 16.30 Paring chisels. The new ones in the centre against the rule are 2in and ⅛in wide – the extremes to which these chisels are made.

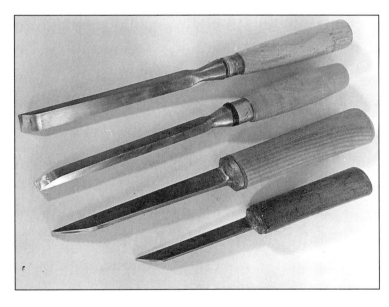

Fig 16.31 Top: sash mortise chisels; bottom: joiner's mortise chisels.

Firmer chisels

The general workhorse on the bench is the firmer chisel. It is robust enough to stand up to fairly heavy work, but is not cumbersome. It is obtainable with a boxwood or plastic non-break handle, as it is often struck with the mallet. The tendency to use plastic handles and to strike the tool with a hammer is not to be recommended.

Bevelled-edge chisels

The bevelled-edge chisel is used for work of a finer nature; it is much lighter than the firmer, and therefore is never struck with a mallet. Because of their bevelled edges these chisels can be used to pare into acute corners, such as those made when dovetailing. If you have new chisels, there may be a need to put some work into sloping the bevels so that only a minute square edge is left up the sides. If this square edge is of any size it will stop the tool from working inside an acute angle. This work can be carried out on a grinder and finished on an oil stone – take your time and do not spoil the tool.

Paring chisels

These chisels have much longer blades than the two types previously mentioned. The best have thin, delicate blades (*see* Fig 16.30). They are used only for paring. The additional blade length makes them very useful for cleaning out shelf housings across the grain, and this length seems to make the tool balance better all round.

Mortise chisels

There are several patterns; Fig 16.31 shows that some are more suited to heavy work than others. If most of the waste material in the mortise is removed by boring it out, there will be little need for heavy chopping.

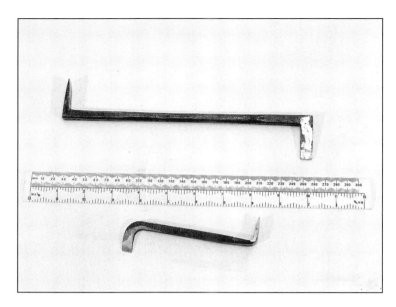

Fig 16.32 Drawer lock chisels are driven with a hammer.

Drawer lock chisel

It is impossible to house a lock inside the front of a small drawer with a normal chisel , as there is not room inside in which to work. This special tool, made in its entirety from one piece of steel, is used with a hammer (*see* Fig 16.32).

Other chisels

Japanese chisels have grown in popularity in recent years, but the would-be user should get only one or two to start with, as good ones are very expensive. The design, which is very different from our Western chisels, is not to everyone's liking.

There are chisels that have special functions like the sash pocket chisel, which is used by joiners to make the pocket in the stile of a box sash window. The swan-necked mortise lock chisel again is used to fit deep mortise locks into the end grain of the door's lock rail. Register chisels are similar to the firmer, but are much stouter and have a ferrule at the top of their handle; they are used for very heavy work. One pattern of chisel that deserves a mention is the cranked paring chisel. This can work in the centre of a job without the handle getting in the way.

BORING AND DRILLING TOOLS

The need to make holes in wood occurs in every workshop. The hole can be for a small panel pin that would otherwise split a delicate moulding, or it may be 4in in diameter to form a recess for a receptacle. Not all the required holes can be made by machine, and even if they could it would be time-consuming to have to set up a machine and jig the work into position. The tool needed will depend on the type of hole required and its size. Screw sinks (mentioned in Chapter 14) are not suitable for use in hand tools as they need to be turned at high speed.

Bradawl

For small holes up to $\frac{3}{16}$in in diameter a bradawl is an ideal tool. There are two distinct varieties: the round-bladed is the most common, and the birdcage maker's awl has a square tapered blade which does not split the wood (as the round one might). All bradawl blades should have the handle secured with a pin through the tang – if there is no pin, it will only be a short time before the handle and blade part company. Round-bladed awls should be sharpened to a chisel edge, not a point. In use the edge is placed across the grain, pressure is applied, and at the same time the tool is rotated a quarter of a turn in each direction. The fibres of the wood are cut cleanly as the tool penetrates. It is recommended to have a set of three bradawls of varying size.

Brace

This is the woodworker's main tool for turning tools that will bore a hole and is obtainable as a plain brace or a ratchet brace. The latter is well worth its extra cost, as it can be used in positions where the plain brace would be useless (*see* Fig 16.33). By setting the ratchet the crank can be turned through part of its sweep and then reversed, leaving the bit stationary, in this way boring a hole in a corner where it is impossible to use the full sweep. The ratchet has a further advantage: when driving screws with a screwdriver bit or boring large holes, it will be found an advantage to use only part of the sweep in a short back and forth movement where most force can be applied.

The size of the brace is given by the diameter of the circle inscribed by the sweep. The better quality of brace has ball bearings in the head; this is a point of high wear and the ball bearings certainly last much longer than the thrust washer on the cheaper tools. Most braces are fitted with replaceable crocodile jaws in the chuck. Keep the rotating parts of the brace lubricated, particularly the ratchet.

Bits

There are many different varieties of bit and drill made for use in the brace, (*see* Figs 16.34 and 16.35). Your choice will be governed by the use to which you will put the tool. Twist bits are sometimes called auger bits.

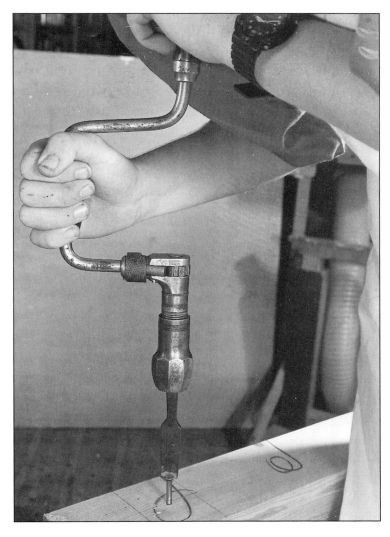

Fig 16.33 Ratchet brace used with a screwdriver bit.

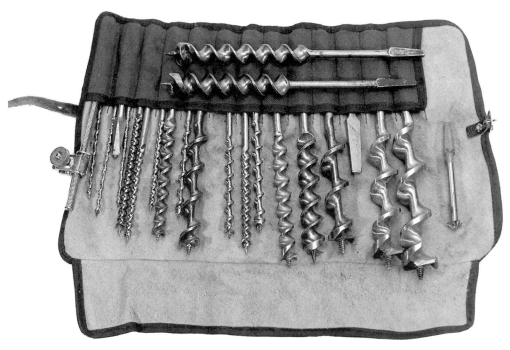

Fig 16.34 Twist bits in a tool roll, with depth gauge at left. The bits laid out separately are a Russell & Jennings and a Gedge.

151

Fig 16.35 Special bits. Left to right: flat head countersink, snail shell countersink. three patterns of screwdriver bit, two rose countersinks..

Irwin pattern twist bit. This is the most common of the twist bits. It has a fairly coarse thread on the screw point. There are two wings at its cutting end, one of which is continued right up the tool to remove the waste wood from the hole. There are single and double spur versions of this tool; the double spur is to be preferred.

Jennings pattern twist bit. This has a fine thread on the screw point, and two wings continued for the full length of the tool. It is designed to cut more slowly than the Irwin bit, but the hole made has a much better finish. This is the cabinetmaker's preferred bit.

Gedge pattern twist bit. This bit is no longer obtainable new; secondhand examples are occasionally obtainable, but inspect

them carefully as bits are easily damaged. The Gedge is similar to the Jennings but is of a much coarser pitch. The cutting ends of the wings are folded over, and there are no spurs. It is easily started at an angle to the work, which is not possible with the Irwin and Jennings bits. The hole is somewhat ragged due to the lack of wings. This bit works particularly well in end grain.

Centre bit. This is a very simple tool which is most useful for holes that have little depth. It is a low-cost tool, and very easily sharpened. It is not however a replacement for the twist bit.

Twist drill. In the past twist drills were made with a square at the top of their shank to fit the brace. They are no longer manufactured, and this is a pity, as they are useful tools.

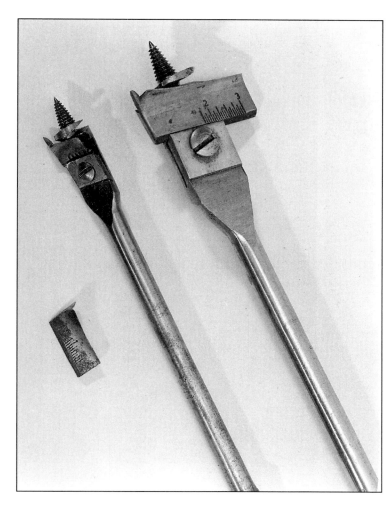

Shell and spoon bit. Although these bits are no longer made, the secondhand market is knee-deep in them. They were only made in smaller sizes, but these are ideal for screw holes.

Screwdriver bit. These bits are very useful, because of the leverage that can be applied to a large screw with this tool in the brace. The screwdriver bit comes in a variety of sizes, and because it is so simple it does not cost much money, and should be in every tool chest.

Expansive bit. This comes in two sizes. The small bit will bore holes from $\frac{1}{2}$in to $1\frac{1}{2}$in and the large tool will bore holes from $\frac{7}{8}$in to 3in. They are very useful because of their ability to be set at any size within their capacity (*see* Fig 16.36). They work extremely well, but are of a rather fragile nature – when the cutter is extended to cut near or at maximum size, there is tremendous strain on the centre clamp. Cutting a 3in hole in hardwood is not to be recommended.

Fig 16.36 Expansive bits.

Fig 16.37 Hand drills: the Stanley 803 on the left is a good modern tool; the Millers Falls in the centre is an excellent old drill; the Leytool on the right is useful for working in a confined space – make sure that the body is cast in aluminium, not plastic.

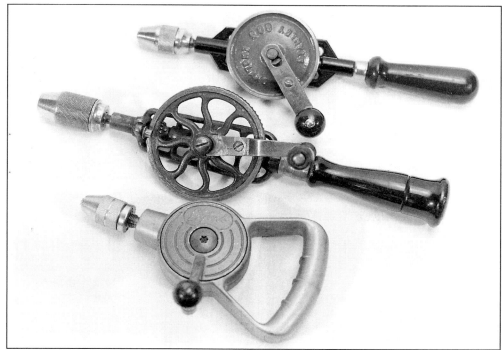

153

Fig 16.38 Metal spokeshaves. The two small tools were made for delicate work, and the larger ones are originals by Preston.

Depth gauge. Over the years, a number of different pattern depth gauges have been made for attachment on the shank of the bit . One is useful to have when blind holes are to be bored.

Countersink bit. There are three patterns of countersink made to fit the brace. The rose countersink has a number of cutting surfaces, and cuts a very clean countersink, even in difficult timber. It was originally designed for countersinking brass and other nonferrous metals. The snail-shell countersink only has one cutting surface. It cuts much faster than the rose countersink but it is inclined to leave a rough surface to the countersink in coarse-grained timber. The flat-head countersink is intended for use on metal; it is inefficient in wood.

Hand drill
While this tool is primarily intended for use to drill holes in metal, it is useful for woodwork (*see* Fig 16.37). The vast available range of sizes of twist drill and the speed at which they cut without any tendency to split the wood, makes them particularly attractive. A set of drills the correct size for screw holes mounted in a block of wood at the back of the bench can save much time. The smaller size of hand drill will also work in confined spaces where it would be impracticable to use another tool.

Spokeshaves
Spokeshaves are made in both wood and metal. The wooden versions have a very low cutting angle, with a very heavy blade, which makes them almost chatterproof, a feature that

cannot be said of the metal variety. There are some very poor metal spokeshaves around; the cutters do not bed down properly and make the tool almost impossible to use. Most woodworkers require at least two spokeshaves, one with a flat sole and the other with a rounded sole. Wooden spokeshaves come in a wide range of shapes and sizes, and are readily available secondhand – the problem is that the blades are often worn out, so inspect them carefully before buying. Prestons made some beautiful spokeshaves; these are fine tools and work extremely well (*see* Fig 16.38).

Routers

Wooden and metal patterns are available. The wooden ones were usually craftsman-made, with a blade from a plough plane as a cutter – this tool is often known as an old woman's tooth. There are two sizes of metal router, and both are useful tools where housings, trenches and other recesses have to be made (*see* Fig 16.39).

Scrapers

The scraper used in the workshop is better described as a cabinet scraper. This is a square of tool steel similar to that from which saw blades are made; the cutting edge is sharpened by putting a burr on it.

There are shaped scrapers called goose necks, for scraping mouldings and curved surfaces. While the scraper is often used by being held in the hands, there are a number of appliances in which it can be installed – some resemble spokeshaves while others are more like a plane.

Fig 16.39 Hand routers.

CHAPTER SEVENTEEN
CARE AND STORAGE OF TOOLS

AN INVESTMENT

The money spent on equipping the workshop with all the required machines and tools should be seen as an investment, and looked after as such. If cared for, most tools will last more than a lifetime; however it does not take much misuse or neglect for a tool to become valueless. One of the best things for tools is regular use – every time a tool is picked up to be used, any rust or damage is immediately seen and can be put right straightaway. Very simple things are needed for the day-to-day maintenance of tools: an oily rag to wipe the tool with, and a piece of fine emery paper for the occasional polish.

When we do any physical work, energy is expended causing heat; we perspire to reduce the body's temperature. Perspiration on bare steel causes corrosion. If the surface of the steel is covered by a thin coating of oil, this moisture cannot reach it. Where a thin oil is used conservatively, it is not noticeable when handling the tool. Camellia oil, sold by shops that stock Japanese tools, is ideal for this purpose (*see* Fig 17.1).

No matter how careful we are, sooner or later some rust will be found on a tool. The best item for removing this is Scotchbrite made by 3M. The finest grade should be used except in the case of heavy rusting, where the coarse grade will work better. Fine emery paper can also be used; do not use a grade that leaves a scratched surface – the ideal surface on a tool is shiny bright.

Fig 17.1 Camellia oil is an ideal dressing for the surface of tools.

Because the surface finish on a tool affects its resistance to corrosion, tools with very smooth surfaces should be chosen. Today's manufacturers are constantly trying to reduce the time spent making a tool. A coarse grinding wheel removes metal much faster than a fine one, so most new tools have deep grinding marks on their surface. Some work on the surface of new tools with various grades of emery paper can change the poor finish to a more acceptable one. The steel on the sides of a cast plane body can be polished to such an extent that it resembles a plated surface; this is very time-consuming, but the surface will last forever with very little maintenance. Start with a fairly coarse paper and change to finer as the work progresses, the last grade used being 1200 wet and dry lubricated with kerosene or white spirit.

Wooden tools such as planes, mallets, gauges, and even chisel and saw handles will respond to the occasional wipe with a little linseed oil. Only a very small amount should be deposited on the surface, and it is best if the tool is polished with a dry rag soon after the application of the oil. A lovely surface patina will take several years to achieve. If you acquire a secondhand wooden tool, do not clean the surface patina off; if the tool is dirty use a piece of Scotchbrite with a liberal amount of linseed oil. When all the dirt has been removed, polish with a dry cloth.

Machines and powered hand tools will require periodic cleaning. An industrial vacuum cleaner is very useful for sucking all the sawdust out of the inaccessible parts. Metal parts should get a wipe over with an oily rag. Careful inspection of flexible cables and plugs is essential in the interests of safety. This inspection is best done to a schedule, i.e. regular dates marked on the calendar – it is too easy to put it off until tomorrow, and of course tomorrow never comes, particularly in the busy workshop. Any damage must be put right before the item is used; this requires a certain amount of self-discipline, but it is very important.

STORAGE

When tools are not in use they need to be put away. If the bench becomes cluttered up the tools knock against one another, cutting edges become nicked and surfaces are damaged. Apart from the damage caused to the tool, searching in a pile of tools and shavings wastes time; tools need to be stored close to where they are used.

It is customary for a craftsman to have a tool chest; the design has been refined over many years. The fitting-out of the chest is very logical, and all the tools are immediately accessible (*see* Appendix B). The outside has traditionally been painted black or grey, and the handles are simple rope loops. The chest is also reasonably portable; I have four large castors on the bottom of my chest that have been a blessing when it has needed moving. In one shop the floor was very uneven and my tool chest used to run downhill at least once a day. This wouldn't have been so bad, except that it threatened to run me over.

Powered hand tools are best stored in cupboards, cramps in open racks where they are immediately to hand, and things like moulding planes in cupboards, which keeps them reasonably free from the ever-present dust.

The best working conditions come about through continual refinement, moving the most used items nearer to hand, making a home for items that are in constant use near the bench. In this way the workshop becomes tailored to your own individual way of working; it will also change if your style of work alters.

CHAPTER EIGHTEEN
OTHER EQUIPMENT

CRAMPS

Cramps conform to Murphy's law: 'No matter how many the shop is equipped with, one or two more will always be needed'. The name cramp is used in the UK, and many other English-speaking countries refer to the tool as a clamp. There are many different designs; some, such as the violin maker's cramp, have very special uses. The best plan is to buy them as the need arises.

In some cases it is possible to contrive a means of holding the job without recourse to shop-bought cramps. A wooden bar with a block screwed on at each end and a pair of folding wedges may not look good, but it is quite effective.

If you are buying secondhand, examine the tool to see if it has been over-tightened – this ruins a cramp, as it pulls out of square when tightened, distorting any work it is used on. Cramps are made to hold work while the glue is drying; they are *not* made to make joints fit by applying extreme pressure. The pressure applied by a fine pitched thread can be several tons per square inch; the inclined plane of the thread magnifies the pressure applied by the hand many times.

T-Bar cramps

The T-bar cramp is the largest and heaviest of the cramp family. It derives its name from the shape of the cross section of its bar (*see* Fig 18.1). T-bars are made in lengths from 2ft – 8ft in increments of 6in, the most usual sizes being 4ft and 6ft. Bars are available to extend the length of the cramp (*see* Fig 18.2).

Sash cramps

For most woodworking purposes where a long cramp is required, this will be the ideal tool. It is made in lengths from 2ft – 6ft, the most common being 4ft. There are lengthening bars made, and a 4ft pair will be found useful in most shops. The pitch of the thread influences the pressure the cramp exerts; this pitch varies.

Cramp heads

These are probably the best buy for the home workshop. They consist of a pair of cramp ends (*see* Fig 18.3). A beam on which the heads are mounted is made in the workshop; in this way several beams of differing

Fig 18.1 The head of a T-bar cramp. The section of the bar can clearly be seen.

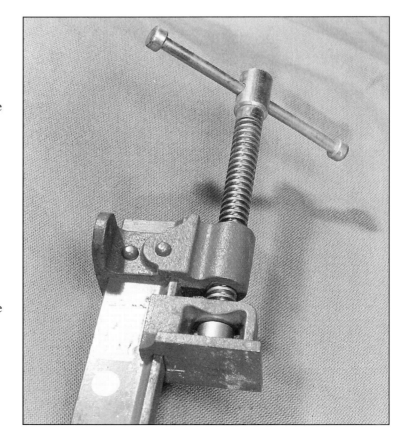

Fig 18.2 The joint on the extension of a T-bar cramp.

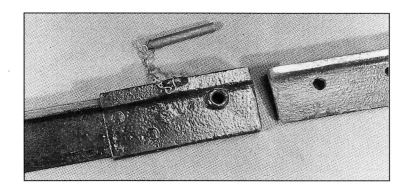

Fig 18.3 A pair of cramp heads.

length can be made for one pair of ends. Some heads made in recent years have very short threads which makes them a nuisance to use – one has to keep stopping to unwind the screw, move the other head up a hole and then reapply the cramp.

G-cramps

Two very similar tools are called G-cramps: one has a tommy bar which turns the screw; this is a true G-cramp. The other has a butterfly-shaped end to the screw; this is a thumbscrew (*see* Fig 18.4). Both of these patterns are made in sizes from 2in – 12in. It is unusual to find thumbscrews in the larger sizes. There is a pattern of G-cramp called

long reach; this has a much deeper frame, so that pressure can be applied further from the edge of the job.

Quick release cramps

These tools used to be known as quick action veneering cramps and have become very popular in recent years (*see* Fig 18.5). They are made in sizes from 4in – 24in, the middle sizes being used most. Because cramps are used during gluing up, they seem to collect any glue that is exuded from the joints. Glue that has set on the cramp needs cleaning off, as this type of cramp relies on the head being a good sliding fit on the bar, and any hard glue on the bar makes it difficult or impossible to use.

159

Fig 18.4 A thumbscrew and a G-Cramp. The G-cramp has a finer thread and a tommy bar.

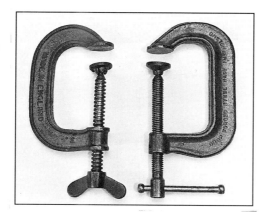

Fig 18.5 A selection of quick-release cramps. The largest is 24in and the smallest is 4½in.

be preferred to the wooden-screwed variety; the jaws can be adjusted to quite a wide angle. With all wooden-screwed tools the screw will need some lubrication, which must be a form of dry material. The best is powdered graphite, also known as plumbago. A soft pencil rubbed over the thread works as an alternative, and flaked graphite, used by engineers as a dry lubricant, can be obtained from some large tool shops.

Handscrews

Although this tool may look out-of-date and old-fashioned, there is no modern tool that can replace it. Its strong point is its long jaws which can be adjusted to pull up parallel to one another or at an angle, thus making it possible to cramp all sorts of awkward shapes (*see* Fig 18.6). Furniture restoration work will keep these tools in constant use, particularly small ones. Jorgenson cramps have metal screws and are to

Mole cramps

There are two patterns of mole cramp. While they have rather special applications, they are useful for certain types of woodwork, particularly in restoration work where small parts need holding while glue sets (*see* Fig 18.7). The mole cramp can be applied with one hand while the other hand holds the part in position. Care must be taken when using these cramps as they can exert extreme pressure and mark the work.

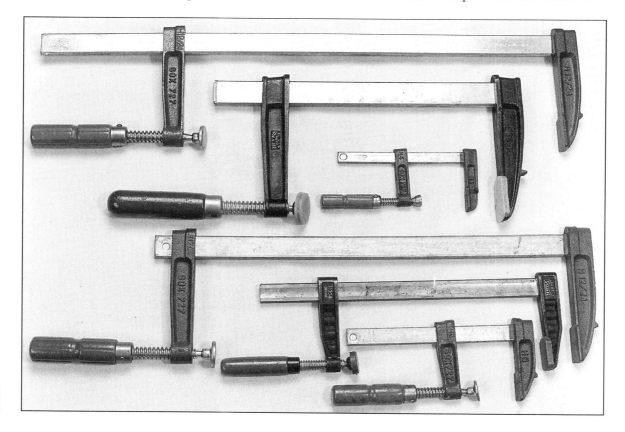

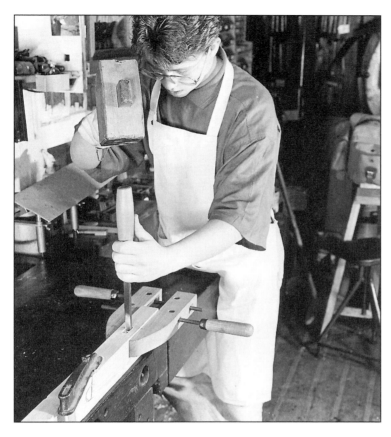

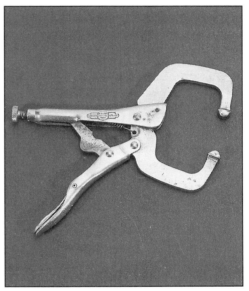

Fig 18.6 A handscrew being used to stop the end of the stile from splitting while it is being mortised. The stile is held down on the bench with a quick-release cramp.

Fig 18.7 The mole cramp, while not being a woodworking tool, can be useful for holding parts together in awkward places.

Edging cramps

This tool is designed with one purpose only, that of holding lipping or edging on to a panel while the glue sets. Unless you have much of this sort of work, the investment is not worthwhile as at least a dozen cramps are needed to edge a single panel of reasonable size (*see* Fig 18.8).

On inspection it might be thought that the tool could double as a G-cramp; this it can do, but it is on the small side to be of general use.

Instrument makers' cramps

These are not woodworking tools and are not often found in the wood workshop. They are very useful for holding small intricate parts, however. They only come in small sizes, and are like miniature handscrews (*see* Fig 18.9). The biggest have jaws 5in long while the smallest jaws are only 3in long.

Frame cramps

Most woodworkers will have a need to hold mitred frames together; picture frames etc. are not easy with normal cramps. There are a number of proprietary items made for this purpose. Stanley make a very simple

Fig 18.8 A pair of edging cramps. At least a dozen are required to be of practical use.

161

device (*see* Fig 18.10) which works quite well, but is difficult to control – one seems to need four sets of hands. The all-plastic tool (Fig 18.11) was bought in a local **DIY** shop; it works very well, but is unlikely to last long. My own make of tool is shown in Fig 18.12; this is solid brass and will be around long after I have gone to work in the governor's workshop. Similar tools to this were made from wood with a metal spindle and ratchet. Some of the old craftsmen-made tools were designed with a particular need and therefore fill the requirement admirably.

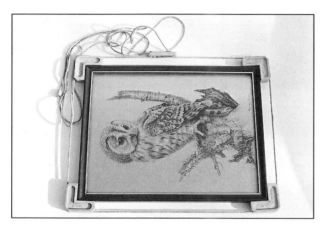

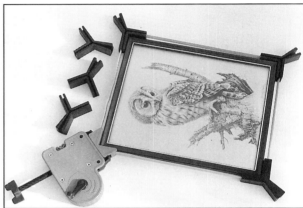

Fig 18.9 Top: instrument maker's cramps. Ideal tools for small work.

Fig 18.10 A cord and toggle frame cramp by Stanley.

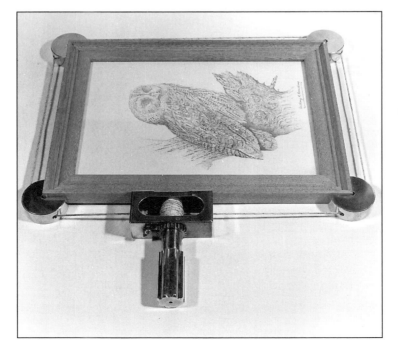

Fig 18.11 A plastic frame cramp. This item is made in Germany but is available in this country. By using the additional plastic corner pieces, six-sided frames can be cramped.

Fig 18.12 The author's own design of picture frame cramp.

Band cramps

Webbing is an ideal material to fit around any shape of frame. With modern materials such as nylon, a webbing strap can be made extremely strong. The webbing is tightened around a spindle that can be turned with a screwdriver or a spanner, and a ratchet holds the webbing once it is tightened (*see* Figs 18.13 and 18.14). This is a modern tool that is far superior to any similar tool made in the past. The only problem I have experienced is one of glue getting in to the webbing and making it stiff.

Rack cramps

These cramps are a fairly recent development. They come in a variety of weights and sizes, the very heavy ones being a favourite tool in the engineering industry for holding metal parts while they are being welded together. They are very robust (*see* Fig 18.15). The lightweight pair are most likely to be used where the head will fit in to a difficult confined space where no other cramp could work.

Jet cramps

These are a proprietary design of cramp, invented a few years ago (*see* Fig 18.16). While they were originally seen as a replacement for the sash cramp, they have been found to have many other uses. The heads may be reverse mounted on the bar so that the tool will force things apart instead of pushing them together; this is an invaluable feature in restoration work. There are many attachments for these tools and comprehensive brochures are available from the manufacturer (see Stockists and Suppliers).

GLUE POTS

While modern glues and resins are superior for many uses, there is still a need in many shops for the old-fashioned hot-melt animal glue. The

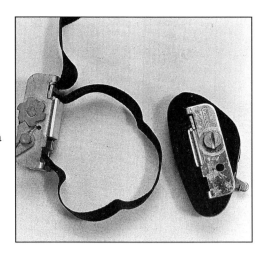

Fig 18.13 Top: band cramps by Stanley's. The photograph shows each side. On one side there is the ratchet and on the other the nut used to tighten the nylon band.

Fig 18.14 Middle: band cramps in use.

Fig 18.15 Bottom: rack cramps come in a range of weights. The heavy ones are favoured by welders for holding metal parts together.

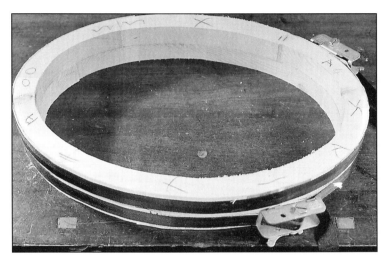

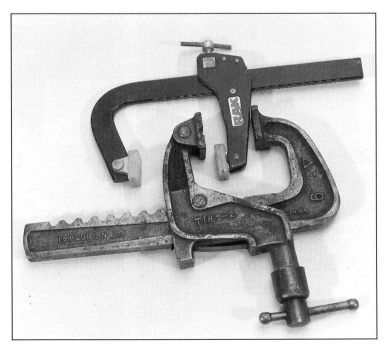

163

Fig 18.16 The jet cramp. The head can be put on to any length of bar. By reversing the heads it can be used for pushing components apart.

traditional cast-iron glue pot has been around for centuries, but it could boil dry and burn the glue, quite a common occurrence for some craftsmen; or it could boil the glue. Glue that is overheated rapidly loses much of its strength. Today we have electric pots, the best of which are waterless. One firm, Barlow Whitney, has specialized in their manufacture, and I can unreservedly recommend them – both their water-jacketed and waterless pots have been in constant use for many years. A glue pot must be made so that no ferrous metal comes into contact with the glue; if it does, the glue will stain the wood it is used on. The best pots have a stainless

steel or copper inner receptacle. Pots are sold in sizes that reflect the quantity of glue they will hold. As glue deteriorates every time it is heated, a pot that will hold sufficient glue for one day's work is the ideal size.

VACUUM CLEANERS

Dust is an ever-present nuisance in the workshop; if it is brushed off surfaces, it becomes airborne and settles again. A vacuum cleaner is the answer to this problem. Some types of dust extraction have an attachment that can be used in place of a separate machine, but a cleaner will be needed in most shops. The types made for normal domestic use are not much good in the workshop, and an industrial machine will be expensive. There are several machines made for the amateur market; these have a large diameter flexible pipe which will not clog up with shavings as a small bore would. I have had a number of cleaners in my workshop over the years. The mechanical parts of the cleaners have not worn out, rather the case and the plastic fittings have given up the ghost first. The Aqua Vac made by Goblin has a powerful motor and is a reliable machine.

Fig 18.17 Improvised cramps.

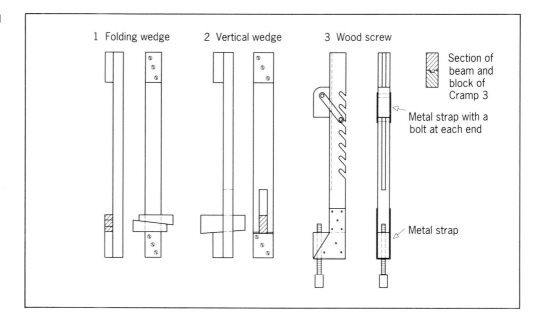

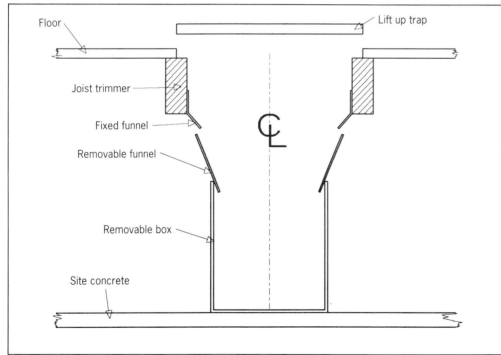

Fig 18.18 Glue pots. Left to right: two old cast-iron pots, water-jacketed electric, and waterless electric.

Fig 18.19 Schematic section through dust box.

OTHER CLEANING ITEMS

Shavings and sawdust are best swept into a heap and picked up with a shovel. A good soft hair broom is required for the fine sawdust. The shavings are best pushed into a heap with a piece of ply about 2ft wide nailed to a handle. A good way of dealing with workshop sweepings if you have a suspended floor is to fit a trap door in the floor about 2ft square and flush with the surface of the floor (*see* Fig 18.19). Make a box with handles to fit under and be lifted up through the trap. When clearing up, the trap is opened and the dust is swept into the box, which when full is lifted out for emptying.

THE WORKING WORKSHOP

THE WORKING WORKSHOP

Everything has so far been described separately, and it must now be seen to come together and work as a whole. The best way to explain this is to describe my own workshop. All important features have been annotated to link this description to the drawings and photographs. As a workshop develops to suit what is produced in it, a description of the work undertaken will be of use. The main product is period furniture – not the usual reproduction type, but pieces made to the style and methods used in the past. The clients for whom the furniture is made are looking for a particular piece that is unobtainable in any other way. Because of the quality and the method of construction the furniture is expensive; the work is very labour-

intensive, it is made on a one-off principle, and it is all bespoke. Some restoration work is carried out for one or two favoured clients, but only on pieces that are worthwhile. I enjoy working by hand with tools made when the trade was at its pinnacle of excellence.

THE BUILDING

The workshop is on the ground floor, in what was once the dining room. The room, in the north-west corner of the house, is 21ft 6in long and 13ft wide (*see* Figs 19.1, 19.2 and 19.3). There is a wooden suspended floor. By modern standards the ceiling is quite high at 9ft 6in; it gives a lot of wall space for cupboards and shelves. Daylight is plentiful and there are four windows and a half glass door, (D1) which is at one end of the shop and

Fig 19.1 Heatherbrae workshop.

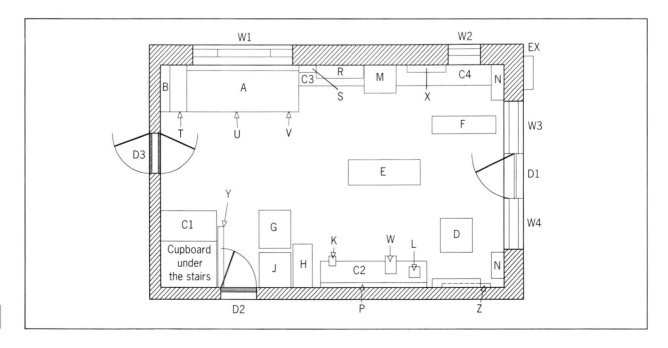

Fig 19.2 The workshop, natural light.

Fig 19.3 View from the bench, natural light.

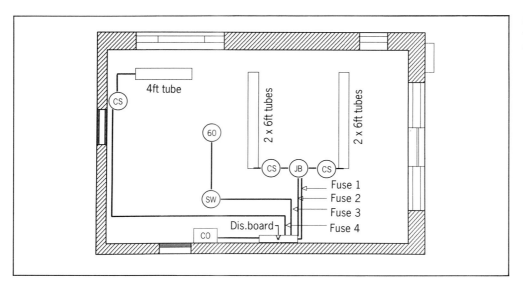

Fig 19.4 Heatherbrae workshop light wiring diagram.

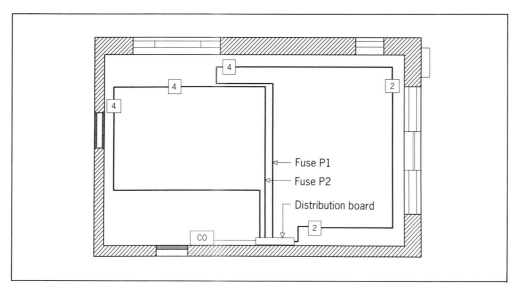

Fig 19.5 Heatherbrae workshop wiring diagram: power rings.

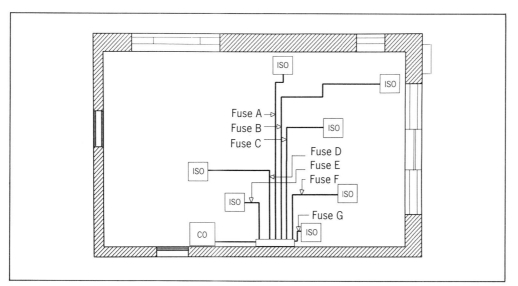

Fig 19.6 Left: Heatherbrae workshop machine wiring diagram.

Fig 19.6a Right: symbols for wiring diagrams.

leads out into a small enclosed garden at the front of the house.

An extractor unit (EX) stands outside and to the left of the doorway. Plywood trunking links the extractor to the workshop through a fanlight window (W3). All the windows are double glazed with ¼in Georgian wired glass which is obscure except for the centre panel of the window over the bench (W1). There are two internal doors; one leads into the hall (D2), the other into the dining room (D3). This last doorway has two doors, one on each face of the lining. The door on the workshop side is soundproofed. The main entrance to the house is through the hall, and this is the way visitors come to the workshop. As the stairs from the hall ascend they take up a small area in the corner of the workshop. There is a cupboard under these stairs.

ELECTRICITY

The electricity supply is single phase only. The lighting circuit supplies two double tube fluorescent units over the machines and one single unit over the bench (see Fig 19.4). There are separate ceiling switches for all of these units. All other lighting is portable and plugs into the ring main. There are several battens fixed at strategic positions to which portable lights can be clipped. The power points in three ring mains and the machines are all fed through one main switch (see Figs 19.5 and 19.6). There is an amp meter in this supply that indicates the total power being used. A residual current circuit breaker is also installed in this supply, together with an earth trip. In all there are sixteen 13amp sockets. The workshop supply is separately fused and switched.

THE BENCH

For me this, marked A, is the most important item in the shop (see Fig

10.5 on page 65). It is placed under a window, and behind it a large mirror under the stair soffit reflects light back down on the bench. The bench top is made from 4in thick Bubinga (*Guettarda sp. [H]*). At the back of the bench and between it and the window is a rack containing two rows of the most used tools – chisels, gouges, bradawls and screwdrivers.

Fitted to the wall at the end of the bench is a series of racks with a shelf at the top (B). In this rack are all my gauges, mortise chisels and drawbore pins. The shelf houses panel pins, string and an electrically heated bending iron. Above my working position, when at the bench, is a batten fixed just below the ceiling, on which all the quick-release cramps are hung. Behind the cramps and at a lower level is another batten running parallel to the bench. Portable spotlights can be clipped on this batten when needed.

To the right of the bench is the sharpening area, with a Sharpenset wet grinder and a small bench grinder with two 6in wheels. To the right of the grinders is a trough holding six Japanese water stones permanently immersed in water. All of these items are on a cupboard (C3) in which the powered hand tools are kept. Over the sharpening equipment is a glass fronted cupboard (R), where most of the moulding planers are kept; others are in my tool chest. A few shelves (S) to the left of the moulding plane cupboard house small planes.

When standing at the bench, the saws are to hand on buttons fixed to the dining room door (D3). Above the saws is a rack with the most frequently used hammers (see Fig 19.7). The tenon saw and dovetail saw are on the wall to the right of the window over the bench. One step back from the bench is a nest of drawers and pigeon holes (C1) where the bulk of the hand tools are stored

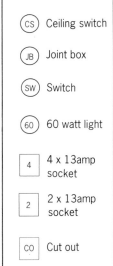

CS	Ceiling switch
JB	Joint box
SW	Switch
60	60 watt light
4	4 x 13amp socket
2	2 x 13amp socket
CO	Cut out
ISO	Isolator

Fig 19.7 Saws and hammers in a rack on the back of a door (which is seldom opened). Note the 150 watt spot light that shines directly on to the vice.

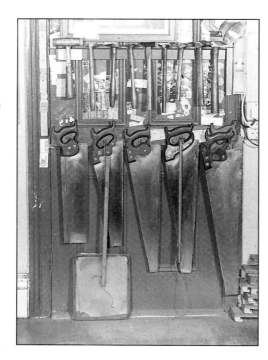

Fig 19.8 The tool storage near my bench.

(*see* Fig 19.8); the planes are in pigeonholes at bench level. There are shallow drawers for carving tools, paring chisels, paring gouges, rules and similar tools (*see* Fig 19.9). Deeper drawers house combination planes, ploughs and bigger items. There is more storage under the bench, with two tiers of drawers (U) and a double door cupboard (T). Bench hooks and short shooting boards live on top of the cupboard, while in the drawers are bits and drills, spokeshaves, scratch stocks, mitre templates and other marking out equipment. The cupboard has one shelf and houses some of the larger items that are not used very often. Under the tail vice end of the bench is a small set of metal drawers (V) in which a stock of abrasive papers is kept.

Entering the workshop from the hall, immediately to the right is a 2ft square engineer's surface plate on a cupboard (J) which holds the stock of clean rag. Next into the shop is the bandsaw (G); this is normally fitted with a 1in wide blade and is used for resawing. By the bandsaw is the pillar drill (H), a 5-speed machine with several chucks. Drills, Forstner bits and screw sinks are stored on a shelf to the right of the drill.

Along the same wall as the drill is a long cupboard about 4ft high (C2). This has a large engineer's quick-release vice mounted on its right hand end (K). On the other end of the cupboard is a 10in disc sander (L) and a scroll saw (W). In the cupboard are metalworking tools and a stock of brass and other fittings. Fixed to the wall over the cupboard is the rack holding G-cramps, with shelves above that (*see* Fig 19.10). These shelves contain all the odds and ends that are kept in bottles, jars and tins, e.g. opened tins of stain, glues, abrasive powders and the million other items which seem to collect in every

Fig 19.9 A nest of drawers for storing carving tools.

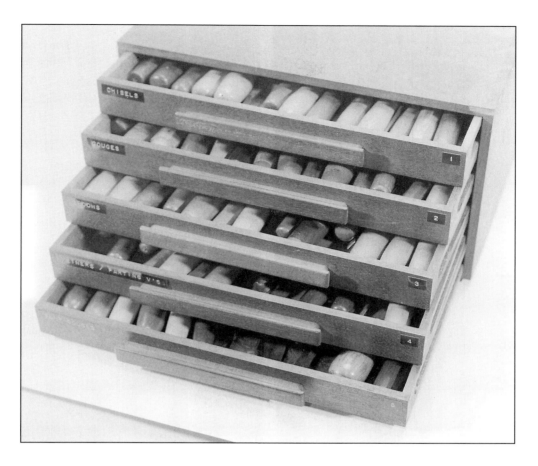

Fig 19.10 My G-cramps in their rack.

workshop and need some form of home.

The next and last item on that wall is the rack of sash cramps (O) (*see* Fig 19.11); cramps up to 4ft long are stored here, and longer cramps are stood in the corner behind the table saw (D). The machines work longer stock than the workshop can accommodate inside its four walls in the following way. The table saw can rip 12ft long lengths of timber; these pass through the saw and out through a trap at the bottom of the window (W4). Fig 12.1 shows the inner window with its plastic strips that keep the warmth in the shop. The outer window is a normal double-glazed sash that is opened when ripping long lengths of timber.

There is always a need for reference books in the workshop. Unless these are stored carefully, the dust and general workshop conditions would soon spoil them. Books are stored in two glass fronted cupboards (N), one each side of the window and door unit (W3, D1, W4). These cupboards are not very accessible, but the books stored here are not in frequent use.

Fig 19.11 The rack containing my sash cramps. T-bar cramps can be seen standing in the corner.

Fig 19.12 Plastic drawers used for the storage of screws and small fittings.

By opening the door (D1), long lengths of timber can be planed or thicknessed. The over and under planer (E), will handle work up to 7ft long without having to open the door. The lathe is strategically placed (F); most of the time there are two attachments fitted on to it, a chisel mortiser and a small bandsaw. By opening the window (W3), a long-hole boring tool can be used, and by opening window (W2), long stiles can be mortised.

There is a small spindle moulder (M) positioned so that 7ft lengths of timber can be machined. This machine also has a bobbin sander attachment. All the machines are connected to the extraction system, and there is also a point over the bench where a flexible pipe can be attached when using the portable router. Screws, different small fittings, tubes of Araldite, washers, and the many small items that can easily be mislaid are stored in plastic drawers mounted on the wall (X) (*see* Fig 19.12). Nails and oval brads, etc. are all in tins on two shelves (Y), fitted well above head height. To keep the workshop at a reasonable temperature there is a radiator (Z) which is connected to the central heating boiler that serves the rest of the house.

Two final points that need mentioning; while these are not part of the workshop, they play a part in its working. Outside in the garden there is a shed 24ft long by 10ft wide, which houses all the timber stock. Next to the workshop there is another large room where furniture waiting to be worked on is kept, along with small stacks of wood that have been prepared ready for a particular job. They live here for several months, and settle down to the moisture content of a centrally heated house. When the family need this room, the workshop becomes congested for a few days.

A BASIC HAND TOOL KIT

While the type of work to be undertaken will determine exactly what hand tools are required, the novice woodworker, faced with a bewildering array, will look for some guidance. The following list is given as a guide for general bench work, such as joinery and cabinetmaking.

BASIC KIT

Jack plane
9in try square
2ft steel rule
Marking knife
26in cross cut saw, 8 or 9 points per inch
10in Tenon saw
Combination mortise and marking gauge
Steel smoothing plane
Firmer chisels $\frac{3}{8}$in, $\frac{1}{2}$in, $\frac{3}{4}$in, 1in
Mallet
Warrington 8oz hammer
Medium oilstone
Screwdriver, 8in cabinet pattern
Fine nail punch
Bradawl
Pincers, 8in
Ratchet brace, 8in or 10in sweep
Twist bits: $\frac{1}{4}$in, $\frac{3}{8}$in, $\frac{1}{2}$in, $\frac{3}{4}$in
Countersink

SUPPLEMENTARY TOOLS

Panel saw 20in, 10 or 12 points per inch
Dovetail saw, 22 or 24 points per inch
Coping saw
Fore or panel plane in metal
Block plane, 60½ or 9½ (both if you can afford them)
Metal fillister record No.778
Bullnose plane, 1in cutter

Shoulder plane, 1¼in cutter
Plough plane or combination with cutters
Router
Bevelled-edge chisels; $\frac{5}{8}$in, $\frac{7}{8}$in, 1¼in
Gouges (obtain as and when needed)
Screwdriver bit
4in and 12in try squares
Mitre square
Sliding bevel
Cutting gauge
Dividers with screw adjustment
Pin hammer, 3oz
Spokeshaves, one flat sole and one round sole
Fine oilstone

The above lists are a representative kit. As the need for additional tools of a more specialized nature occurs, they

Fig 20.1 My tool chest. Note the rope handles and the plain painted appearance. Only the inside is embellished.

can be purchased. Most good quality woodworking tools last for several lifetimes, and many secondhand tools, made when the trade was at its zenith, are far superior to some of those being manufactured today. Keep your eyes open for the secondhand bargain.

When you start to acquire your kit of tools, they will need somewhere to live; what better than the traditional tool chest? The photographs and drawings are of mine, a traditional cabinetmaker's chest, which has developed over several centuries and has remained unchanged for the past 100 years. The case is made from good quality pine and painted black on the outside. The inside is fitted out in mahogany, and all the skills of the craftsman are displayed here, including marquetry on the inside of the lid. The rope handles are traditional, and are far kinder to the hands than any metal contraption.

Fig 20.2 The inside of the lid of my tool chest showing the marquetry. The hinges were salvaged from the scrapped case of a grand piano. The lock is antique and stamped 'William III'.

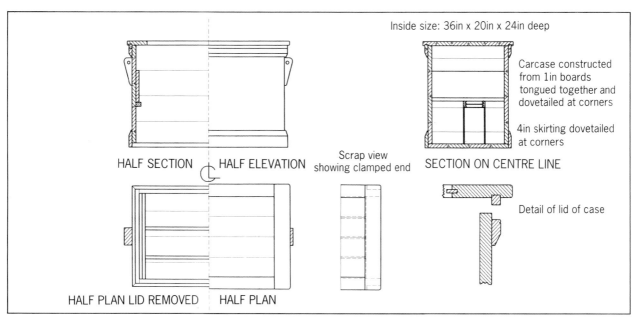

Fig 20.3 Tool chest carcase (with tills removed).

Inside size: 36in x 20in x 24in deep

Carcase constructed from 1in boards tongued together and dovetailed at corners

4in skirting dovetailed at corners

HALF SECTION   HALF ELEVATION

Scrap view showing clamped end

SECTION ON CENTRE LINE

HALF PLAN LID REMOVED   HALF PLAN

Detail of lid of case

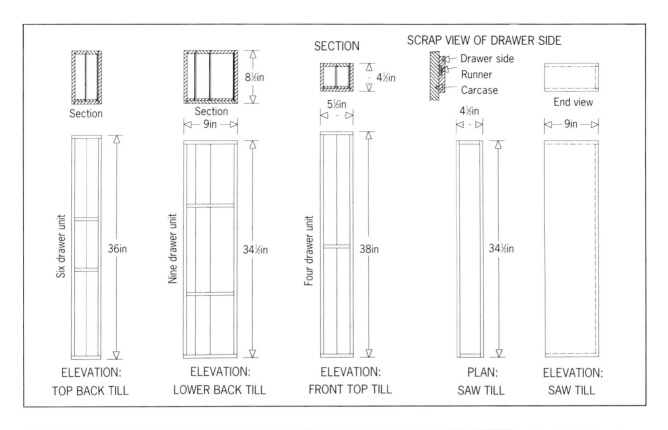

Fig 20.4 Tills for tool chest.

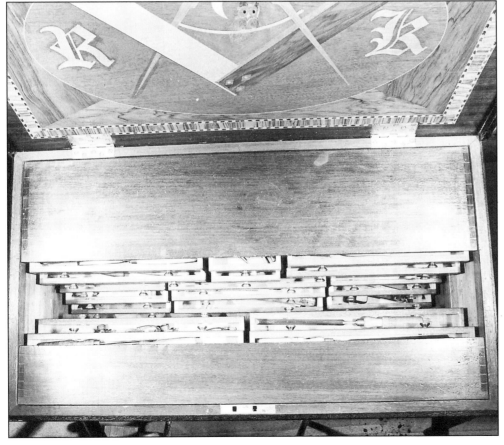

Fig 20.5 Looking inside the chest with all the drawers open.

Fig 20.6 Drawer units moved to show the saw till and space below for long tools.

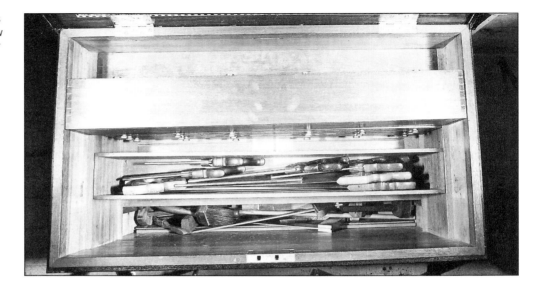

Fig 20.7 Looking into the chest with drawer units moved to show planes in the bottom of the chest and the saw till.

Fig 20.8 Drawer units moved to show moulding planes stored at the back bottom of the chest.

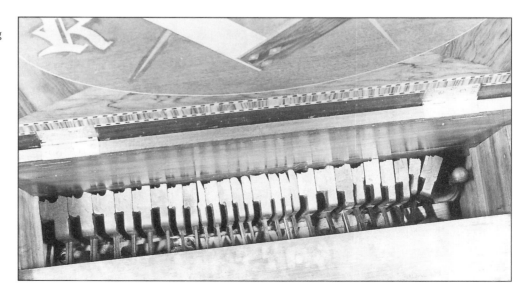

STOCKISTS AND SUPPLIERS

PREFABRICATED BUILDINGS

Southern Sectionals International Ltd, Maltings Road, Battlebridge, Essex SS11 7RH

D W Pound, Rock, Kidderminster, Worcs DY14 IBR

Passmores Portable Buildings Ltd, Canal Road, Strood, Rochester, Kent ME2 4DR

County Precast Ltd, Globe Works, Rectory Road, Grays, Essex RM17 6BD

Arrow Buildings, Hollin Farm, Appleton, Richmond, North Yorkshire DL10 7QZ

A E Headen Ltd, Marshmoor Works. Gt North Road, North Mymms, Hatfield, Herts AL9 5SD

Davis and Clifford Ltd, Beta Works, Oxford Road, Tatling End, Gerrards Cross, Bucks SL9 7BB

W S Hodgson and Co. Ltd, Cotherstone, Barnards Castle, Co. Durham DL12 9PS

MACHINERY MANUFACTURERS

AEG (UK) Ltd, 217 Bath Road, Slough SL1 4AW

R S Brookman Ltd, Parkside Works, Rothley, Leicester LE7 7NS

Dodd Machine Tools Ltd, Woodham Halt, South Woodham Ferrers, Chelmsford, Essex CM3 5NH

Dominion Machinery Ltd, Denholmegate Road, Hipperholme, Halifax HX3 8JG

Black and Decker Professional Products Division, Westpoint, The Grove, Slough, Berks SL1 1QQ

Robert Bosch Ltd, PO Box 98, Broadwater Park, North Orbital Road, Denham, Uxbridge, Middlesex UB9 5HJ

Electra Beckum, 10 Willment Way, Avonmouth, Bristol

Sanlin, 23 Church Street, Toddington, Dunstable, Beds LU5 6AA

Interwood Ltd, Stafford Avenue, Hornchurch, Essex RM11 2ER

JKO Cutters Ltd, Hughenden Avenue, High Wycombe, Bucks HP13 5SQ

Luna Tools and Machinery Ltd, 20 Denbigh Hall, Bletchley, Milton Keynes MK3 7Q

W J Meddings (Sales) Ltd, East Way, Lee Mill Industrial Estate, Ivybridge, Devon PL21 9LL

Multico Machinery Ltd, Brighton Road, Salfords, Nr Redhill, Surrey RH1 5ER

Nu-Tool (Machinery Sales) Ltd, Carcroft Industrial Estate, Wellsyke Road, Adwick-le-Street, Doncaster, S. Yorks DN6 7DU

Wm Ridgeway Ltd, Parkway Works, Sheffield

J J Smith & Co. (Woodworking Machinery) Ltd, Unit 10, Trident Industrial Estate, Blackthorne Road, Colnbrook, Slough, Berks SL3 0AX

Wadkin Plc, Green Lane Works, Leicester

Kity UK, 6 Acorn Park, Charlestown, Shipley, W Yorks BD17 7SW

Startrite Machine Tool Co, Waterside Lane, Gads Hill, Gillingham, Kent

TOOLING

Whitehill Spindle Tools, Union Street, Luton, Beds LU1 3AN

Vanguard Cutting Tools Ltd, 102 Harvest Land, Sheffield S3 8EG

E Crowley & Sons, Bentalls, Pipps Hill Industrial Estate, Basildon, Essex SS14 3BY

Clico (Sheffield) Tooling Ltd, Unit 7, Fell Road Industrial Estate, Sheffield S9 2AL

WOOD WASTE BURNING STOVES

Talbott's Heating Ltd, Drummond Road, Astonfield Industrial Estate, Stafford ST16 3HJ

DUST EXTRACTION

P & J Dust Extraction Ltd, Unit 1, Lordsword Industrial Estate Chatham, Kent ME5 8PF

P M Walker & Co. (HX) Ltd, PO Box 22, Gratrix Lane, Sowerby Bridge, W Yorks HX6 2AW

Fercell Engineering Ltd, Unit 60, Swaislands Drive, Crayford Industrial Estate, Crayford, Kent DA1 4HU

Wood Waste Control Engineering Ltd, Unit 6, Soho Mills, Woodburn Green, Nr High Wycombe, Bucks HP10 0PF.

DIAMOND WHETSTONES

Starkie & Starkie Ltd, 118 South Knighton Road, Leicester LD2 3LQ

JET CRAMPS

TMT Design Ltd, Queensway Trading Estate, Leamington Spa, Warks CV31 3LZ

BIBLIOGRAPHY

Chudley, R., *Construction Technology,* Longman

Corkhill, Thomas, *A Glossary of Wood,* Stobart & Son

Feirer, J.L. and Hutchings, G.R., *Advanced Woodwork and Furniture Making,* Chas. A. Bennett

Feirer, John L., *Cabinetmaking and Mill Work,* Chas. A. Bennett

Greenhalgh, Richard, *Joinery and Carpentry,* New Era Publishing

Hayward, Charles H., *The Complete Book of Woodwork,* Evans Brothers

Hayward, Charles H., *Tools for Woodworking,* Evans Brothers

Odate, Toshio, *Japanese Woodworking Tools,* Taunton Press

Powell-Smith, Vincent and Billington, M.J., *The Building Regulations,* Blackwell

Salaman, R.A., *Dictionary of Tools,* Allen & Unwin

Sellens, Alvin, *The Stanley Plane,* Early American Industries Ass.

Sellens, Alvin, *Woodworking Planes,* privately printed

Voisey, Nigel S., *Wood Machining,* Stobart & Son

Wearing, Robert, *Woodwork Aids and Devices,* Evans Brothers

METRIC CONVERSION TABLE

INCHES TO MILLIMETRES AND CENTIMETRES						
MM = Millimetres CM = Centimetres						
INCHES	MM	CM	INCHES	CM	INCHES	CM
⅛	3	0.3	9	22.9	30	76 2
¼	6	0.6	10	25.4	31	78.7
⅜	10	1.0	11	27.9	32	81.3
½	13	1.3	12	30.5	33	83.8
⅝	16	1.6	13	33.0	34	86.4
¾	19	1.9	14	35.6	35	88.9
⅞	22	2.2	15	38.1	36	91.4
1	25	2.5	16	40.6	37	94.0
1¼	32	3.2	17	43.2	38	96.5
1½	38	3.8	18	45.7	39	99.1
1¾	44	4.4	19	48.3	40	101.6
2	51	5.1	20	50.8	41	104.1
2½	64	6.4	21	53.3	42	106.7
3	76	7.6	22	55.9	43	109.2
3½	89	8.9	23	58.4	44	111.8
4	102	10.2	24	61.0	45	114.3
4½	114	11.4	25	63.5	46	116.8
5	127	12.7	26	66.0	47	119.4
6	152	15.2	27	68.6	48	121.9
7	178	17.8	28	71.1	49	124.5
8	203	20.3	29	73.7	50	127.0

ABOUT THE AUTHOR

Jim Kingshott was born in 1931 in Surrey, where he still lives. He is a professional cabinetmaker who served his apprenticeship in the late 1940s and gained experience by working in a wide variety of posts, ranging from undertaking to aircraft construction; in more recent years he has been involved in the training of apprentices.

He has been a regular freelance contributor to woodworking magazines for a number of years, and he has also made a study of the history of woodworking and the tools associated with it; this led to his first book, *Making and Modifying Woodworking Tools*, published by GMC Publications in 1992.

INDEX

TITLES AVAILABLE FROM GMC PUBLICATIONS LTD

BOOKS

Woodworking Plans and Projects	GMC Publications	Making Dolls' House Furniture	Patricia King
40 More Woodworking Plans and Projects	GMC Publications	Making and Modifying Woodworking Tools	Jim Kingshott
Woodworking Crafts Annual	GMC Publications	The Workshop	Jim Kingshott
Woodworkers' Career and Educational Source Book	GMC Publications	Sharpening: The Complete Guide	Jim Kingshott
Woodworkers' Courses & Source Book	GMC Publications	Turning Wooden Toys	Terry Lawrence
Green Woodwork	Mike Abbott	Making Board, Peg and Dice Games	Jeff & Jennie Loader
Making Little Boxes from Wood	John Bennett	The Complete Dolls' House Book	Jean Nisbett
The Incredible Router	Jeremy Broun	Furniture Projects for the Home	Ernest Parrott
Electric Woodwork	Jeremy Broun	Making Money from Woodturning	Ann & Bob Phillips
Woodcarving: A Complete Course	Ron Butterfield	Members' Guide to Marketing	Jack Pigden
Making Fine Furniture: Projects	Tom Darby	Woodcarving Tools and Equipment	Chris Pye
Restoring Rocking Horses	Clive Green & Anthony Dew	Making Tudor Dolls' Houses	Derek Rowbottom
Heraldic Miniature Knights	Peter Greenhill	Making Georgian Dolls' Houses	Derek Rowbottom
Practical Crafts: Seat Weaving	Ricky Holdstock	Making Period Dolls' House Furniture	Derek & Sheila Rowbottom
Multi-centre Woodturning	Ray Hopper	Woodturning: A Foundation Course	Keith Rowley
Complete Woodfinishing	Ian H osker	Turning Miniatures in Wood	John Sainsbury
Woodturning: A Source Book of Shapes	John Hunnex	Pleasure and Profit from Woodturning	Reg Sherwin
Making Shaker Furniture	Barry Jackson	Making Unusual Miniatures	Graham Spalding
Upholstery: A Complete Course	David James	Woodturning Wizardry	David Springett
Upholstery Techniques and Projects	David James	Furniture Projects	Rod Wales
Designing and Making Wooden Toys	Terry Kelly	Decorative Woodcarving	Jeremy Williams

VIDEOS

Dennis White Teaches Woodturning
Part 1   Turning Between Centres
Part 2   Turning Bowls
Part 3   Boxes, Goblets and Screw Threads
Part 4   Novelties and Projects
Part 5   Classic Profiles
Part 6   Twists and Advanced Turning

Jim Kingshott   Sharpening the Professional Way
Ray Gonzalez   Carving a Figure: The Female Form

GMC Publications regularly produces new books and videos on a wide range of woodworking and craft subjects, and an increasin' number of specialist magazines, all available on subscription:

MAGAZINES
WOODCARVING   WOODTURNING   BUSINESSMATTERS

All these publications are available through bookshops and newsagents, or may be ordered by post from the publishers at 166 High Street, Lewes, East Sussex BN7 1XU, telephone (0273) 477374, fax (0273) 478606.

Credit card orders are accepted. Please write or phone for the latest information.